Of Exile and Music

Of Exile and Music
A Twentieth Century Life

BY

Eva Mayer Schay

To Bobby and Fay
with happy memories of the
Europa!
And love from
Eva

Purdue University Press
West Lafayette, Indiana

Library of Congress Cataloging-in-Publication Data

Schay, Eva Mayer, 1931-
 Of exile and music : a twentieth century life / by Eva Mayer Schay.
  p. cm.
 ISBN 978-1-55753-541-2
 1. Schay, Eva Mayer, 1931- 2. Exiles--South Africa--Biography. 3.
Exiles--Great Britain--Biography. 4. Exiles--Germany--Biography.
5. Women violinists--Biography. 6. Violinists--Biography. 7.
English National Opera--Biography. I. Title.
 CT788.S33A3 2010
 787.2092--dc22
 [B]
                                          2009008126

Dedicated to the memory of my mother, whose courage, determination, and devotion made all things possible; and to my husband, who brought my years of exile to an end.

Contents

Part Four—Work, Politics

Part Five—England

Acknowledgments

I should like to express thanks to my mentor, Sonia Ribeiro, creative writing tutor at The East Finchley Institute for Further Education, who set me on this path, and without whose guidance this book would not have been written; to the Irish author Brian Gallagher, whose encouragement at a crucial time enabled me to finish writing it; to Professor Joseph Haberer of Purdue University for his faith in it and his unfailing support; to retired publisher Barry Shaw for his unstinting, hugely appreciated help; and to my friends Sidney Buckland, Martha Baker, Edwina Leapman, and Margaret Musset for their invaluable feedback.

⌒ Introduction ⌒

In 1923 my Uncle Rudi, a left-wing journalist, interviewed Adolf Hitler, at the time a prisoner in Landsberg gaol. Ten years later, Hitler became Chancellor of Germany. As political editor of the *Dortmunder General-Anzeiger*, Rudi wrote a scathing article about the Nazi party and was hounded out of the country. He managed to send his family to Paris the day the Reichstag burnt down and followed some time later. At the border he was severely beaten up by a group of Hitler's Brownshirts. In 1935 he left Paris for Manila on the invitation of his uncle Emmanuel Haberer, who had already assisted his twin cousins Fritz and Joachim Haberer to emigrate to the Philippine Islands, where they had begun to make a life for themselves.

My father too was hounded out of Germany, though in a less dramatic way. He had written a textbook on income tax, which was widely used in Germany but was banned as soon as the Nazis came into power. He was falsely accused of fraud at a bank he worked for in Cologne, but at the trial the evidence was clearly in his favour—still possible then—and he was exonerated. In July 1933 he received an official letter debarring him from practicing his profession as tax consultant, on the grounds that he was not of "Aryan" descent.

Unlike so many of their contemporaries, my parents were in no mood to wait in the hope that things would change for the better, and in no mood to put up with the daily indignities to which Jews were subjected. They decided to leave Germany.

Wondering where to go, they spread out the map of Europe on their living room floor. Spain, which had expelled the Jews centuries earlier, was now eagerly inviting them to return. The island of Mallorca, untouched by war for a hundred years, was known as the Island of Peace. That was where they decided to emigrate with their baby girl, to build a new life in safety. But first they spent a few months in Paris, where Rudi was slowly recovering from his wounds, before the two brothers went their separate ways, never to meet again.

In the intervening years before World War II, my mother's elder sister, her brothers and cousins, and my father's half sister all emigrated either to Palestine or the United States, thus joining the mass exodus from Germany and beginning their hard years of exile. And so the family was dispersed, as were so many other Jewish families, and joined the ranks of "rootless cosmopolitans" so despised by Stalin.

But the fate of those left behind was worse than the worst imaginings.

1

```
   Der Vorsitzende                    Köln,den 1.Juli 1933
des Grundsteuerausschusses            Gereonstrasse 44
   Katasteramt    I

    ▲   293
    -----------------

                    Herrn

                        Alfred   S c h a y

                                    Köln -Sülz
                                    ---------------


    Auf Grund des Artikels I § § 1 und 3 des Gesetzes über die Zu -
lassung von Steuerberatern vom 6. Mai 1933 ( Reichsgesetzblatt I,
Seite 257 ) dürfen Personen,die im Sinne des Gesetzes zur Wieder-
herstellung des Berufsbeamtentums vom 7 . April 1933 nicht arischer
Abstammung sind,als Steuerberater für Staats - und Gemeindesteuern
ab 6. Mai 1933 nicht mehr zugelassen werden.

    Anträge,die von Ihnen ab 6. Mai 1933 eingereicht sind,können da-
her nur dann erledigt werden,wenn der Eigentümer sie während des lau
fenden Rechnungsjahres hier auf dem Katasteramt I unterschreibt oder
sie durch schriftliche Erklärung zu den seinigen macht.
```

Official letter debarring my father from his work, 1933.

I was too young to remember Germany, to feel the pain of separation from my homeland, or the disillusion that my parents felt about a country that had so cruelly disowned them. I had no feeling of connectedness at all with Cologne, the city of my birth. My exile was from somewhere quite different.

Throughout my childhood I would look back with longing to those early years in Mallorca: my lost Paradise, my home, where life and friendships had been simple, and where I had been truly happy.

For many years I felt a stranger in South Africa, our adopted homeland, and yet just at a time when I had at last begun to put down roots and feel at home, it became a moral necessity for me to go into exile once again.

Two little Mallorcans, Eva and friend.

Part One

 EUROPE

Chapter One

☞ A Childhood Idyll—Mallorca, 1933 to 1936 ☜

"Mamma! Why are you throwing water at Pepita?"

I was about three years old, upset and bewildered by the scene I had just stumbled upon. Pepita, my mother's devoted maid, lay writhing and screaming on the kitchen floor, maddened with jealousy because my mother had engaged a second maid, Maria, to help with the workload. "Cold water will bring her to her senses," said my harassed mother. As far as I know this therapy worked, and Pepita never held it against her.

Yet for all their rivalry and devotion to my mother, neither Pepita nor Maria was prepared to venture out in the midday sun if some last-minute cooking ingredient was missing, and she would simply have to go out and buy it herself. Every now and then I would hear screams from the kitchen: my mother had once again burnt herself. Sometimes she could scarcely cope with this little girl around her knees. Yet I do not recollect being much affected by the various domestic crises, immersed as I was in the many impressions of my own little life.

High above the sea, we lived in a white, elegant, and modern villa, just below the woods surrounding the Castell de Bellver in Palma de Mallorca. A short flight of steps with a banister led up to the front door. There was a large balcony on the first floor and a flat roof above the second. The garden was hedged in by mauve, purple and or-

Pension *Schay.*

My father's residence permit Mallorca, 1934.

ange bougainvillea, oleander, and prickly pears. It had an almond tree, fig trees, and hibiscus. Geraniums and masses of nasturtiums lined the pathway to the front steps. I followed my father around as he tended the garden. On one occasion when watering the flowers, he gently turned the watering can on me, declaring I was a flower too.

At the time he was attempting to earn a living as photographer. He took good photographs, but most people were unwilling to pay for them. Having practiced as a chartered accountant in Germany, he eventually decided to study Spanish accountancy law on the mainland, in Barcelona, coming home to Palma during the holidays.

For my parents, Mallorca was a haven. For me, it was simply home, where my friends were, and where life was happy and uncomplicated. My mother ran a *Pension*. We had guests of all nationalities, including a retired British army major who wrote novels and said he had put my mother in one of them; a Chinese gentleman who taught her how to cook rice; and a Frenchwoman with her little Spanish-named daughter Conchita, of whose father we knew nothing.

Conchita was my dearest companion. We played, slept, bathed together, and never tired of each other. For six months each year, Conchita and her mother disappeared to Monte Carlo, where her mother mysteriously earned enough money to keep them for the rest of the year. I would feel desolate when they left, longing for their return, but each time they came back to Mallorca, Conchita had forgotten every word of Spanish.

One evening after their most recent return from Monte Carlo, her mother was bathing us both. Suddenly she called out, "Madame Schay, Madame, *venez vite!*" and ran to get my mother, busy as ever in the kitchen. "*Écoutez!*" she exclaimed, and there I was, chatting away to Conchita in fluent French. The two mothers fired questions at me in French, and I replied to them all.

Apart from Conchita and my kindergarten friends, I had two other playmates: one was Puchee Olivér, a handsome little boy with dark-brown eyes and hair as blond and straight as mine was dark and curly. ("How does a little German girl come to have such dark hair?" the German lady tourists used to ask my mother. "Oh, that comes from looking so much

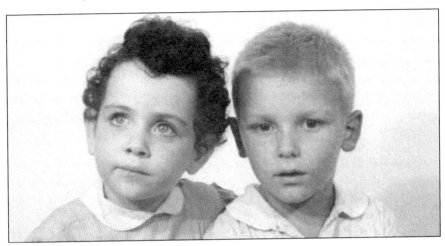

Eva and Puchee, 1935.

Eva, Pünktchen, *Conchita, and Puchee playing with roll film.*

at Spanish children!" my mother would reply—or so she told me.) The other was nick-named *Pünktchen*, German for "little dot," because she was so tiny. She annoyed me, and to my shame, I pushed her down a flight of stairs. She was surprisingly unharmed. Later there was also young Sven Treitel who played with me in our sandpit. His parents hailed from Laupheim, my mother's hometown, and his grandfather had been the rabbi of its Jewish community.

Some months after starting his studies, my father returned from Barcelona on va-cation. He was appalled at the arrogant and inconsiderate manner in which some of the newer guests behaved toward my mother. Greatly puzzled, I watched from the window as my kind and gentle father, whom I had never seen angry before, unceremoniously threw them out—and with them, my mother's hard-earned income. Yet I never heard her com-plain. I think she understood how bad he felt that for the time being she was obliged to be the sole breadwinner.

My bedroom overlooked the backyard, where a turkey lived, until it was slaughtered for dinner. At night it invaded my dreams, pecking at me from under my bed in revenge. I cried and cried until my mother promised me never to have a turkey slaughtered at home again. She kept her promise, and I was thankful, though I well knew that the turkey on my plate had met with a similar fate elsewhere, and for that I was sorry.

During the summer my bedroom would become oppressively hot, and some nights I could not sleep. Then a bed would be made for me on the flat roof, and I was allowed to sleep blissfully out in the open, caressed by cooling breezes.

Behind our house was a wood. We used to walk there and enjoy the cool air, the sounds of cicadas and birdsong, the scent of cedars and pine, eucalyptus and carob trees. When our cat Mimi died, I rallied my friends, and we took her in a long funeral procession and buried her deep in the wood.

Palm trees lined the seafront. I spent many hours on the hot, sandy beach beneath the vivid blue Mediterranean sky. A thousand diamonds sparkled on the sea. My lips tasted salty, and I could smell the ozone in the air. And there was the cinema: *Ali Baba and the Forty Thieves*, which terrified me; Charlie Chaplin sliding in and out of metal tubes in *Modern Times*; and several films with Shirley Temple, whom I adored and envied. "Why is Shirley Temple so pretty and Eva so ugly?" I asked despairingly, looking in the mirror. Major Charles Gilson, too, was a fan of Shirley Temple. In general, he hated children and thought they were a "bloody nuisance"—including me. One day my mother sent me up to his room to deliver his newspaper. "But she's charming!" he said to her later, and from then on he had two favorites: Shirley Temple and Eva, my mother told me.

Somehow my parents managed to do a little traveling for pleasure. We visited Vall-demossa, where Chopin had lived, joined for one winter by George Sand, as she recorded in *Un hiver en Majorque*. We had short holidays at a farm in Cala Ratyada. There I used to get up at five in the morning to watch the cows being milked while eating a breakfast of bread in one hand and cheese in the other, doubly enjoyable because so different from how I had been taught to eat.

Little Mallorcan Eva.

This idyll came to a brutal end. In July 1936 the Spanish Civil War broke out, and General Franco conquered Mallorca long before the final outcome of the war. When Republican bombs began to fall on Palma, my parents took me back to Cala Ratyada for safety, but it was not long before the bombs followed us there. The Island of Peace it was no longer.

A fascist soldier drove us back to Palma in his brand-new Mercedes Benz. He was all oily politeness, but I was violently sick in his car, much to my mother's glee. The bombs fell fast and furious over Palma. "Tell them not to hurt Eva!" I begged my mother, and she set me to washing dishes noisily, in order to distract me. At night there would frequently be loud knocks on the door, long after we had gone to bed. It would be the Nationalist police demanding to know whether we were harboring any Communists. In fact, my mother later told me that we were, but both my parents strenuously denied it. It was all rather frightening for a four- soon-to-be five-year-old.

Sven's father, I learned much later, was arrested, falsely accused of spying for the Communists and on the verge of being executed. His frantic mother rushed to see the German consul and pleaded with him to intervene. Mercifully he did, putting the family on the very next German freighter, bound for Naples.

We must have been the last of our small group of German-Jewish refugees to leave. The Republicans, with whom my parents sympathized, briefly regained a foothold in Mallorca in August 1936, but were beaten back by the Nationalists, aided by Italian Fascists. We were no longer welcome. Neither side wanted to be responsible for the blood of foreigners in this ghastly war. My parents wanted to go to England but were refused entry; a great number of British expatriates were returning to their home country, and we could not be included.

Our kind Mallorcan neighbors promised to guard the belongings we had to leave behind until—they hoped—our eventual return. Pepita and Maria, now fast friends, bade us a tearful farewell.

And so we were shipped off, back to the land we had come from, back to Germany.

Chapter Two

RETURN TO GERMANY—AUGUST 1936

As we stood on the quayside on the morning of our departure, we watched a crane lifting the larger pieces of luggage onto the small German warship that was to take us away from Mallorca. Suddenly, a cabin trunk burst open, and a huge carving knife came crashing down. "Bloody Communist!" somebody muttered next to my mother, little knowing that the knife was hers, from the kitchen of *Pension Schay*, hastily packed in case she might need it in whatever future life had to offer. My poor mother was petrified. Fortunately, no one was hurt. Somehow the trunk, with most of its contents, was closed up, and no questions were asked.

We were strange passengers to be on a German warship, and my parents must have wondered anxiously what would happen when the crew realized that we were Jewish. In fact, we met with nothing but goodwill. I even made German newspaper headlines, my mother discovered: "Youngest Traveller on German Warship."

The sea was rough, great waves breaking and crashing down over the bow of the little ship, which pitched and rolled mercilessly. I was violently seasick several times over; each time the sailors made me comfortable on a deck chair and covered me with blankets so that I could sleep. Each time I would find a box of chocolates by my side on awakening. I do not remember ever having so many adoring young men dancing attendance on me at the same time, and I, not quite five years old, lapped it all up. My other memory of that ship is of going below deck for lunch and having my first taste of delicious, cold cherry soup.

Later we had to transfer on the high seas to a large passenger liner that would take us to Genoa. We said farewell to our friendly sailors, our trunk was hoisted up, and we climbed a ladder up the steep side of the ship. For the first time I became aware of other passengers; I suspect now that they were German expatriates from the Spanish mainland, bound, like us, for Germany. They stared at us with unveiled contempt. It was as if we had walked into a wall of silent hostility, which I did not understand but which, even at that age, I sensed. It made me shrink inwardly.

In Genoa, my parents' errant cabin trunk was nowhere to be found. We were packed, trunkless, into a train bound for Munich. The carriage in which we traveled was locked. There was no escape and no food or drink to be had, until, somewhere in Switzerland, my parents were able to buy some milk from a platform vendor through the window. All through my subsequent childhood I—who loathed milk—remembered Swiss milk as the most sublime food.

Our arrival in Munich was a confusion of events beyond my understanding. My mother later told me that there were banners across the station platform saying: **"Welcome to the Refugees from Communism."**

This was directed at the majority of free passengers on the train, but for those of us in the locked carriage, it was quite another matter. My father, for one, was immediately arrested and kept in custody overnight. He was given an ultimatum: leave Germany the following day, empty-handed except for a train ticket to Milan for himself and his family, or go to an *Erholungslager*, Convalescent Camp, which he well knew to be a euphemism for Concentration Camp. The choice was obvious.

Meanwhile, my mother had just one night in which to visit her parents in the little town of Laupheim in Upper Swabia, to show them their young grandchild, and to say farewell before rejoining my father and traveling to Milan.

I had a lovely time in my grandparents' little house, where I felt surrounded by loving-kindness. I awoke there on the morning of my fifth birthday, August 24, 1936, to the aroma of a grape tart that my grandmother had baked especially for me. I was given a wonderful doll that had belonged to my mother as a child and had my mother's own real brown hair, eyes—with eyelashes—that opened and shut, and fully mobile joints in arms and legs. Best of all, my four-year-old cousin Albert, who lived next door, came over to recite a birthday poem for me. I was so touched.

Too soon it was time to leave: "Goodbye Mother, Goodbye Father, take care, be safe, we'll be thinking of you. When we are settled we will send for you!"

"Goodbye Hermine, goodbye Little One, blessings on you, travel safely, write to us!" Parting felt very sad.

Thirty-two years later, on tour with the orchestra of Sadler's Wells Opera, I made the acquaintance of a fellow violinist, an elderly Maltese gentleman, who was soon to retire. He was fascinated with the workings of the human brain, had studied hypnotism, and had become quite adept.

He persuaded me to let him hypnotize me, and because I had a tendency to fly into a rage when provoked, which I dearly wanted to conquer, I agreed, perhaps against my better judgement. He kept repeating that my right arm would rise of its own accord, which I didn't believe, until it actually happened. At this stage, perhaps in order to find out how and when this tendency to lose my temper originated, he asked me to go back to my fifth birthday. He knew nothing at all of my background, and he and I were equally taken by surprise when I burst into tears. I wept and wept, uncontrollably. That was the end of his attempt to hypnotize me, but when he asked me the reason for this unexpected outburst, I told him about my fifth birthday, about the farewell to my grandparents, whom I scarcely knew, whom I was never to see again, and about their end. He tried to comfort me and to reassure me: "It was not your fault." But that had no meaning for me. What astonished me was the depth of sorrow that had been unconsciously stored up in me for so many years, as well as the feeling of guilt that we had not been able to save my grandparents and my youngest aunt, who had remained with them.

And so to Italy.

Chapter Three

Italy was not a happy place for us. Although Mussolini was not yet persecuting the Jews, he had ruthlessly invaded and conquered Ethiopia, was Franco's ally, and was increasingly under Hitler's influence. The omens were bad. Added to that, we were miserably poor. My father went to work every day, but his earnings were meager. We lived in one room in a run-down block of flats in a poor district of Milan and had barely enough to eat.

Yet I have pleasant memories, too. I made friends with the caretaker's daughter and soon learned to speak Italian. Every morning my mother would take us to the *Jardini Publici*. She made boats for us out of the fallen chestnut leaves on the lawns, and we floated them on the lake. One day though, when I turned around from the lake, I was alarmed to see a policeman speaking severely to my mother. She was almost arrested for letting us play on the lawns, which were out of bounds, but when she conveyed to him that she had been unable to read the Italian notices, he gallantly let her off. I remember, too, standing with a group of people in front of a shop window, seeing my first television set. It had a small screen, at most about ten inches wide and six inches high, and I was amazed to see what appeared to be live people moving about in it.

Undernourished, I eventually developed painful mouth ulcers and other symptoms. By now my life had been so derailed that I began to have nightmares. Although my parents did all they could to hide their anxieties from me and protect me from the knowledge of the evil that was striding across Europe, fear seeped into me. I cried so much at night that neighbors, fearing my parents were maltreating me, sent the police to investigate. My wonderful, loving parents. I felt so ashamed.

A few years earlier, much as my parents loved Mallorca, they had found earning a living there such a hard struggle that my father had written to his aunt Ilse, who had previously settled in South Africa, to inquire about the possibility of our going to live there. She was the widow of his artist uncle Oscar Haberer, whose painting student she had once been, and the mother of the twins Fritz and Joachim, who had emigrated to the Philippines ahead of Uncle Rudi. Now she was earning a meager living painting portraits in Johannesburg. She had seriously advised against immigration to South Africa because of the pro-fascist

Nationalist government in power at the time. (However, the Nationalists were to lose the general election in 1939 to the United Party, led by General Smuts, and so South Africa was to fight together with the Allies during World War II.)

Now, in 1936, the situation had changed, and it had become imperative to get out of Europe. My mother wrote to Carl Laemmle, the eminent Hollywood film director who came from her hometown—Laupheim—but received no reply. Many years later, I learned that he had dealt with an enormous number of such requests. She wrote to several others but never with any result.

One morning, having just finished reading a book about South Africa by a Czech author, she announced, "We're going to South Africa!"

"You're crazy!" said my father. "We have no one to sponsor us. We've no money. How do you suppose we'd get there?"

"I don't know, but I know we'll get there! I'm sure of it!" she replied.

Later that very day, a letter arrived from Johannesburg from Tante Ilse. When the Spanish Civil War had broken out, she had reproached herself bitterly for discouraging my parents from coming to South Africa. She had no money herself, but her wealthy aunt, Tante Mendelssohn, was willing to lay down the £100 guarantee required by the government to ensure that new immigrants did not become a burden on the country's economy. At the time, £100 was a lot of money. I later learned that she had helped many refugees in this way. Tante Ilse's letter had followed us around Europe and had taken almost three months to reach us.

Day after day my mother and I packed our few belongings and waited eagerly for my father to come home with tickets for a passage to South Africa. Day after day we were disappointed. There were just too many people trying to leave Europe at the same time.

At last, a berth was found for us on the *Duilio*, our fares paid by a Jewish aid organization. It was the second last ship to reach South Africa before that country's doors were finally closed to refugees. (The *Duilio*, we read some years later in a Johannesburg wartime newspaper, was sunk by the Allies in World War II.)

A few days before she was due to sail, we left Milan for Genoa. My parents took a walk along the quayside one evening and there, completely abandoned under an archway, stood a familiar-looking cabin trunk. Tentatively, they approached to inspect it more closely. Marvel of marvels, it was the very trunk they had lost in Genoa on the way back to Germany. "Eyes front," they said, each picking up one side by the handle, and they carried it away. Next day they arranged for it to be sent to us, care of Tante Ilse, in Johannesburg. I still remember the excitement, after it finally arrived, of unpacking forgotten treasures, including many of my father's evocative photographs of Mallorca and of my early years.

In October 1936 my uncle Rudi was well settled in the Philippines and able to help his and my father's parents to follow him to Manila. By great good luck we managed to meet my paternal grandparents in Genoa on their way to the Philippine Islands. My grandmother had made me a blue and white gingham dress embroidered with red cherries, which I continued to treasure long after I had outgrown it. I wrote them a thank you letter after our arrival in Johannesburg, signing off with the words, "*gute Besserung*," the German for "wish you better." They were not ill, but I had got it into my head that that was how you were supposed to end a letter.

On the *Duilio* my parents made friends with several other German-Jewish refugee families, whom we continued to see after settling in Johannesburg. There was also a wealthy, childless couple who offered to adopt me, and who were disappointed when my parents turned down their promise to give me a "good life." And there was a man who gave me a coral necklace because I—a five-year-old—reminded him of his wife. I still have that necklace.

But the attentions of most of the grown-ups were a trial to a small child whose life had been disrupted and who had become shy and withdrawn. I remember one who teased me and another who tried to make me curtsey: "Come now, it's more ladylike!" he said. I positively refused. There were no children that I remember, or perhaps by that time I had grown too shy and unsure to approach any, and I was lonely. I learned to play games with imaginary playmates and with my dolls. It seems to me that I was a little mentally deficient for, remembering that my mother "thinned" my too thick hair when she cut it, I thought I would do the same for the doll with my mother's precious hair. I cut off a layer of it and wondered why it did not grow back as mine always did.

The journey seemed to last an eternity, but at last, on the fifteenth day, Table Mountain came into sight with its "tablecloth" of cloud. We had arrived at Cape Town.

Italian ticket to Cape Town.

Part Two

SOUTH AFRICA

Chapter Four

☞ South Africa, the Early Years—October 1936 to September 1939 ☜

"Freedom at last!" my mother exclaimed, breathing a huge sigh of relief.

I was amazed to see a host of little brown boys swimming toward the ship, diving for pennies that the passengers threw to them, and struck with wonder at the skill with which they retrieved them in their mouths. Later my mother described the intense gratitude she felt when she first saw Cape Town, nestled in the embrace of Devil's Peak, Table Mountain, and Lion's Head—names we only subsequently learned—and when we finally docked in the harbor, late in October 1936. That harbor in time came to epitomize romance and adventure for me, an opening to another world full of possibilities. Cape Town seemed to welcome us with its Mediterranean climate, lush vegetation, and woods, which reminded me of the Europe I already missed. To this day, the cooing of doves brings back to me that feeling of love for Cape Town's Botanical Gardens, and of the nostalgia it evoked in me as a small child and newcomer.

After a few days, with the help of the local branch of the Jewish aid organization that had helped us to leave Italy, later conscientiously repaid by my parents, we took the thirty-six-hour-long train journey to hot and dusty Johannesburg, where Tante Ilse met us at the station. On the way there, my parents had decided it would be better for their relationship if my father were to become the chief wage earner. However, the first thing Tante Ilse said was: "Alfred, you can forget about finding a job in this country—there's far too much unemployment." Their hearts sank.

"Then what are we to do?"

"Well, it will be up to Hermine to find ways to support the family," she said.

My mother did all sorts of things she hated, including door to door collecting for charities, just to make ends meet, but it was not long before my father succeeded in finding a job after all, as accountant for the large electrical firm of Westinghouse. During the time he worked there, he was able to buy my mother an electric waffle iron as a birthday present, and for many years after, whenever guests came to tea, they would be regaled with freshly made waffles and honey or preserves.

Our first home was a nightmare. We had a room in the small, cramped house of an

Afrikaner couple who owned about a dozen smelly, yapping Pekinese dogs that got under our feet wherever we went. I hated it.

Soon after, we moved into a flat in Elfreda Court in Doornfontein, an inner-city suburb that had seen better days, where many German-Jewish new immigrants lived. We were quite a community. There was Hirsch the shoemaker, Apfel the grocer, Speier's Confectionery, Strauss the kosher butcher who lived next door to us with his wife and daughter Marianne, and an ice cream parlor where we occasionally went for treats and where my parents met with their cronies for coffee and conversation. Everybody spoke in German.

Marianne and I sometimes played together. One of the grown-ups gave us each an apple, and I immediately bit into mine. Marianne's apple was in pristine condition when we arrived outside her bathroom door, and she asked me to hold it while she went inside. "Don't you dare eat it," she warned.

I felt affronted. "Of course not," I said, "Why should I? I've got my own apple! What do you think of me?"

She took her time. I was always a dreamy child, and after a while I forgot which hand held Marianne's apple. I looked down and was mortified to discover that neither apple was any longer in pristine condition...

Our flat overlooked the Jewish Government School, where later Hans, my cousin twice removed, went to school. Meanwhile, he and I were sent to Fraulein May's Kindergarten. She assured our parents that after a year with her we would all be speaking fluent English. In fact, her own English—which our parents were unable to judge—was so appalling that we learned absolutely nothing, except for some mispronounced nursery rhymes, which nobody understood. And among ourselves we spoke in German.

But I have one tender memory of my first morning at Miss May's, when a little boy called Lutz gallantly drew up a chair for me to sit beside him. I never received such gentlemanly treatment from my cousin Hans, who teased me mercilessly and turned down my proposal of marriage at the age of six, on the grounds that I was a year older than he was. Once he told me that the Devil was a black creature with horns, which lived just underground.

Hans and Eva, 1938.

"Yes, really," he said. "I'll prove it!" and started digging.

Ever gullible, I was terrified and pleaded with him to stop. Yet I was fond of Hans and nearly burst with fury and a sense of injustice when I once saw his mother slap his face. We played together regularly, and our parents took us for Sunday outings together until we reached puberty, when he became sulky and withdrawn, and I felt puzzled and hurt.

After a year at Miss May's, in October 1937—springtime in South Africa—my mother took me to Barnato Park School with the intention of enrolling me as a pupil there the following January, the beginning of the school year. Mrs. Daniel, the headmistress, regretted that she could not possibly accept me as a pupil then, as my English was atrocious. She recommended a year's attendance at Mrs. Poulteny's Kindergarten nearby, and we moved to Yeoville, in part to be nearer this kindergarten and the school.

We rented a house on Percy Street. It had a large garden and a tree that a friend and I used to climb, with a platform that served as a tree house. There we ate the irresistible Marmite sandwiches my mother regularly produced for us. It was a happy time. On Sundays, his day off work, my father made breakfast. I remember him relaxing with visitors on the veranda, looking handsome and debonair in his creamy-white duck suit. We had a large basement where, together with some women of her acquaintance, my mother formed a *nähstube*, sewing room, where they worked as alteration hands, altering clothes, running up curtains and the like. For a while, she kept paying guests. There was a jolly, plump, comforting sort of lady whom everybody called "Bobba"; Herr Gottschalk a painter-decorator; and a family Blumann. Frau Blumann was rather excitable and self-willed, as I remember her. Ruth, the elder child, was clearly the favorite. But already then I favored the underdog; my heart bled for her little brother Johnny, and I tried to make up for the love I felt his parents denied him. He had a toy broom with which he used to sweep the floor in imitation of our African servant, singing a tune he had heard him sing and which I remember to this day. When he developed whooping cough, he was kept in quarantine in a room all by himself. I would hear him coughing his heart out in the dead of night, and I would sneak into his room to try to comfort him. I did not catch whooping cough.

Like Johnny, I picked up tunes wherever I heard them and sang them lustily wherever I happened to be—in my bath, in our garden, when painting pictures, whenever I felt contented—sang the marching songs my father taught me when we were out walking in the country, the lullabies my mother had sung to me since ever I could remember, and the canons, such as "Frère Jacques," which she taught me to sing with her. I wept over the fate of "Das Heidenröslein," the little wild rose that, despite her pleadings, was plucked by a careless boy. The poem is by Goethe, and my mother taught me two settings, the best known of which is by Franz Schubert. I learned and loved both versions. With nostalgia I remembered hearing a group of young people laughing and singing "La Cucaracha" to guitar accompaniment in a boat on a river in Mallorca, and I sang it for many years without knowing it was a humorous song about a cockroach.

We had a dog, a black pointer called Rinja, and a fluffy, gray cat with which I was besotted. She used to wait for me when I came home from kindergarten, and later from school, hiding behind the far corner of the corridor. As I approached she would leap out to surprise me. It was a game she regularly played with me. In my infatuation I nicknamed her

Kittylausischen, rascally little Kitty, (from the German *lausbub*, young rascal). Kitty came home late one night with terrible lacerations after a fight. My mother cleaned and dressed her wounds, and we kept her in the cool of the basement to recover. There I devotedly fed her and comforted her until she was well enough to venture out again.

It was during this period of our lives, in the summer of 1938, that my father took me on our first holiday in South Africa. We spent a week at a guest farm in nearby Parys (an Afrikaans name pronounced "Parace"), a little village set in dry, empty countryside as unlike the city of Paris, after which it was named, as one can imagine. Helen McGregor, who was renowned throughout the land for her excellent marmalade, owned the farm. I was proud to know someone so famous. We went for walks and swam in the muddy Vaal River. While my father read in the garden, I would sit drawing and painting in the shade of a eucalyptus tree.

Here, on Helen McGregor's farm, my father first talked to me about death. The knowledge that life came to an end for all of us, that it meant total extinction, which no one could escape, came as a great shock. My father would have no truck with comforting ideas of life after death.

"But aren't you afraid Daddy?" I asked.

"There's nothing to be afraid of," he said. "You don't feel anything, you don't know anything—it's just nothing. How can you be afraid of nothing?"

But I was. And I went on being afraid for many, many years.

My mother regularly collected me from Mrs. Poulteny's at lunchtime. On one occasion, waiting outside the playground among a group of mothers, she noticed a vaguely familiar, middle-aged woman staring intently at her. Later, she told me she had mistaken her for an acquaintance, Frau Hohenstein. "What a surprise, how good to see you!" she said. "Do come home with us for lunch!"

The invitation was eagerly accepted.

"Who *is* she?" I whispered to my mother with distaste.

"Shhh! I'll tell you later. I thought she was someone else. I've invited her to lunch. We'll just have to go through with it," she replied.

It was some time before we discovered Frau Witchik's real name—at least that's what I was told it was. I never quite believed it because it seemed too good to be true: she seemed so much like a witch to me. Poor woman, she was quite mad—another fractured refugee life—and my mother hadn't the heart to turn her away. She would frequently arrive just in time for lunch, and she bored us to distraction. It took years before we managed, somehow, to lose her.

Yeoville was a lower middle-class suburb within walking distance of, or a tram ride away from, Barnato Park School. A family Graff lived near us, and I made friends with their daughter Ella. She was born in Johannesburg, and her parents were of Russian-Jewish descent, having come by way of Holland and England. They were good, warm-hearted people, but I don't think Ella and I really liked each other. Our frequent stand up fights would begin in play, but we would invariably end up trying to kill each other.

One day I came home to my mother and said scornfully, "Ella is so funny. She talks about next year as if she knows she'll still be living here!" My mother was dismayed that I had come to regard fleeing from country to country as inevitable.

Around this time I had a nightmare that I have never forgotten: I dreamed that my mother was at home cooking, waiting for us, while my father and I were standing in a long queue in the Johannesburg City Hall. At the head of the queue was a large cauldron. I asked my father what we were waiting for. He told me that when we reached the head of the queue we would be put in the cauldron together with all those people and boiled alive. In my terror I fell out of bed and awoke on the floor. For all my parents' efforts to protect me, I had clearly absorbed some of their dread of the Nazis and their murderous hatred of us Jews.

At the end of my year at Mrs. Poulteney's I spoke English as well as any of my peers, without a trace of German accent, but I had forgotten my Spanish, French, and Italian. Ella and I started school together in January 1939, though she was a year younger than I. Through her, on our first day at school, I met Sarah Klempman. She, too, was South African born, her parents having emigrated from Russia. Sarah was pretty and vivacious, with dark-brown sparkling eyes and short, dark straight hair with a fringe. She played the piano, which filled me with admiration and envy. Until then I had never known anyone who played a musical instrument, apart from guitar accompaniments to Spanish songs. We did not possess a radio or gramophone, and Sarah's playing was my first conscious encounter with instrumental music. Among other pieces, I remember she played me a little Mozart sonata, which I thought quite wonderful. I still feel saddened that she gave up playing after a few years.

The three of us were inseparable, yet deep down I felt lonely. My school report said: "Eva is a bad mixer." How different from my carefree time in Mallorca. I had a sort of detachment from my classmates, saw them as being only half-awake and unaware. Admittedly, I was several months above the average age, but the main difference, as I look back, was in our early experiences. The majority of girls at our school were South African born. The few German-Jewish immigrant children had come direct from Germany to South Africa, and their parents had managed to bring most of their possessions. Their timing had been more auspicious. They too had been uprooted, but not several times over. For all that, however, like my parents, most of them had no more than one child. Emigration and its trials were not compatible with bringing more children into the world, my mother said, when I asked with longing why I had no sisters or brothers.

Though I thought of myself as awake, I daydreamed constantly. I dreamed with longing of having a sister or a close friendship with a truly kindred spirit, and I dreamed endless stories. Yet I remember sometimes wondering whether we were, all of us, not quite real, merely playing a part in someone else's dream.

In my first year at school I experienced a few frightening walks home, twice being caught in a locust storm, the horror of which I have never forgotten, and once in a hailstorm of such violence that I was driven to seek shelter in the house of complete strangers. Yet I also remember moments of carefree contentment. I see myself, a small girl walking home from school, picking honeysuckle blossoms from the hedges as I went, sucking the nectar, and singing loudly and unselfconsciously, tunes that I'd heard our African servants sing as they worked, Afrikaans and English folksongs I'd learned at school, and the German lieder my mother had taught me from infancy.

Throughout our six years in the prep school, Ella, Sarah, and I were constant companions. Then circumstances separated us, though we remained in touch and would meet now and then. Ella remained in South Africa, and we lost touch, but Sarah now lives in Haifa with her husband and two daughters, and we have discovered over the years that we have more in common than we ever realized all those years ago as schoolmates.

Chapter Five

Throughout the Spanish Civil War my parents followed news reports and were dismayed at General Franco's final victory early in 1939. Even though I was so young, I felt I understood and shared in their distress. Later in the same year, on September 3, World War II began. I had just turned eight.

My father immediately lost his job at Westinghouse, classed as an "enemy alien." For the next six years, whenever we left Johannesburg on vacation we had to register with the local police. At the cinema there was an unremitting flow of horrifying American newsreels showing the fighting in Europe. Our own South African soldiers were sent "up North" to fight in the desert, and we schoolgirls were set to knitting socks and balaclava helmets for them. How well I remember the newspaper headlines shouting: "Avenge Tobruk!"

Our teachers warned us not to pick up stray objects in case they were booby traps and exploded on us. We had air-raid drills: a loud siren was the signal for us to walk as fast as we could to the nearest shelter. I always ended up with a violent stitch in my side. The perceived threat was from German South West Africa, now Namibia. Rationing was introduced, and I envied the girls whose parents took them on holiday to Lourenço Marques, in the Portuguese colony of Mozambique: they were able to get chewing gum there—not that I would ever have been allowed to chew gum at home.

My father attempted various jobs. The first was as a waiter. He felt so humiliated when patrons tipped him that he gave it up after one evening. We could no longer afford the house in Percy Street and had to move again. What had become of the paying guests I do not remember. I minded desperately having to part from our animals, for which we had to find other homes. Rinja went to live on a farm where I was assured he was happy. We paid him a visit, and he jumped all over us with joy and excitement. Kitty, too, was given away and disappeared from our lives forever. Except for a couple of tiny tortoises, which lived on a balcony, I was never able to keep a pet again.

My mother had made the acquaintance of a wonderful woman, Annie Kaufmann, whom everybody called *Mutti*, German for Mummy. She was a slender woman, with short gray hair and dark eyebrows, which emphasized the strength of character in her face. She had no personal vanity, and during the summer she had only one cotton dress, which she washed every evening and wore the next day. She had temporarily left her husband in London, where they had emigrated from Germany, to live with their two daughters in Johannesburg, one married, with a little girl called Marianne, the other unmarried. They lived in a flat in Yeoville and shared it with another immigrant couple, the Rosenfeldts, and their toddler daughter, Marion. Mutti said we were to move in with them all: they would make room for us. Each family of three had one bed-sitting room, and Mutti shared a room with her unmarried daughter Illa. She also gave classes in that room: remedial gymnastics for children, in which I was allowed joyfully to participate. All eleven of us shared one kitchen and bathroom, yet under Mutti's beneficent influence all of us managed to live together in peace. My mother later told me that living with Mutti had permanently influenced her for the better, in her attitude toward life and other people.

I have a memory of finding little Marion sitting on the kitchen floor, happily biting into every single one of a crateful of tomatoes—which was pretty disastrous considering how poor we all were—and of my delight when she asked, "*Hat die Kuh ein Pyjama an wenn sie in's Bett geht?*": "Does the cow wear pajamas when she goes to bed?" Many years later I visited my paternal grandmother in a Jewish retirement home in America, where to my surprise I found that the matron was none other than Frau Rosenfeldt. We threw our arms around each other in joyful reunion.

There was only one Jewish teacher in our school, Mrs. Stern, the only teacher who was married. She was our class mistress in 1940. I was in my second year at school, the only year we had religious instruction. She had a brisk but warm personality, was far less formal than our other teachers, and I liked her. Her voice was a little husky; she was short and slightly plump, with blue eyes and straight blond hair, which she wore in a braid around her head. Hitler would have seen her as the ideal "Aryan."

I have always remembered our first day of Religious Instruction. The majority of girls went to another classroom to learn about the New Testament while we few Jewish girls remained behind with Mrs. Stern. The first thing she said to us was, "Before we learn about Bible history, there is something very important, which I want you all to remember. Wherever you go, always behave well. You have a grave responsibility. If a non-Jewish person does something bad, he is blamed for it, but if a Jew does something bad, *all* the Jewish people are blamed for it. People think and say it's *because* he or she is Jewish that they've done wrong, even though we know it isn't true. Don't let that happen because of something *you* have done!"

As it was impossible to find a job, my parents took out a loan and bought a fish and chip shop in Vrededorp, a short train ride away from Johannesburg, in a "poor white" area. It was the only way they could think of earning a living. For five long years they were slaves to that shop, saving to pay back the loan plus hefty interest. During that time, my mother never bought a new dress or any luxury for herself, but I never lacked essentials. I knew we were poor, but it never eroded my sense of worth, despite the fact that many of my classmates were from wealthy homes.

My father was a fastidious man, repelled by the many drunks who used to lurch into the shop to try to sober up with fish and chips. They called him "The Professor" because of his air of remoteness. He was tall and slim, with a slight stoop that increased as the years in the shop went by. My mother was short and plump, more adaptable and extroverted. She managed to keep smiling and joking with the customers, knowing intuitively how to please them, and so they kept returning. Her courage kept us going; without it we'd have been lost. She had a delicious sense of humor, infecting everybody with her laughter. And yet she had her darker side, was easily hurt, and had a quick temper, though she forgave readily and was not above asking for forgiveness herself. I felt so secure in her love that I was happy to share it with my friends, who bathed in her warmth and encouragement.

Because the shop demanded increasingly more of their time, my parents arranged for me to spend afternoons at a local kindergarten, which was open after school hours for children whose parents worked and could not be at home for them. I had read boarding school stories, was longing to experience boarding school myself, and eventually persuaded my parents to let me spend nights in the dormitory of this unusual kindergarten.

By now my father had rented a dreary one-room *pied-à-terre* in Vrededorp, coming home only on weekends, his clothes reeking of fried fish. My sleeping away from home enabled my parents at last to spend more time together. Sadly, this arrangement lasted for only one week, by the end of which I was suffering from a high fever and a screaming earache. I didn't know how to bear the pain, so I kept walking up and down the length of the dormitory in an effort to distract myself. One of the girls in the dormitory told my mother: "She kept walking up and down the room. She looked like a little old woman!" By the time my mother was called it was almost too late. I had to go into hospital to have a mastoidectomy, in those days performed with hammer and chisel, leaving a gaping hole behind my left ear and some hearing loss. To add to the misery, I contracted chicken pox—probably from a visitor to the ward—soon after I left the hospital, and it spread into the hole behind my ear, which the doctors and nurses were keeping open for regular cleansing and dressing.

During my time in hospital my parents moved yet again, away from Yeoville, into a bachelor flat on the fifth floor of Geraldine Court, at the corner of Quartz and Wolmarans Street, in Hillbrow. It was only a short walk through lovely Joubert Park to the railway station where they caught their train to Vrededorp, and it was near the General Hospital, where they visited me, and which I continued to attend for months afterward as an outpatient. Yet another home to get used to; but I had come to regard these upheavals as a normal part of life.

When I came out of the hospital I found myself in a tiny room just big enough for my bed. A corridor led to a bathroom and then a kitchenette, which opened to my parents' large bed-come-living-room facing Quartz Street. Later, when they could afford to pay more rent, we moved into a larger, two-roomed flat with a balcony, on the third floor of the same building, facing the great Wolmarans Street Synagogue. There was always something going on at the corner of that street: the evocative sound of the penny whistle played by little black boys, the terrible sound of a crash as cars raced the wrong way down one-way Quartz Street, or a bloody inter-tribal fight ("Daddy, *please* stop them—they'll kill each other!" I shouted frantically, but he said that any interference would be bitterly resented). Sometimes I watched as a Jewish bride all in white emerged from a limousine, or posed for a photographer after a wedding ceremony in the synagogue.

But now we were facing Quartz Street, and there was a kindergarten across the road below us. At eight years old, I craved the company of other children, and the three months' convalescence away from school felt like an eternity. My parents were both away working, and I was left in the care of a young woman who tried her best to keep me amused, but who was unable to fill my aching loneliness. I used to wait eagerly, kneeling on the sofa beneath the living room window, for 11 a.m., when the children from the kindergarten below came out to play: then I would delightedly watch and listen to them, until they went indoors again, and I returned to my loneliness. The girls in my class were all made to write letters to me wishing me better, and that gave me great pleasure, especially one from a girl who accidentally signed herself Barbarbara Jones.

Emmy Cohn, my father's young cousin, had arrived in Johannesburg with her parents, Onkel Willy and Tante Lina, soon after us. She was ten years older than I, and she had three more years at school after their arrival. I admired her beautiful botanical drawings and thought her quite wonderful. Almost as soon she left school she was engaged to be married, and I was supposed to be a flower girl at her wedding. However, to me she was just an older girl, not a grown woman, and I thought of her engagement as preposterous affectation.

During my convalescence she came to visit me with her fiancé, Ernst Wenger, all self-important, as I saw it, playing at being grown up and changing my world. I flew into a rage and ordered them to leave. Anne, the pleasant young German-Jewish woman in whose care my parents had left me, was overcome with embarrassment. "You surely don't wish to be so impolite," she tried to reason with me. "They only want to be kind. You will hurt their feelings if you turn them away."

"They're only showing off! I don't want them here. Go away and leave me alone!" I ordered. And thus I threw them out. In later years I often wondered how, at the age of eight, I found the courage to do it; and yet, how I could have been so careless of their feelings. Needless to say, I was not allowed to be a flower girl at Emmy's wedding. I believe she forgave me, but her father, Onkel Willy, never did.

At long last I was able to return to school. I took the Twist Street tram, often in the company of a girl called Isabel. When we were a little older we would take a pleasant twenty-minute walk to school, picking up Trudy and Ruth on the way. Isabel and I would play in the park playground together, sometimes joined by Chonny, a boy with Down's syndrome, whose mother doted on him and was determined he was going to be a doctor or a lawyer when he grew up. He died instead, and she was inconsolable. We felt awful.

Ella's parents, Mr. and Mrs. Graff, turned out to be staunch friends. I was allowed to spend every Saturday with them while my parents were at the shop, and I well remember their warm hospitality and loving kindness. Sometimes Ella took me to their synagogue; the only time I enjoyed that was on Simchas Torah, when the children were given fistfuls of sweets... There was always roast chicken, carrots and peas, potatoes, and rice for lunch. I was impressed that Ella's naughty little brother, Cyril, whose parents never ever seemed to control him, invariably thanked his mother politely for the meal. Afternoons were often spent at the cinema—bioscope, as we knew it—visiting Sarah, or all three of us playing at Ella's house.

I was still only eight when I decided to disobey my parents' injunction not to travel alone on the train. They had to spend all available time at the shop, and I was lonely. I had a little pocket money, so I walked to the station, bought myself a ticket to Vrededorp, and turned up—surprise!—at the shop. They were not angry as I expected them to be, but relieved and delighted that I had proved my independence. Thereafter I visited them frequently. Sometimes my father took the opportunity of leaving the shop in my mother's hands and taking me for a long walk. Eventually, after one of his long discourses, we would return to the shop to relieve my mother.

He talked at length about life, ethics, and religion. He quoted extensively from Josephus, was extremely well read in theology and the Scriptures, but only, it seemed to me, in order to discredit religion. Yet he had great respect for the ethics of Judaism, by which he lived, and he gave me a Bible. He inveighed against racism in all its forms. From the start of our life in South Africa he made me aware of the injustices perpetrated against the black people, comparing them to the persecution of the Jews, although at that time we had no idea just how terrible that persecution had become in Europe. We Jews, of all people, he said, had no right to condone these injustices, which caused so much suffering: we, who could so well empathize with the victims of discrimination and oppression. So I learned to respect all people, regardless of the color of their skin or how menial their work. For the majority of Africans at the time, there were no opportunities for equal education or training, nor any choice but menial work.

Despite the hardships and having to report to the police wherever they went, my parents managed to go on several holidays—never together, because one of them always had to attend to the shop—but always taking me along. My mother took me to Durban to help me recuperate after the mastoid operation. We stayed at a modest family-run hotel a few streets away from the beach. I was thrilled to be by the sea again, thrilled by the wildness of the breakers, by the once familiar smell of the ozone, and the taste of sea salt on my lips. We visited the aquarium on the beach, and every afternoon there was a Punch and Judy show, which I never missed. There was a fancy dress competition, for which my mother made me a "grass" skirt of sisal and a garland of bright-red paper carnations to hang round my neck, with another carnation in my hair. I won second prize as a hula-hula girl. The next time we visited Durban, my mother took along my old traditional Mallorcan costume, altered to fit my new height, but it won no prizes.

The owners of the hotel were a kindly old couple whose son and daughter-in-law helped them to run it. They had a little three-year-old boy called Rodwin—a composite name, after his parents, Rodney and Winifred—with dark-brown eyes and a mop of curly brown hair. He fell in love with me, and every morning I would find him sitting on the floor outside our bedroom, waiting for me to emerge. I was a good deal taller and five years older than Rodwin, but he called me Little Eva. My mother took us both down to the beach every morning. On the way, she would stop at a bakery and buy us each a warm, crusty, poppy seed roll to eat when we arrived there. Rodwin delighted and charmed us both.

On our return, my mother took me to my first symphony concert. At the age of eight I heard my first Mozart symphony, and I fell in love with his music.

Chapter Six

⟡ Music Lessons—1940 onward ⟡

My first symphony concert was attended by *Ouma* (Grandma) Smuts, as she was affectionately called. She was the wife of South African Prime Minister General Smuts, who had taken us into World War II on the side of the Allies and was to remain leader for the duration of the war. I was impressed that such an important lady appeared to be so modest. She was slight and elderly, with short, gray, curly hair, and she wore a simple black dress, with a sparkling V for Victory diamond brooch. She gave a rallying speech. So many impressions on one evening—it was a thrilling occasion.

Apart from the then rather mediocre orchestra of the South African Broadcasting Corporation, there was no professional orchestra in Johannesburg at the time, and an amateur orchestra, the Johannesburg Symphony Orchestra, gave the concert, conducted by the strikingly handsome Joseph Trauneck.

There was, however, a professional string quartet in Johannesburg, led by Harold Ketèlby, brother of the composer Albert Ketèlby, of *In a Monastery Garden* fame. My mother took me to their quartet recitals. They played in a darkened hall, with only a standard lamp in their midst to light up the music. It lent their faces an intimate glow, and the effect was magical. I was enraptured as I listened and watched.

One day my mother told me, "When you were still a baby inside my tummy I went to lots of concerts, because I hoped you would hear the music and come to love it." She got more than she bargained for.

The crucial moment came with an American film called "They Shall Have Music" about a music school for deprived children, in which Jascha Heifetz played, among other pieces, Saint-Saëns' *Introduction and Rondo Capriccioso* and part of Mendelssohn's Violin Concerto. Oh, what bliss; I was transported with joy. Soon after this we saw a film about a children's holiday camp in which a girl violinist kept complaining, "But I want to go to the seaside!" and I thought how strange it was that she should complain when she had everything I wanted.

On the way home my mother said, "It must be wonderful to play the violin. You can take it with you wherever you go, and you hold it so close, it must feel like part of your body." This remark only intensified what I was already feeling.

"I wish I'd learned to play a musical instrument," she mused. "I had a few lessons on the zither when I was a young girl. I played in a village concert, but…my teacher hadn't taught me to tune the zither…and I didn't *know* it went out of tune. It made such an *awful* noise that my father fled, he was so ashamed. I wanted to sink through the floor. Can you imagine how I felt?"

"Oh how dreadful!" I exclaimed, picturing the scene, feeling her humiliation and helplessness.

"Mommy, I want to play the violin. Please will you let me learn?" I pestered both my parents from then onward, but we had barely enough to live on; there were regular payments, including interest on the loan for the shop, and there was nothing left over for violin lessons. "You'll have to wait. Be patient," they said.

In the meantime, I went to art classes every Wednesday after school at the state-subsidized Technical College, where I was happy drawing, painting, and modeling in clay, singing as I worked. But it could not satisfy my hunger for the violin.

Perhaps realizing the part she had played in arousing this longing, my mother eventually turned for advice to a piano teacher we used to meet on social occasions at Onkel Willy and Tante Lina's. Rosa Geisenberg—another German-Jewish refugee—had the most extreme hunchback that I have ever seen. Socially, she overcame this handicap with a sparkling and attractive personality. Everybody loved and respected Geisi. Rather than give advice on violin lessons, Geisi offered to teach me to play the piano at a much reduced fee. "Even if she learns to play the violin later, the piano will give her a much better foundation," she told my mother. "I know you're not in position to buy a piano now, but she can practice on mine, every day. I always go out at five, and I'll give you a key to my flat. We live near enough to each other. Eva can let herself in. I'd love to teach her."

It seemed she was kindness incarnate and doted on me, so nothing prepared me for the monstrous transformation of Geisi as piano teacher. The first two lessons went well, and she managed to convince me that nobody in Johannesburg taught a piano method equal to hers. Then came the shock of lesson number three: "But you have forgotten everything I have told you!" she scolded. "*This* is how you must hold your hands—no *don't* drop your wrists!—and keep your fingers curved! No, no, *no*! Can't you read the notes? Have you forgotten them too? *Now* what is your left hand doing? Concentrate!"

It was an unrelenting onslaught. By lesson five she was slamming my fingers down on to the keys. I dreaded this, and my fingers trembled above the keyboard as I was getting ready to play. "Look how your hands are shaking! Have you no self-control?" she sneered. My parents never hit me, and I was quite unprepared for such violence. I developed a stomachache before each lesson, but I continued to go. Despite her persistent interruptions, bitter reproaches, mocking, and scolding, Geisi had convinced me there was nobody else who could teach as well as she did.

Eventually this treatment reduced me to tears. Then out came her lace handkerchief to dry my eyes, little round chocolate discs covered in multi-colored "hundreds and thousands" to comfort me, and sweet words of flattery to bind me to her. Each week she wrote, in an exercise book, all the faults I needed to correct, and scrawled the word "CONCENTRATE!" in capital letters across the page. All that this conveyed to me was a kind of mental cramp. My father tried to persuade me to leave her, but I stubbornly refused. She must, after all, have taught me something good, because when I accompanied my friend Ella, who also took piano lessons for a short while, to her lesson, her teacher asked me to play a piece for her and appeared very impressed with how well I played.

The time came when Geisi went too far, and humiliated me in front of another pupil, an older girl called Nana Levin, who was more advanced than I, and whose playing I admired. Poor, beautiful Nana. Little did I know then that Geisi would systematically set about destroying her, as—I learned much later—she did all her pupils. "You'll never see me again!" I shouted, as I strode out and slammed the door, trembling with rage.

My mother was appalled. "I know we wanted you to leave Geisi, but not like this. Look how good she's been to us. Please go back and apologize," she begged.

"I can't! I won't!" I exclaimed.

"I beg you, don't leave her like this," said my mother. "It isn't right. I'll even give you a tickey if you go!" A tickey was a tiny silver coin worth three pennies.

"I don't want your money. I'm not going!" I declared.

But in the end she persuaded me, and full of fear, I knocked on Geisi's door. She opened it, exclaiming, "You don't need to say a word!" and embraced me. I was back in the spider's web.

This nightmare went on for about eighteen months.

There was a violinist living in Geraldine Court whose wife had some months previously, on March 18, 1942, given birth to a baby girl. My mother used to meet him in our lift with the baby, Joanie, and observed how tender and affectionate he was with her. She told me that she had thought: *"Here's someone who is kind to children. I'll ask if he'll give Eva violin lessons. It's the only way to get her out of Geisi's clutches without hurting her feelings: she knows Eva's wanted to play the violin all along."*

Hermann Abramowitz was another of Hitler's casualties. He had been considered a child prodigy, had enjoyed something of a solo career, and had played in the major orchestras in Germany: the Leipzig Gewandhaus and the Berlin Philharmonic, under Artur Nikisch, Bruno Walter, Furtwangler. Then came the Nazi oppression; he lost his job and left Germany for South Africa. At the time there was no professional orchestra of any standing in Johannesburg, so he made do with playing interval music with Charles Manning and his Band at the Colosseum Cinema. Harold Ketèlby led, Abramowitz sharing the front desk with him. After the war, when London West End musicals toured South Africa, it was Charles Manning's band that accompanied them. Meanwhile, Hermann Abramowitz had little to do other than take a tram ride once or twice a day to the Colosseum, play for fifteen minutes, and come home again for *kafeeklatch*, coffee and cake and gossip with the ladies. Sadly, his wife did not encourage him to practice. Yet he used to dazzle me with pyrotechnics on the violin: Paganini, Wieniawski, and especially Sarasate's *Zigeunerweisen*, reflections of his past glory. Although we failed to realize it at the time, his musical life was in a state of collapse, and he was thoroughly demoralized. After the war, when visiting artists came on tour to South Africa, he could not even bring himself to go to the concerts, could not bear the pain.

Nevertheless, he agreed to teach me, found me a reasonable factory-made violin, bow, and case—my eleventh birthday present from my parents—plus music and stand. He gave me a little introductory talk on the beauties of the violin, and his charm and good looks captivated me. At last my dream of learning to play the violin was about to come true. Geisi reluctantly let me go, and we remained on visiting terms.

And then I was subjected to a new kind of torment.

My mother had explained how Geisi's repeated commands to "CONCENTRATE!" had served only to make me tense, so Abramowitz told me *not* to concentrate, but to relax. He took to shouting "RELAX!" loudly into my ear, which had, not surprisingly, exactly the opposite effect. I had absolutely no concept of what either of those two words meant. It was years later that I learned that paying attention was a quiet, simple thing to do, without strain and without fear. The one word he should have used and never did was "Listen: Listen to the intonation and to the quality of sound you are producing; listen *for* the sound you want to produce." Instead, he stood over me during every lesson shouting "Sharp! Flat!" until I started to pull faces—a difficult habit to shed—just to show that I knew what was wrong, just to stop him shouting at me.

After my second lesson—only my second lesson—he said to me, "It doesn't look very hopeful, does it?" and I stood on the landing between his floor and ours and wept. *"But I want to be a violinist! What will I do if he decides not to teach me anymore?"* I worried.

One day soon after, I announced with pride that I had practiced for two hours the previous Sunday. "Why kill yourself?" he asked, instead of being pleased. "Half an hour a day is enough!" There was no question of my parents pushing me to practice: As we had no garden, they were concerned that I should get enough fresh air and exercise and kept sending me off to play in the park.

I saw another film in which Jascha Heifetz played, this time the Tchaikovsky Violin Concerto. The film was called "Carnegie Hall." I had never heard such ravishing sounds, and I nearly died of longing and envy. *"Will I ever be good enough to become a violinist?"* I agonized. It didn't occur to me that I didn't have to be as good as Heifetz, especially not at that stage, that I could only go one step at a time. Possibly, it didn't occur to Abramowitz either.

"You're the worst pupil I've ever had!" he railed at me again and again. I sometimes wondered about the pupils he may—or may not—have had in Germany. I was certainly his only pupil at the time. Eventually a new pupil, Adrian, arrived on the scene, and Abramowitz said to him: "Unless you practice like Eva, you'll never get anywhere!" Kurt Abramowitz, his brother, sometimes popped in for a visit. "Come Eva, let's play one of our duets for Kurt," he would say. "Listen to this, Kurt—isn't she good!"—that, after a lesson of shouting insults at me. I was utterly confused. I always believed the insults and doubted the compliments. The miracle was that I persisted.

It was not long before Adrian gave up. I was completely isolated with my violin. Nobody in our class played a musical instrument, other than some half-hearted attempts at the piano. At school I felt that the other girls regarded me as a bit of a freak. Their main interest was in sports, and not until they were much older did a few of them show any interest in classical music. They were nonplussed by my passion. Abramowitz felt that adherence to an examination syllabus would interfere with the progression of studies and pieces he wanted to teach, so he did not enter me for any violin exams, nor for any competitions or music festivals. I was thus deprived of the opportunity of performing in public, of socializing with other music students, and of measuring my rate of progress against theirs. Visitors sometimes asked me to play for them, but I was far too shy to comply. When my mother and I paid one of our visits to Geisi, another visitor asked if I hoped to become a concert violinist. Geisi answered for me: "No, of course not—she's much too shy!" Little did she know that I dreamed of nothing else!

Eventually, at the age of fourteen, thanks to an introduction by Miss Starke, our school music teacher, I joined the newly formed children's orchestra at the Teachers' Training College. It was founded and conducted by the college's head of music, Miss Maria Boxall, an elderly, warm-hearted woman. I did play for her, and she made me leader of the second violin section. I'll never forget the thrill of playing my first ever orchestral pieces, the "Mazurka" from Delibes' ballet, *Coppelia*, followed contrastingly by Corelli's *Christmas* Concerto.

The star of the orchestra was the flautist, Alex Murray, who had come to South Africa as a wartime evacuee, and went on later to become the brilliant first flute in the London Symphony Orchestra. We had an excellent trumpeter who performed the *Trumpet Voluntary* and Haydn's Trumpet Concerto with us on several occasions. The leader of the first violins was Derek Osche, a handsome young boy, whose piano-teacher mother carefully nurtured his talent and drove him to orchestra rehearsals from their home in the town of Rustenberg every Saturday morning. His violin teacher was Harold Ketèlby. I envied and admired Derek but was too shy to talk to him until I met him again seven years later.

Eva, schoolgirl, playing violin.

Chapter Seven

☙ THE LATER WAR YEARS—UP TO MAY 1945 ☙

When I was ten or eleven I made friends with Mickey Ross, the caretaker's granddaughter, and her best friend Hazel Lipman. To my astonishment, Hazel later married my cousin Hans and went with him to live at Kibbutz Tzor'a in Israel, where I have often visited them since.

Geraldine Court had a laundry, a small, separate building on stilts, partly covered, partly open, where Mickey, Hazel, and I used to play. It overlooked a *cheder*, where Jewish religion and Hebrew was taught outside school hours, and we used to taunt the boys when they emerged in the playground for their afternoon break, throwing missiles at them from our vantage point. The time came when they'd had enough. "We're coming to get you!" they shouted, and we clattered down the laundry stairs and banged on the adjoining door of the menservants' compound, pleading with them to open it. No white person was meant to enter there, but they were kind to us and let us in. That was when I saw how our African menservants were expected to live.

Separated from the wives and families they had left behind in their tribal homelands, they lived in an enormous, dark dormitory. There was a long row of beds along each wall, and at the end nearest the door, a huge cauldron for cooking their staple food, *mielie pap*, a porridge made of coarsely ground maize.

Etian was older than the average "boy," as they were disrespectfully called, gray-haired and dignified. He came every morning to polish our parquet floors and once a week to clean the windows. After I had penetrated his usual reserve, he used to grumble to me about the pass laws, and he allowed me to sketch his portrait. Alphius, a youth from rural Zululand, came some years later. He had strong principles and refused to accept a tip from me for doing an extra job despite his low wages, and he lectured me seriously that I ought to get married and have children instead of going off to study.

The men's services were included in the rent. The maidservants, who dusted and laundered and cooked, were privately employed and lived in faraway townships. They had to leave their children and their homes incredibly early to catch monstrously overcrowded trains in order to arrive at the expected time in Johannesburg. There was one lift for us in the block of flats, and one lift for them, which as often as not was out of order. If they dared to use our lift and were caught, they would be severely reprimanded. I would be filled with shame and embarrassment.

In the park, most of the benches were for "Europeans only." At the bus stop outside the General Hospital, where we would wait when visiting friends in the suburbs, there would be three or four white people waiting for ten minutes or so for a bus. Alongside, there was a stop for "non-Europeans," with scores of black people patiently waiting for perhaps an hour, perhaps more. The injustice of it made me ashamed and angry. None of this was as bad as seeing the police manhandling a black man into a police van. Nor as bad as standing at our small, local post office counter, partitioned into "Black" and "White" areas, yet served by the same one man behind the counter, and hearing him say to an African on the other side of the partition, "You're no better than a monkey off a tree!"

Besides errands to the post office, my mother regularly sent me to the nearby dairy with an empty jug for milk and an order for a little butter and cheddar or "sweetmilk" cheese. The latter tasted like a cross between mild Dutch Gouda and Edam. Meat and bread were rationed during the war, imported food was not available, and the only chocolate to be had was made in South Africa and tasted rough and bitter. Fruit and vegetables were freely available and inexpensive. Mr. Patel, the greengrocer, came around with his lorryload of fruit and vegetables once a week, and I always went downstairs to pick good avocado pears, oranges, pineapples, pawpaws, guavas, and granadillas. Whenever visitors were expected I would walk down to our old haunts in Doornfontein to buy a cake from Speiers' Confectionery, and I always came away with a present of one or two of my favorite meringues. I took our shoes to be repaired by Hirsch the shoemaker, and I sometimes popped in to visit Hans' family on my way back home. Hans had by now acquired a pretty little sister, Yvonne, who in my memory was nearly always knitting when I visited.

When the fish and chip shop was better established and my mother found it possible to spend more time with me after school and on weekends, she was able to return some of the hospitality I'd received from the Graffs. On many Saturdays, Ella and Sarah visited me, and the three of us would play in Joubert Park, as always carried away by our imaginations. We had just entered the park one Saturday morning when Sarah suddenly exclaimed: "Hey! Look at that man! I bet his walking stick's got a sword inside it. Let's follow him. He looks like he's up to no good!"

We were three sleuths, about to expose a dangerous criminal. We followed him closely, all the way to the exit at the far end of the park, terrified that he might turn around. However, he walked out through the gate, and we gave up the chase and went on to our usual haunt: the Art Gallery. This was situated in the park and had reputedly the best collection of paintings—chiefly Dutch and Flemish, Italian Renaissance, and French Impressionist—and sculpture, including a Rodin and an Epstein—in the southern hemisphere. The curator, an elderly Afrikaans gentleman with a goatee beard like General Smuts', followed us around suspiciously for a while, expecting us to get up to some mischief. When he saw that our interest was genuine, he took us under his wing. He pointed out details that we might have missed in the paintings, such as a tiny insect on a plant in a still life or the texture of some article of clothing, sometimes bringing out his magnifying glass. He often took us to the storerooms at the back of the gallery to show us paintings that were not on display, and he showed us the sculpture he was working on himself, as he was preparing for retirement. He was our friend, and it never occurred to us not to trust him, but instinctively we did not tell our parents about him until years later. My mother said she would have been out of her mind with worry that he might abuse us, which of course he never did.

Sarah, Ella, and Eva on art gallery steps, 1944.

Every year during the long school vacation my mother and I went away on holiday. My most vivid memory is of traveling by train through the night. We traveled second class, six people to a compartment. By day we sat in two rows of three, facing each other. In the evening, the Cape Coloured attendant—the attendants were always mixed-race Cape Coloureds, as they were known, and always pleasant and efficient—came to take down the bunks and roll out our beds. I clambered up to the top bunk and stayed awake half the night, watching the myriad brilliant stars in the deep black sky through the top of the window, listening to the regular rhythm of the train along its track: tocketok, tocketok, tocketok. When we came to a halt, I became aware of the ceaseless sound of crickets, and occasionally heard a group of farmers singing Afrikaans folk songs to concertina accompaniment.

Although my mother and I got along famously, I missed my father on these holidays away from him and eagerly anticipated our reunion. I clearly recall at age eleven, after another holiday in Durban with my mother, a moment of heightened awareness on the return journey. Standing in the passage outside our compartment, I watched the passing scenery, smelled the smoke from the engine, and listened to the familiar rhythm of the train on the

track. We were nearing Johannesburg. My father was going to meet us on the station platform, and I knew, as never in my life before, that I would always remember this moment.

In the springtime we
enjoyed the glorious bright-
yellow mimosas that lined
the streets of Johannesburg,
and my mother and I would
take a day's outing to Pretoria to admire the mauve jaca-
randa blossoms outside Union
Buildings and along Pretoria's
Avenues.

Occasionally she would
take me to the Moon Hotel,
a blissful, isolated place, set in
the countryside not far from
Johannesburg, a couple of
miles' walk to the nearest village store. It had a swimming
pool and tennis court, and indoors, a large hall for ballroom
dancing that took place every
Saturday evening. I sat at the
top of the staircase and looked
down, entranced, at the danc-

My father, 1941.

ing and at the lovely ball gowns. My mother had political debates and played tennis with
Mrs. Tilly First, an ardent Communist and mother of Ruth First, later renowned as a tremendously courageous anti-apartheid activist. Ruth endured arrest and detention without
trial in 1963, and was in solitary confinement for 117 days. In 1982, she was blown up in
Mozambique by a parcel bomb from the South African Police, a dreadful shock to all of us
who admired her. She was married to Joe Slovo, who was to play an important part in helping to establish a new order in South Africa together with Nelson Mandela, many years later.
But at the time she was a young girl of nineteen, on holiday with her mother and younger
brother, Ronald. Initially it was good-looking Ronald who made my heart flutter, and I still
have a mental picture of him lying on his stomach beside the swimming pool, so lean that
every vertebra of his spine stood out. Then I developed a crush on his beautiful and already
charismatic sister. After our return to Johannesburg I wrote her a letter to tell her how much
I admired her, and I received a charming reply.

Meanwhile, the war continued relentlessly. We followed the news with great anxiety. For
a long time it looked as if the Germans were winning. "The trouble is they are just too efficient," my father said. "If Hitler wins, he will make slaves of us all," and he did not only
mean the Jews.

One day, Shirley, a girl in our class, received a letter from her German grandmother. It was miraculous to have reached South Africa at all during the war. Nobody at home could read it, so she brought it to school, knowing there were a few German-speaking girls in our class. Miss Ireland, our class mistress, gave it to Lore Levine to translate out loud. Lore read: "All our troubles are caused by the accursed Jews. But our wonderful Führer has promised to get rid of them for us!" Lore stopped reading, aghast.

Miss Ireland said, "That's enough. Poor woman, she'll realize her mistake soon enough, won't she?" And so she tried to cover up everyone's embarrassment.

I was afraid of Miss Ireland. She seemed to be forever scolding me, and I dreaded weekends coming to an end and having to face her again on Monday mornings. This continued for three years. When I first came into her class in 1942, she called for my mother and complained that I never paid attention during lessons, was always looking out of the window or daydreaming. "Mrs. Schay, I have to warn you that if your daughter doesn't pull her socks up she'll probably fail at the end of the year," she said.

"I think you'll find you're mistaken," said my mother, and she refused to reprimand me. In fact, she did not even tell me of this conversation until long after I came first in our class at the end of the year. Not that this endeared me any more to the dreaded Miss Ireland. Beatings were unheard of at our school, and the only time any teacher touched me was when Miss Ireland crept up from behind me, looked over my shoulder at my work, and thumped me hard on the head. I nearly jumped out of my skin with shock and had no idea what had caused her displeasure.

She had two little black Scotch terriers, and she sometimes brought them to school. They sat quietly in their baskets next to her desk, and during the morning break some of the girls made an adoring fuss over them. Not I. I couldn't wait to get away to the playground.

The combination of nervousness and hilarity, finding Miss Ireland absurd and yet being afraid of her, led to uncontrollable outbursts of giggling on my part. On one such occasion Miss Ireland angrily sent me out of the classroom. My mother had chosen that particular day to drop in and see her to inquire how I was doing. She came upon me sitting disconsolately on the bench outside our classroom. "What are you doing out *here*?" she asked in surprise, so I told her. She laughed. "I'm going home!" she said, and that was the end of it. On another occasion, Miss Ireland asked, "Who is it who is All-Powerful, before whom we must tremble, whose laws we must obey?" and poor German-Jewish Anne Silberberg said, "Adolf Hitler!" Miss Ireland was outraged and sent her out of the classroom, thinking she had committed a terrible blasphemy. My heart bled for Anne. I think I was the only girl in the class who understood her mistake, but I was not articulate enough to defend her.

After her retirement from school some years later, Miss Ireland and her retired teacher friend Miss Cochran—who used to take turns with her looking after the two little "Scotties"—bought a guesthouse in the Magaliesberg, in the Transvaal. My mother and I frequently went there for weekend retreats. The setting, high up in the mountains, was beautiful and peaceful. We got on perfectly well with Miss Ireland then. She was the ideal hostess, and all the old animosity was forgotten.

The war continued throughout my prep school years and my first few months in the high school. During that time, we had very little contact with our scattered relatives in Germany, Palestine, and the Philippines, though my mother did receive a few letters from her older sister Rosa in the United States. I remember how proud she was of her nephew Albert—the same little boy who had read me a birthday poem in Laupheim—and of his progress at school. Apart from that, we had hardly any personal news, and we had no idea of the full extent of Hitler's "Final Solution," though we knew enough to be very afraid for the Jews left behind in Europe. And I continually had newsreels of the fighting, the killing, and the suffering in the war, going around in my head.

Yet in 1944, with the war raging and our fears for our people intensified—though we little knew at the time what torments of hell they were suffering—I experienced—really experienced—my first spring. Joubert Park was alive with blossoms and they filled me with euphoria. Everything was new. At the entrance to the park stood a large tree covered in snow-white blossoms, which I named "the Bride." It took my breath away. There were pink and white blossoms everywhere in the park. At the center was a pond with benches around it, each one within a bower covered in heavily drooping, divinely scented lilac. In the evenings my parents and I sat there, enjoying the peace and beauty surrounding us. And in the pond the frogs mated and croaked to their hearts' content. I was intoxicated with joy.

On June 6, 1944, my mother's birthday, Britain and America joined forces to invade Normandy: D-day, which marked the turning point of the war in Europe. We were filled with hope and excitement. The following year, after almost six terrible years, the Allies won the war in Europe. I was in my first year at high school. Amidst general jubilation we were given a day's holiday. There were two dissenting voices in our class, those of the twin nieces of a prominent Nazi-sympathizer who was to become a cabinet minister in the Nationalist government of 1948. The rest of us were overwhelmed with relief and happiness.

The costing came later.

Chapter Eight

☞ My Father's Death—August 24, 1945 ☜

The war in Europe ended on May 7, 1945, though the war with Japan was not over until mid-August. During the preceding year my father had gradually built up an accountancy practice, working at home in the evenings, after closing time at the shop. My mother assisted him, doing the more mechanical work. She was no accountant and merely followed his instructions.

There were some ugly incidents in the shop, when my father had to defend himself against drunken assailants. He was under enormous pressure.

At last the shop was sold, almost simultaneously with the end of the war in Europe. The accountancy practice was now large enough to support us, and the debt for the shop was finally paid. My mother never forgot the relief she felt when she closed the shop door behind her for the last time.

But all was not well. For over a year my father had experienced ever-increasing difficulty swallowing his food. He was sent from doctor to doctor. "Mr. Schay, you should learn to relax, the trouble is with your nerves," they said. His back had become bent with weakness. Anxiously we watched his jaws working with the pain of "indigestion." He took to having his meals alone in a darkened room to soothe his nerves. He lost weight, and he became irritable with my mother.

She telephoned his doctor one day, after he had returned from a visit to the surgery. "Have you weighed my husband?" she asked. "Are you aware that he has lost nine pounds in one week?"

Shaken, he replied, "I'm very sorry I overlooked it. You must realize I'm suffering from a heart condition. I could drop dead any day."

"Then you shouldn't be having patients in your care!" she retorted.

I could not understand the changes in my father and longed for the days when he had been younger and handsome, philosophical and humorous. "My Daddy," who had taught me to wash and dress and to brush my teeth and gargle, while my mother slaved away in the kitchen of *Pension Schay*; who had spent long hours teaching me to roll my Rs, Spanish style, in place of the guttural German Rs; who had defended me when I was fractious and said I was only tired; who had played marbles with me when I was older, and allowed me to read

45

to him while he was having his bath. My Daddy, with whom I had gone for regular evening strolls in Hillbrow, or together with my mother when the air was balmy, in Joubert Park. My Daddy—where had he gone? Who was this suffering, irritated being who had taken his place? He never let out his irritation on me, but why did he snap and snarl at my innocent, patient mother? Why did she never snap back? What had happened to her fiery spirit? I bitterly resented his treatment of my mother, and one day I decided I no longer loved him. He asked me to come for an evening walk with him, as so often before, and I refused. Just once. And for that once, I suffered agonies of grief and remorse for years afterward.

By the time his cancer was diagnosed it was too late to save him. He was told he had a stomach ulcer and needed an operation. In fact he had two operations in close succession. I feel certain that if he had been told that he had cancer, instead of being made to feel guilty because of "nerves," over which he apparently had no control, he would have accepted it with equanimity. At that time it was usual to keep patients in ignorance of the fact that they were soon to die, and the word "cancer" was hardly ever mentioned. Not even my mother was told. She had to go to the reference library to find out what the words on the report sheet at the foot of his hospital bed meant, and the nurses scolded her for reading it at all. How alone she must have felt. However, she was allowed to sleep in the hospital, so that she could always be near him. She told me later that he'd said that whenever he saw the blue of her dress coming through the door, he felt reassured and comforted.

I had no warning. Nobody told me he was mortally ill. It was the very first time that the death of someone close was staring me in the face, and I had no previous experience to relate it to—so I simply didn't believe it. Yet I must have feared it after all, because I had worked out a magic formula. Every night at bedtime, while he was still at home, I had said to my father, "Good night, sleep well, and wake up nice and fresh tomorrow morning"— the salient words being "and wake up." But once he was in hospital I could no longer say the magic words to him, I lost the power to keep him alive.

"When can I go and see him?" I kept asking.

"Not yet," said my mother, "perhaps on your birthday." She had only one aim at the time: to look after my father, to give him comfort and courage and protect him from the knowledge that he was going to die. She was afraid that if I knew, or saw how ill he looked, I would be unable to hide my feelings from him, and she was probably right.

On the morning of my fourteenth birthday, August 24, 1945, I telephoned my mother at the hospital, expecting to be allowed to visit my father that day. It was all I had been looking forward to. "How's Daddy?" I asked. "Still conscious," she replied. "He bought you a birthday present before his operation. A pair of slippers. You'll find them in a box at the bottom of the wardrobe."

What did she mean, "Still conscious"? She'd never said anything like that before. I didn't care about the present; I wanted to see him. Gloomily, I walked to school. It was a Friday, and our first period was singing. The music unleashed a flood of tears. Miss Starke asked me to sit with her, keeping me back after the class had left, to ask what the trouble was. "My father's ill in hospital…" I said, and choked. I got no further. I dared think no further.

Mr. Abramowitz, my violin teacher, lived in the flat above us with his wife and little daughter, and they had kindly invited me to share their meals. We were about to sit down to supper when there was a knock on the door, and I was sent to answer it. My mother stood there, looking pale and spent. "He's gone," she said. Just those two words.

"Gone? What do you mean 'gone'?" I asked.

"Dead. Your father is dead."

My first thought was, at last his suffering is over. My second thought was, now I can have his penknife. I had coveted this penknife, yet I never ever used or wanted it after that moment. My third thought was, my Daddy is gone, gone forever, and I could not even say goodbye or "I'm sorry"! And the full weight of my loss came crashing down. I threw my arms around Mrs. Abramowitz' neck and wept. Somehow I did not dare go near my mother. She seemed a tragic and holy figure to me, and I kept her at a distance and put her on a pedestal.

My mother went to our flat to rest. I stayed behind, expecting to sit down to the meal already on the table, but of course I could not eat. I followed my mother to our flat, but I went to my own room and lay with my face to the wall, longing for oblivion.

The pain and anguish did not leave me. Every night I dreamed that my father was alive, that it had all been a nightmare. I would imagine seeing him in a crowded street; again and again I thought I saw him. Suddenly I was faced with real existential problems, which had been mere theory to me in the past, and the only person in the world who could answer my questions was dead and gone. I would not, could not, speak of him. Years later, my poor mother told me she had thought I blamed her for his death, when all I'd blamed her for was not warning me. The person I really blamed was myself, for having refused that one time to go for a walk with him, for having judged him without knowing how mortally ill he was. She tried to reassure me that he never held anything against me, that he loved me and was proud of me, and proud, too, of my violin playing, but no words could heal me.

Tante Ilse took the trouble of having a special illuminated manuscript made for me, of the Jewish anniversaries of my father's death for the next fifty years, to show that they did not coincide with the secular date of my birthday. "The child must be able to celebrate her birthday!" she declared, but to me that was cheating, and it was many years before I really appreciated Tante Ilse's kindness or consented once more to acknowledge my birthday.

Chapter Nine

⌒ The Aftermath—after August 1945 ⌒

"Mrs. Schay, be sensible and take Eva out of school. It's time she earned a living and took some of the weight off your shoulders," various acquaintances and clients advised my mother. "I'd be happy to employ her in my office," said Mr. Cahn, who owned a paint factory. But my mother told me she had no intention of taking such advice or kindly meant offers.

"I was just fourteen—same age as you—when I was taken out of school," she told me. She was a bright pupil, and her school had offered her a scholarship to the *Gymnasium*, the high school, insisting that she should continue with her education. "I begged my parents to let me go to the *Gymnasium*, but they wouldn't listen. They thought the scholarship was charity, and they were too proud to accept—never mind how it would affect my life—and that was the end of it!" She'd had to do the clerical work of no less than three men, as they had all been sent off to fight in the Great War. "All my life I've been trying to make up for the education I missed. I can't let that happen to you," she said.

She kept on the accountancy practice, at first with hardly an idea of what she was doing. Most of the clients she had inherited were remarkably loyal. She attended evening classes at the technical college, took extra-mural courses at the University of the Witwatersrand, and slept with the *Government Gazette* under her pillow at night in the hope that she would absorb the tax laws in her sleep... She gained new clients and became so good at her work that they all came utterly to depend on her. But it took a toll on her health and on her social life, and I felt terribly indebted to her. Her interests were in the arts, her passion was literature, and accountancy went against all her natural inclinations. I was in awe of her determination, energy, and success. She discussed her insecurities and her problems with me, and I know I was a support to her; but I could also be headstrong and difficult, so much so that I decided never to have children of my own in case they turned out to be like me.

In addition, without any faith to give a framework or meaning to life, I found the pain of losing my father and the irrevocability of death, unendurable.

"*I'm never going to get married,*" I decided. "*It must be the worst thing in the world to be a widow! And I don't want to have a child, to let it suffer so much pain. I don't ever want to be* reproached with: 'Why did you bring me into the world? Nobody asked me whether I wanted to be born!'"

Some months later, at the end of a fine early-summer's day, my mother and I were washing dishes in the kitchen, when I burst out, "Mommy, tell me, *please* tell me, why are we alive? What's it all for, what is the meaning of life?" I longed for an intellectual answer, such as I would have expected from my father. My mother was a much more instinctive person. "This morning I walked through the park," she said. "I smelled the freshly turned earth and the newly mown grass…the flowers were in bloom, the birds were singing. The sky—the sky was clear, clear blue…just a few puffs of cloud. I thought, '*That's* why I'm here!' Who says there's got to be a purpose? It's a *privilege* to be alive!" At the time her reply gave me no satisfaction. Today, I feel it was the best reply she could have given me.

A few years back, Mutti Kaufmann's younger daughter Illa, a qualified children's nurse, had been asked to go to Cape Town to look after a newborn baby, a little boy called Kenneth, whose mother had died in childbirth. The upshot was that she married the baby's father, Frederick Marcus, whom she soon brought to Johannesburg to meet all her friends. When Illa and Fred heard of my father's death, they immediately invited my mother and me to spend the summer holidays with them in their beautifully situated home in Cape Town, and they treated us with generous hospitality. My mother and I walked in the woods, bathed in the warm Indian Ocean at Muizenberg beach with Illa, Fred, and little Kenneth, and in the cold Atlantic at Sea Point. We visited the harbor and watched the comings and goings of ocean liners and cargo ships. Except for our grief over the loss of my father, it was a marvelous holiday. Fred was an excellent cook and delighted in serving us gourmet food. Only one thing spoiled the visit for me: the lascivious way in which he used to ogle me across the dining room table. I felt threatened and annoyed, and eventually told my mother, who in turn explained how I felt and asked him to watch himself. He told her that he was in love with me and was going to marry me when I was twenty.

"Don't be ridiculous!" said my mother. "In the first place you are already married, and anyway, what makes you think that she's going to be interested in marrying a man so much older than herself?"

After that Fred let me be, and so I began to trust him sufficiently to help him a little in the garden, until he said to me there, "From now on I want you to regard me as your father."

"Nobody can take the place of my father" I said, loathing him for his crass insensitivity. In later years I learned to respect other aspects of his personality a little: his generosity, his intellect, and his love of music.

I wrapped my life around my mother. When I served a meal I would always give her the choicest portions, not because I was good, but because I was afraid of losing her too and afraid of having to reproach myself yet again. I turned down all weekend invitations from my school friends, however tempting they were, so that my mother would not be alone. In all my high school years I only remember going to one party, when I was just sixteen, given by my friend Ella. I wore a navy taffeta dress with a flared skirt, fitted bodice, puffed sleeves, and sweetheart neckline, together with a coral-colored suede belt, a coral necklace—the one that had been given to me on our journey from Italy—and matching lipstick, my first ever. I coiled my black plaits around my head and looked in the mirror; my gray-green eyes looked back at me, and I was pleased with the effect. My mother and Ella's mother said I looked stunning, but the only person to ask me to dance was an "old man" of twenty.

Sometimes on impulse my mother and I would take a walk to Yeoville and visit Tante Ilse, who invariably said, "I was *just* thinking of you. Truly! It must be telepathy. I *knew* you would come!" She almost always had a dish full of luscious, slightly brown, soft-centered meringues floating in whipped cream, which she knew I relished, ready to serve us with coffee. Then we would settle down to a game of rummy, which she had taught us, and there was always joking and laughter. She was good company, funny, and kind.

However busy my mother was, she always found time for our weekly visits to the public library in the center of town. I felt more relaxed there than anywhere else. As a special treat on our way home, she would sometimes take me to the Waldorf Café, where we would have supper of the most delicious souffléed Welsh rarebit I have ever tasted.

The library was also my favorite place at school. I was invited to join a small bookbinding group before morning assembly, rebinding book covers that had become worn. I liked the feeling of peacefulness in the library, the smell of the leather bindings, and the friendly, relaxed atmosphere among us girls before school began. On the whole I did not feel all that relaxed with my peers at school, and I remember the astonishment I felt when Miss Fenwick, our Afrikaans mistress, said: "Eva, yesterday when I passed this classroom, I saw you chasing another girl around the class with a ruler and laughing! Why can't you be like that when I'm here? Why are you always so quiet? Don't you like me?" I was astounded on two counts: that I had ever been so much at ease with my classmates as to have done something so spontaneous and carefree, and that instead of reprimanding me, Miss Fenwick was actually encouraging a bit of unruliness from me. On school Open Day, when parents were invited to meet the staff, I was surprised how many of them said, "Mrs. Schay, your daughter is a pleasure to teach." It genuinely was news to me.

While I was so seemingly inept at my violin lessons, at school I was always considered outstandingly musical. I was invited to sing in the descant choir almost as soon as I entered high school. This meant that I had the privilege of sitting up in the gallery every morning at assembly, looking down at the majority of the girls and the teachers, seeing all, yet not being seen. I loved the singing and had no problem with the hymns, as they were ecumenical and tactfully chosen with—I imagine—the minority of Jewish girls in mind. In our weekly music classes I sailed through the aural tests, to the astonishment of my classmates. "Never mind, she can't help it!" Miss Starke, our music mistress said, to comfort them.

My mother's chief form of relaxation, apart from reading, was going to the cinema. "I wish you'd come to the bioscope with me," she said, "I really need it for relaxation. When I'm watching a film I forget all the sadness and strain in my life. All the hard work and worries of the past week just disappear. Do you good, too. Why don't you come?"

I struck a deal with her. If there was a film I particularly wanted to see, I would come. Otherwise I'd walk with her to the Bijou—the cinema closest to where we lived and the one she frequented most often—then go home to practice the violin, paint, or do my homework, returning to collect her when the film was over. We would walk through Joubert Park, past the Noord Street entrance to the railway station—cautiously, as it had a reputation for violence and thuggery—past the African street vendors, selling bright-yellow, boiled *mealie* cobs straight from their cauldrons, and turn right into Plein Street. This was the nearest street in town, and viola! there was the little Bijou cinema. When I did join her, I could see for myself just how my mother could lose herself entirely in whatever was showing on the screen. If it happened to be a comedy, how she would laugh. It was the most infectious laughter I ever came across. I have seen her set whole rows of audience off, rocking with laughter.

When eventually the British film of Bernard Shaw's *Pygmalion*, starring Wendy Hiller and Leslie Howard, came to Johannesburg, she was enchanted. "This you *must* see," she declared. "I just know you'll enjoy it—and I'm coming with you—I've got to see it again!" So we went together.

"Mom," I said, "Do you realize I'm going to have to see that film all over again! You were laughing so much, I didn't hear a single one of the funny lines. I doubt anyone else did either!" In fact, I saw it three times.

As soon as it became possible after the war was over, my mother took out South African citizenship, and I, being a minor, automatically became naturalized with her. We were profoundly grateful that my father had lived to see the end of the war. However, after the war, we began to see horrifying pictures of dead and living skeletons at Belsen and to hear of the appalling extermination camps, including the gas chambers at Auschwitz. It was beyond anything we could have imagined.

My mother heard from her closest friend, Gretl Gideon, who had lived in Switzerland throughout the war. From infancy they had been next door neighbors in Laupheim, and a close friendship had existed between the two families. Gretl had, via the Red Cross, kept up a correspondence with my mother's parents and also with my mother's younger sister, Selma. I have found two increasingly desperate telegrams from my grandfather to my parents' "fish restaurant" address, also through the Red Cross, saying how long it was

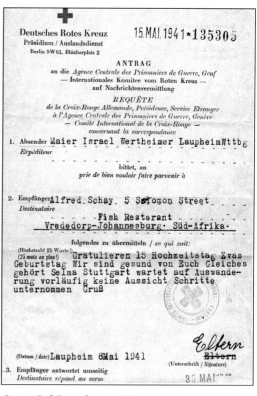

German Red Cross telegram, 1941.

taking to get permission for Selma to leave Germany. She never made it. The letters to Gretl were at first from a Jewish Old People's Home—in fact, the house that been the rabbi's house for generations, which the Nazis had requisitioned for this purpose—from 1940 to 1942. My grandparents, together with all the other Jewish Laupheimers of their generation, had been herded into it. After this, they were taken to Theresienstadt, the "model" concentration camp, and Selma chose to go with them, to care for them. She sent only postcards, written in blunt pencil. Never a word of complaint, just news of friends who were sharing their fate, anxious enquiries after the rest of us scattered around the world, and profuse thanks for any news and the few food parcels that they had received. In October 1943, she wrote simply, interspersed with minor news items, "My parents have died." In March 1944 she was on her way to Auschwitz, never to be heard of again.

My grandparents in forced old people's home, 1940. My grandmother wearing white collar, seated second from the right.

Gretl sent copies of the letters to my mother. My father was no longer there to support her, and she had to bear the news without him. In her distress she destroyed them all. Later Gretl sent her the originals, and although she tried to protect me by hiding them, I eventually found them. I found some of the script too difficult to read, but I could read the "address of sender" quite clearly. Puzzled, I asked my mother why both my grandmother, whose name was Lina, and her daughter, my aunt Selma, had the same second name of "Sara"—for I knew it was not done in Jewish families, to name a child after a living parent. I was also surprised that my grandfather, Meier, had a second name of "Israel."

"All Jewish women were made to attach the name 'Sara,' and the men, 'Israel,' to their names, so that they could easily be identified as Jews," she told me. "It was like having to wear armbands with a yellow Star of David on them. It was meant to be shameful, nothing was considered lower than being a Jew, only fit to be exterminated," she said bitterly.

I noticed that all the letters had been censored, the envelopes taped together with the word *GEOEFFNET*, opened, stamped brutally across, in large, bold letters. The postcards from Theresiensadt were stamped across with the words, in German: "Reply only on open postcard in German language." My blood boiled at all these indignities heaped so senselessly on these defenseless people. It was so sad, sad, sad.

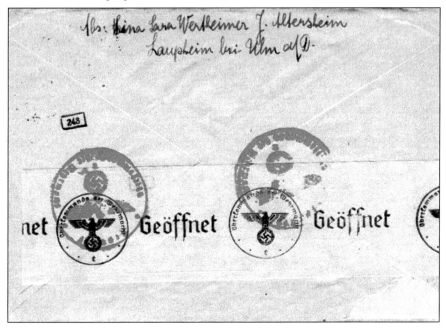

Back of my grandmother's envelope, 1941.

My mother said, "I feel ashamed for what the Germans have done. Can you understand that? *I* feel ashamed for *them*!" And she quoted from the poet Heine, also of Jewish blood: *"Ich hatte einst ein schönes Vaterland*, I once had a beautiful fatherland." No more. Never again.

My mother's two brothers, as well as two of her closest cousins, had emigrated to Palestine before the war, as had my father's beloved half-sister. They and their families suffered incredible hardship there, but at least they were relatively safe, living where they wanted to live. They, as well as my parents, had tried desperately to rescue my grandparents and Aunt Selma from Germany, but to no avail. It was to be many years before we surviving members of the family met again.

Late in 1945, after the war with Japan came to its horrifying end with the atomic bombs over Hiroshima and Nagasaki, my mother had news from the Philippines, which had been occupied by the Japanese.

"At least your father was spared this," she remarked sadly.

Both my father's father and his brother Rudi had died of meningitis, not having been able to get the penicillin that might have saved them, during the Japanese occupation. Tante Ilse's twin sons, Fritz and Joachim, had been administering first aid during a bombing raid when a bomb killed Fritz outright. Two years later, I met Joachim for the first time, when he visited his mother in Johannesburg, and over the years we became close friends.

After a distance of several years he was able to talk to me about that time. "I've never got over my brother's death," he said, "He was killed in the very act of giving first aid. I still see it happening in front of my eyes, and I have nightmares about it every night." He told me, too, of the suffering and fear during the Japanese occupation, and of my cousin Ruben, Rudi's son, who joined the guerrillas until the American army liberated the Philippines and he was old enough to join the regular army. And he told me about my uncle Rudi, what an intelligent and good person he was, and how I would have loved him had I known him.

Joachim was one of the kindest, most charming, and funniest, people I ever knew. He helped everybody he could, much as a result of his wartime experiences. After the war he took my grandmother—my father and Rudi's stepmother, their real mother having died when they were little boys—to the United States and settled her in a pleasant retirement home in Newark, New Jersey, where I visited her nineteen years later, in 1964. On that first visit to the United States I also met my cousin Ruben, Rudi's son, for the first time since our emigration in 1933, and my cousin Albert, who had recited a poem for my fifth birthday, in my maternal grandparents' home in Germany in 1936.

Chapter Ten

⚘ RUTH—1941 TO 1953 ⚘

I thought I could guard against future occasion for remorse. Vain hope.

To tell my story about Ruth I must go back briefly to the early 1940s, after our move to Hillbrow. She was considered the dunce of our class in the prep school. I came to know her better as a result of the move, for she lived in a block of flats just two streets away from us. She was a fairly plump little girl, with short, straight, mouse-colored hair and pretty features. She was more than a year younger than I. We used to visit each other and walk to school together, sometimes in the company of Trudy or Isabel.

Ruth's mother had died in childbirth, and her father had vowed always to remain faithful to her memory. He told my mother that in order to avoid temptation he had never engaged a young nurse to look after Ruth when she was a baby or to help bring her up. When I was old enough to think about this it seemed symbolic to me that he stood and walked always with his hands clasped firmly behind his back.

I was struck by the contrast between their flat and ours. My mother had made attractive curtains and matching bedspreads, with piping around the edges to give them a tailored appearance, and matching bedrolls, into which we stuffed quilts and pillows each morning. This turned the simple divan beds into smart sofas for daytime use. She was a real homemaker, and had a knack of turning the simplest materials into cheerful and pleasant objects. She even made me a dressing table out of two orange boxes, painted and nailed together, with a curtain in front and a mirror above.

Ruth's flat was full of dark, heavy, expensive furniture, which her father had managed to bring from Germany, and thick curtains that let in hardly any light. A grumpy old aunt of his lived with them and kept house. I never saw her smile, and her presence seemed to add to the gloom of their home. His sister, Ruth's aunt, lived on her own in the same block of flats.

Ruth's father was a devout Orthodox Jew, who attended the Wolmarans Street Synagogue regularly and kept a strictly kosher home. It seemed to us that he was concerned only with the bare bones of Jewish law, without the spirit of compassion and loving-kindness that runs through Judaism. His sister, however, was an avowed atheist and tried to influence Ruth against everything her father taught her. Although I was brought up without religion, I thought this disloyalty outrageous. Ruth felt torn and confused. Her aunt had an abrasive personality, beside which the old great-aunt seemed almost kind. However, I never saw any of them give Ruth a hug or a smile or softly stroke her as my mother used to do to me. Nor did she have any pictures to brighten up her life, and hardly any books other than schoolbooks or those I lent her. Despite my irreligious background, Mr. Franck seemed to consider me a "good influence."

"Why do you let them think you're stupid at school?" I asked her, "I know perfectly well you're not!"

"It suits me," she said cunningly, "that way the teachers don't expect anything of me. I don't have to work so hard."

At the end of our prep school years, a girl I hardly knew called Maureen tied with me at the top of the class. She had fallen out with her closest schoolfriends, and she took me home one day after school and made me swear that I would always be her friend. We didn't seem to have much in common, and I had misgivings, but I was too polite to refuse. As it turned out, Maureen proved to be a loyal and devoted friend throughout our high school years, defending me against accusations of "madness" by some of our classmates because they could not make me out at all. We shared teenage anguish and reflections, and also fun.

When Ruth discovered I had a new friend, she was beside herself with jealousy. She could put up with Ella and Sarah because they had been in the picture all along. But Maureen? "How can you do this to me?" she shouted. "You're *my* friend, not hers! Now you won't have time to come and see me anymore! I won't let you be her friend!"

Instead of reassuring her that there was no threat to my friendship with her, I reacted angrily. "How dare you tell me who I can be friends with! How dare you interfere!" And we had a terrible row.

The following morning I did not walk to school with her. Isabel said to me: "Ruth says the row you had yesterday will blow over in no time!"

If only she hadn't said it. If only I had not been so full of false pride. I thought: *"Oh does she indeed? I'll show her!"* And I refused to speak to Ruth for the next five years and more.

Mr. Franck implored my mother to persuade me to relent. My mother in turn implored me. On several occasions I was on the verge of making it up with Ruth, but my mother *would* bring the subject up just at the crucial moment, and I simply couldn't do it.

Poor, lonely Ruth, whose only fault was to be too fond of me, and a little too possessive. At least Ella and Sarah took pity on her and befriended her. They tried to bring us together, but I would not relent. I was insufferable. When my father died, they brought her to me in the school playground—we were no longer in the same class—and Ruth nervously rattled off: "I just wanted to say: I'm sorry your father died."

I was taken by surprise and answered, "It's alright," which it wasn't, and she vanished as quickly as she had come.

And so our years in high school went by, and after school I went to university. My mother heard from Mr. Franck that Ruth had suffered a nervous breakdown and was at Tara, a hospital for nervous complaints. I was shocked, and after Ruth came home, I finally went to see her. We had a long and serious conversation, the first serious conversation we'd ever had.

"All my life," she told me, "my father's stopped me from doing what I wanted. Do you remember that time when we were children and your mother offered to take me along to the opera with you? There was a visiting opera company here—remember? My father said, 'No.'"

"Yes, I remember—he said that if you were allowed to enjoy everything then, there'd be nothing left for you to enjoy when you grew up!"

"So I was never allowed to enjoy anything, and now it's too late!"

"What do you mean, too late?" I asked.

"When I left school there was only one thing I wanted to do. I wanted to be a nurse. My father wouldn't let me, because it would've meant working on Saturdays."

"But didn't he realize that saving a human life is more important than anything else in Judaism?" I replied. "And you'd have been saving lives as a nurse."

"All he cared about was that I shouldn't work on the Sabbath. And maybe he just didn't want me to be happy! So he found me a job as a clerk in the office of a friend of his. You've no idea how I hated it! Being cooped up in a tiny office, when all the time I wanted to be a nurse. Honestly Eva, I just couldn't stand it! And so, I landed at Tara. And now I'm back here, still living under my father's roof, and the awful thing is—I now realize how much I hate him. I *hate* him and can't get away."

Not one word of reproach for all the years I had withheld my friendship. And I hadn't the courage to bring it up myself and ask for her forgiveness.

I was in England when I received a letter from my mother telling me that Ruth had suffered another breakdown and had been sent to the mental hospital in Pretoria. I wrote her a long letter. After she came out of hospital she happened to meet my mother. She told her about my letter and how she treasured it, and took it out of her handbag to show that she kept it always with her.

And then, my mother wrote again: Ruth had been admitted to the hospital for the last time. She was given electric shock treatment, which in those days was a much more brutal affair than now, when techniques have been greatly refined.

One day Mr. Franck told my mother that Ruth had telephoned him from the hospital. "Take me away from here!" she had begged him. "They're killing me!"

"What shall I do?" he asked my mother.

"If that were my daughter I would fetch her straight away!" she said.

But Mr. Franck had an unquestioning belief in authority. When Ruth was at school, the teacher always "knew best." Now he was convinced the doctors "knew best." He did not answer Ruth's call for help.

After one more shock treatment, Ruth was dead. An embolism in her lungs, he was told. I was filled with horror at the news and overcome by sadness and regret.

None of Ruth's friends spoke to her father. He told my mother that he could not understand why they did not offer him their condolences. They told her that they considered him to be a murderer.

And in my heart I wondered how much of a murderer I had been, how much my rejection had added to the unbearable stresses in her short life. Even now after all these years I long to ask for her forgiveness.

She was not yet twenty when she died.

Chapter Eleven

GROWING UP—1947 TO 1949

"Hey, that's bloody good—where did you learn to paint like that?" A tall honey-blond man suddenly stood over me as I was trying to capture in watercolor the landscape at Ruigtevlei, on the beautiful Garden Route in the Cape Province, where I was on holiday with my mother. I made some polite reply, but unfazed by the presence of the stranger, I continued to paint. In contrast to my inhibitions about letting others hear me play the violin, which had become tied in my mind to so many knotty problems, drawing and painting were so natural to me that nothing disturbed my concentration, and I remained unself-conscious and relaxed.

Lake Pleasant Private Hotel was situated by a brackish lake—part sea water, part fresh water—called Ruigtevlei, and my mother and I had been attracted by the advertisement promising beautiful scenery, proximity to the beach, and freshly caught fish from the lake. Every evening we had ordered "Selected Fish" from the menu—and every evening it had turned out to consist of nothing but tinned pilchards.

That evening we were seated at the same table as the tall blond man, Gordon Vorster, and his bride, Yvonne. Although they were on honeymoon they didn't seem to mind sharing a table with us, and the only fresh fish we ever had was what Gordon caught in the lake and asked the chef to cook for us. We were surprised that they chose to spend so much time with us, taking us rowing on the lake, driving us down to the beach to bathe, and taking us for a drive to wonderful Knysna Forest. We were even more surprised that the friendship continued after our return to Johannesburg. I was fifteen and they were to play an important role in my growing up years.

Gordon had recently been demobbed from the army, where he had started to paint, and was at the beginning of a great career as an artist. His work became highly prized in South Africa, and I remember how proud he was when he was first invited, some years later, to exhibit at the Venice Biennale, the international exhibition of contemporary art held in Venice every two years

They adored my mother, who in their Afrikaans fashion they called "Aunty"; they were drawn to her European culture, and they loved her cooking. Gordon gave her several of his paintings, which are still in my possession; the first was inspired by one of my father's Mallorcan photographs. A multi-talented man, Gordon became artistic director at Killarney

Film Studios in Johannesburg, and he also did some acting. He once gave me a job playing solo violin for an advertising film to be shown in Rhodesia.

Tall and well built, he had honey-colored, curly hair, light-blue eyes, a snub nose, and a square chin; later he grew a beard. Yvonne was blond and blue-eyed, gentle, and sweet. I treasured their friendship. On weekends they frequently took my mother and me on country outings. Later, whenever I played in public they always supported me. But above all, Gordon encouraged my drawing and painting and lent me many art books, showing the work of important contemporary artists. When it became clear that I was set on a career in music, he tried his best to persuade me to become a painter instead.

"Don't you know we *all* want to be violinists?" he asked. He shared a studio at the time with several other painters. "You should see us," he said. "Every now and then one of us steps forward and makes as if

My father's Mallorcan photo that inspired painting by Gordon Vorster in 1947.

he's playing the violin," and he gestured accordingly. "But we do what we're meant to do— paint!"

I laughed. "You're making it up Gordon!"

"No, honestly, we're all crazy like that!"

"But that's just it—I don't want to end up a frustrated violinist like all of you!" I parried.

It was as if my life depended on my becoming a violinist, even if it was the most difficult choice. I thought I should die otherwise.

Another couple who gave me unstinting moral support were Walter and Marion Rothgiesser. Marion worked as secretary for a firm of interior decorators who were my mother's clients. Periodically, Marion and my mother's work threw them together, and they became friends. Walter, her husband, was at the time a taxi driver. He was one of the kindest men I ever knew. By dint of hard work and determination they had made a good life for themselves in Johannesburg. Both had been members of the Communist Party in Germany. They had been lovers before the Nazis had imprisoned them, separately. After three years, Walter was miraculously released and able to join his brother who was already living in South Africa. Marion, a strikingly attractive woman, had meanwhile given birth to the child of another man, in prison. She was allowed to keep it for three months, after which time the prison authorities would automatically have given it away for adoption had not her mother—who had kept her distance from Marion's political involvement—come to the rescue and taken the baby. Marion also was eventually released from prison, and she wrote to Walter asking if she might join him in South Africa, with a child who was not his. Without hesitation Walter said he would adopt the baby as his own, and they were married. He doted on both Marion and Hazel, his adopted daughter. They subsequently had another daughter together named Jeanette, whom we knew as Netty.

I loved going to their house in Orange Grove. It had a living room the width of the entire house, with French windows giving on to the back garden and a porch where we would sit having coffee and chatting. The living room walls were of natural brick, lined with bookshelves. The fine wooden furniture was modern, with uncluttered lines; there were handmade rugs, beautiful handmade pottery jugs and bowls, and best of all, a radiogram and a large collection of records. I was let loose on the records and spent hours listening greedily to music while the "grownups" sat outside talking. Oh, the joy of discovery. It was Paradise. I particularly remember listening, in ecstasy, to Beethoven's *Emperor* Concerto. As evening drew in everybody came indoors, and Marion produced delicious open sandwiches and more coffee. Conversation was always interesting and animated, and I never wanted to leave. When they visited us, they always encouraged me to play to them. I had a habit of sabotaging my own performances, but they had endless patience and compassion for my psychological hang-ups, as well as belief in my talent. They simply urged me to play again, until I stopped stumbling and gave them a performance.

It was at their home that my mother and I met the distinguished pianist, Bruno Raikin, whose playing we had often heard and admired in the Johannesburg City Hall. He was supposed to be giving Hazel a piano lesson but was kicking a football around in the garden with her instead. My mother took the opportunity of consulting him about my obsession with becoming a professional violinist, against the advice of my violin teacher.

"Anybody who wants to be a musician as passionately as she does *must* have talent!" he declared. "Don't stand in her way." I was to be forever grateful to him for those words. Little did we suspect that fourteen years later he and I would form a sonata partnership that was to last for nearly forty years.

Bruno left South Africa in 1948, and he settled in London.

In January 1948, my mother and I went on holiday to Hermanus in the Cape Province, where the sea hurled itself against enormous, rugged rocks, producing huge white plumes of spray. It was a glorious sight.

I kept a diary, and I wrote:

> We went to the beach and found ourselves a shady spot under some rocks. The
> bathing today was superb—large waves, which knocked us down, helpless. Some-

one had a pet penguin, a darling creature! It swam over the smaller waves and then tottered on to the beach like an old man. Then it crept under a baby's pram for shelter from the sun. It was quite tame and let itself be patted and petted by the little children.

After lunch my mother rested, and I would take my sketchbook down to the rocks and try to catch the wonderful seascape in watercolor and charcoal.

My head was filled with romantic notions. On our last day there, I wrote in my diary:

> I remembered that I had been longing, ever since we came to Hermanus and saw the rocks by the sea at high tide, to play my violin on these rocks, to the sound of the sea. I made up my mind to do so now, as it would be my last chance. It *was* high tide, and I've never ever seen such a beautiful sea. The spray was higher than the highest rocks—magnificent! I was trembling with excitement as I took out my violin, and then—how could fate be so spiteful?—my bow snapped, and nothing I could do would tighten the hairs. I tried and tried to fix it, but I couldn't. Then my violin strings started breaking in that humidity, first the E, then the A. The only thing to do was to pack up as quickly as possible, before any more harm was done!

1948 was my second to last year in high school, and I won a battle with our headmistress to be allowed to drop maths, at which I was hopeless—despite, or because of, the fact that both my parents were wizards at maths—and take music for matric instead. Therefore, when Abramowitz went away on tour for three months with a West End musical, he felt I should not be left without a violin teacher for so long, and passed me on to his old colleague, Harold Ketèlby, for the time being.

Ketèlby had retired from Charles Manning's band and was an experienced teacher. I used to love going to his house in the pleasant suburb of Parktown. Unlike Abramowitz, he did not stand over me during lessons, but sat at a distance, letting me play without interruption. He did not bully me as Abramowitz did, and yet he was far more demanding. He made me play a new study from memory each week, as well as learn Bach's E Major Concerto, which I adored, and Kreisler's *Praeludium and Allegro*. He gave me motivation and encouragement and made me feel I could achieve anything with hard work. But Abramowitz returned, and stupidly, I felt honor-bound to return to him.

I played a trick on him on April Fool's Day. We used to have occasional earth tremors in Johannesburg, which could be quite alarming. The whole building would shake, pictures rocked on the wall, and crockery rattled in the kitchen. It was said that explosions in the gold mines surrounding Johannesburg, the largest of which was Crown Mines, caused these tremors. On April 1, I telephoned Abramowitz, put on a false voice, and said, "This is Crown Mines speaking. I'm ringing to let you know that we have to do some major dynamiting in half an hour's time. There will be a tremendous explosion, and I've been ordered to warn people to vacate their homes. Thank you," and put down the receiver. I felt sure that however hard I had tried to disguise it, he would recognize my voice. The next day he told us of the terrible fright he'd had. He had torn down to the caretaker's flat to tell her of the warning. She had laughed and said, "Somebody's having you on," but he didn't believe her.

I had sounded too convincing. When I confessed that it was I who had made that phone call, he at first didn't want to believe me, describing this pert young woman's voice that was quite unlike mine. When I finally convinced him, he was not amused.

That year Abramowitz introduced me to Joseph Trauneck, who eight years earlier had conducted the first concert I had ever attended, and I joined the amateur Johannesburg Symphony Orchestra, for "grown up" orchestral experience. Rehearsals took place every Monday evening. Trauneck, another émigré from Germany who, though not Jewish, had made common cause with us Jewish refugees, was made in the same mold as Abramowitz, incessantly shouting at the orchestra, losing his temper, sneering, stamping his feet. One Monday evening his foot went right through the rostrum, to everybody's delight. The orchestra laughed, and he looked embarrassed, unable to apply his customary sarcasm. Yet he had his good points: He took us to several African townships to give concerts, which were enormously appreciated, and he inaugurated a series of Concerto Festivals, giving young music students, who had to pass auditions to an independent panel, the opportunity to play concertos to a large public audience in the University Great Hall. Later I, too, participated as soloist.

It was time to give up playing in the children's orchestra at the Teachers' Training College. When I told Miss Boxall, who conducted the orchestra, she gave me half a dozen children to teach on Saturday mornings while the orchestra was rehearsing, and a room to teach them in. The college was situated in Braamfontein, a rather poor residential area, and none of the children's parents could afford the normal fees for lessons, so I taught them for very little. I myself had been given lessons at reduced fees, and I was glad for the opportunity to pay something back; all the same, I was earning money for the first time. And so, at age sixteen, my teaching career began. Of all the children, one stands out in my memory: a little freckle-faced, carrot-haired boy called Errol. He was the least gifted, and I became frustrated and shouted at him the way Abramowitz shouted at me; I knew no other way, until my lessons with Ketèlby. Errol was such a good-natured little boy; he never seemed to hold it against me. Eventually I realized that my shouting only served to confuse him; that patience, gentleness, and encouragement were preferable teaching aids, and I felt ashamed. I really loved that child and sketched his portrait, so that I should never forget his face.

Trauneck went abroad for several months, later in 1948. The young Ernest Fleischman conducted our first concert after his departure. He was a gifted and vibrant conductor, and I have never forgotten how thrilling it was to play Smetana's *Vltava* under his baton. I was disappointed to learn that he was studying accountancy and not aiming to be a professional conductor, and I surmised that perhaps he, too, had been got at by well meaning advisors to choose a profession that was remunerative and safe, rather than to risk becoming a musician. However, he seemed to have found a way to combine both skills, for he later became the extremely successful manager of the London Symphony Orchestra, and later still, of the Los Angeles Symphony Orchestra.

After that first concert, a young Afrikaans conductor named Anton Hartman took over until Trauneck's return. On November 1 of that year we gave a concert in Alexandra Township on the outskirts of Johannesburg. It was enormously appreciated by the African inhabitants. They were not allowed to attend regular concerts at the Johannesburg City Hall, and Trauneck, who had organized the concert, did all he could under the circumstances to redress the situation. I was shocked at the foul-smelling, open sewers, and the general poverty of the township, but impressed by the eager attention of our audience.

Hartman gave me a lift to and from Alexandra Township, together with two of our girl instrumentalists and a professional timpanist from the SABC Symphony Orchestra, who had been engaged to help boost the orchestra. On the way back, we had a slight accident involving another car, the driver of which was unnecessarily rude to Hartman. The timpanist said, "What do you expect, she's Jewish!"

I flared up. "So what! I'm Jewish too!" but he seemed not to hear.

Both cars drove to the nearest police station to report the accident. While Hartman was in the police station, Ratface—I did not know his name and I thought his face looked ratlike—went on: "You know what these Jews are!"

When we arrived at Geraldine Court I got out of the car, thanked Hartman politely, and then turned on Ratface. "As for you," I said, "I hope I never have to see you again!" Invective streamed out of me. "How do you think Goebbels was able to convince people it was alright to murder millions of Jews? Because for years they'd been listening to prejudiced, unthinking people like you! The war's hardly over, yet you can still talk like this!" I slammed the door and walked away. It was only one of many incidents of anti-Semitism that I met, and I boiled over every time, from fear and rage. Ten years later I discovered that I had not spoken in vain.

The newly formed Johannesburg City Orchestra, consisting mainly of post-war immigrants of a high professional standard, from France, Holland, and Belgium, gave a symphony concert at our school, an unprecedented event. What happened after the concert was equally memorable. The young principal double bass player, a blond Adonis called Willem van der Klaauw, was the most glamorous and handsome man any of us had ever seen. The whole school, all six hundred girls, mobbed him as the orchestra tried to leave the school, and prevented him from getting on to the orchestra bus for as long as they could. I should say five hundred and ninety-nine girls, for I disdained to be one of the crowd. Besides, I had a passionate crush on our games mistress, and no mere man was going to turn my head. Again, ten years later I had reason to remember that day.

We had a history lesson immediately after the bus left, and to my surprise, our history teacher admitted that she felt just as attracted to the double bass player as we girls were, but the next day at assembly our headmistress scolded us roundly for our "display of bad manners."

Miss Starke taught our small group studying music for matric, the theory, harmony, form, and history of Western music. Of the five in our group—all studying piano except for me—I remember only Myra Tannenbaum, who sometimes took me to her home in one of the wealthier suburbs of Johannesburg for lunch, and played me gramophone records of Kreisler, Heifetz, Menuhin, and Szigeti, violin playing which filled me with admiration and delight. Then she made me sing Schubert lieder to her piano accompaniment. Those afternoons were a wonderful treat for me, a joy to have a friend with whom at last to share the passion for music.

Despite the difficulties of Schubert accompaniments, she considered her piano playing not advanced enough to play sonatas with me, and apart from a middle-aged amateur-pianist acquaintance of my mother's—of very limited ability—I had no pianist to work with until my matriculation year. Then I was introduced to a university student whom I had heard perform Beethoven's Second Piano Concerto at a Concerto Festival. Her name was Shora Sherman, and she was kind enough to work through all my twenty-four matric pieces with me at regular weekly rehearsals throughout the year. Miss Boxall, conductor of the children's orchestra I had played in, accompanied me for the actual examination, which took place at the Teachers' Training College. Miss Starke heard me play before the examination and gave me much praise and encouragement.

However, Abramowitz said, "You'd better give up this silly idea of becoming a professional violinist. It's no career for a woman. Anyway you're not strong enough! You haven't got the stamina. And you're much more gifted at art. Why don't you become a commercial artist?"

"I'm not going to become a commercial *anything*!" I declared. The more he opposed me, the more determined I became.

He then tackled my mother. "I'm sure you're too sensible to agree to this nonsense!" he said. "Women are terribly discriminated against in the musical profession. She should learn how to earn a decent living and be a help to you."

My father was no longer alive, and my mother didn't know which way to turn. Then he tackled my mother's friends. "For goodness' sake, persuade her not to let Eva take up music as a profession. Let her keep it as a hobby," a remark I heard more than once, and which made me see red. Looking back now I think perhaps his concern was genuine, but at the time I saw his attitude as one of treachery and jealousy; jealousy for my youthful enthusiasm and for having a life of music still ahead of me, while his was over.

I remember with gratitude how on cold winter days he always took my hands in his, one at a time, and rubbed them briskly until they were warm, before I began to play. I remember the many complimentary tickets for concerts he obtained for me, which made me wild with joy, and an outing to the zoo he treated me to, with his wife and little daughter, Joanie. After a day's fishing on the Vaal River, his favorite pastime, his musical voice would ring out outside our flat announcing the carp he was bringing my mother from the day's catch. Above all, I remember the moral support he gave us when my father died. He was a good friend and neighbor, and I remember him with affection, yet whenever the opportunity arose, he lost no time in saying something to undermine my violin playing, even after I had stopped having lessons with him, and always with devastating effect. He was the only one of our neighbors who ever complained that my practicing disturbed him.

For many years I was unable to forgive the damage he inflicted on my self-esteem. Despite my determination to overcome his negative influence, it bit deep. When I see young violinists perform today, how calm, poised, and focused they are, I think how their teachers must have nurtured them, and wish he could have done the same for me. I tried desperately to impress him, until I finally realized that he would never be impressed—not, at least, until many years later, when I no longer cared, and it no longer mattered.

I was incredibly naïve. There was a new, dynamic conductor in Cape Town, a Spaniard, Enrique Jorda. I wrote to him during my second to last year at school, explaining my circumstances: that I needed to earn a living and aimed to be a professional violinist. I asked whether he would give me an audition to play in the Cape Town Symphony Orchestra after I finished school. He invited me to play to him during the Christmas holidays. My mother came with me and waited anxiously outside. As soon as I stopped playing he said, "Coffee?" and I knew bad news was coming.

"How many hours a day do you practice?" he asked. With matriculation exams ahead at the end of the following year, I said I was only managing about half an hour a day.

"At your age youngsters in Europe are practicing five to six hours a day!" he said. "My advice to you is to practice really hard this coming year—five or six hours *every* day. Come and play to me again in a year's time, and then I'll have a clearer idea of what you can do."

He couldn't have been kinder, but I felt crushed, defeated. I'd had no idea how far I fell short of the required standard. It seemed there was no hope.

My mother came to the rescue. She was not going to leave me in such despair. "Come!" she said, "we're going to take a bus to the College of Music!" She winkled out the principal, the formidable Dr. Eric Chisholm, and asked what chance there was of my being accepted there as a student after my matriculation. He sought out an accompanist and auditioned me straight away.

"Your daughter is very talented," he declared. "We'd be happy to accept her as a student, and I can already guarantee her a scholarship."

What an unexpected turn of events, to be so readily accepted after my terrible failure. I have always been grateful to my mother for what she did for me that day. To have the prospect of studying music in such glorious surroundings and to be together with other music students: here was Life at last.

Part Three

STUDENT YEARS

Chapter Twelve

Pierre was a tall, handsome man with a head of rich brown hair and brown eyes, immensely charming, and with a refreshing breadth of vision. He was exactly twice my age, extremely happily married, and I adored him.

For after all, I did not go to Cape Town. It was said that I could find a better violin teacher in Johannesburg. I announced to Abramowitz that, come what may, I was going to study music. "I know you disapprove," I told him, "and I wouldn't dream of asking you to compromise your principles, so I shall have to find another teacher."

To my surprise, he became helpful and sat down with me to discuss the possible alternatives. Between us we decided on the Belgian violinist, Pierre De Groote. He was one of the musicians who had come from Europe after the war to form the Johannesburg City Orchestra, and he led a string quartet whose excellence had taken Johannesburg musical life by storm. Apart from their superb performances of the classical repertoire, they were actively involved in bring-

Pierre De Groote.

ing contemporary music, including works by Darius Milhaud, Béla Bartók's six String Quartets, and Olivier Messiaen's *Quartet for the End of Time*, to a conservative audience, with remarkable success.

I was his first pupil in Johannesburg. To begin with, he came to our flat to teach me, driving his tiny Fiat Topolino, which he named Fifi. Abramowitz insisted on speaking to him alone before my first lesson on October 21, 1949, so I took Pierre up to his flat and introduced them, leaving them to it. Both men were great talkers. When Pierre returned to our flat all he said, dryly, was: "He won."

Abramowitz was always "Mr. Abramowitz" to me, but De Groote soon became "Pierre," thanks to the informality of his English wife, Joyce.

Pierre gave me my last few lessons before my practical music examination for matric, because Abramowitz was again away on tour. I passed with Distinction, the first Music Distinction ever in our school, which caused some excitement. He opened up a great new musical world for me. It amazes me now, but all this time I had been playing on a factory-made violin. Fortunately for me, Pierre had a Giovanni Battista Grancino (late seventeenth to early eighteenth century), a "lady's size" violin, which was of no use to him, and which he sold to me very cheaply. It was badly cracked but had been well repaired. Above all it had a sweet tone, encouraging me to produce as good a sound as I possibly could, and I loved it.

"It really is a shame," said Pierre, "that someone with your talent is so isolated. You should be studying in Europe. You'd have other violin students to compete with, and you'd hear world class performances. You're missing so much of student life and musical stimulation."

I felt I had an enormous amount of catching up to do and wanted to work exclusively at the violin, but Pierre said, "Go to University and broaden your horizon, I beg you; don't end up like most of my colleagues in the orchestra. They have nothing but violins and motor cars to talk about."

The question was settled when I was awarded a scholarship by the Chamber of Mines, for study at the University of the Witwatersrand, commonly known as "Wits," where I enrolled for a Bachelor of Music degree.

Matriculation results were published in the national press and when in the lift I met our GP, Dr. Lester, who lived at Geraldine Court, he congratulated me on my First Class pass. "I assume you'll be enrolling at Medical School," he said. I answered no, I was going to study music, and he was enraged. "Do you realize how many students want to become doctors and are being kept out of medical school because they haven't got your matric results? What a waste!" he fulminated.

I had never played for a violin examination before matric and had never performed in public. Now I had to get used to performing. Dizzy with nervousness and fear I took part in many Eisteddfodau, organized by Welsh members of the community, and other music festivals. Shora accompanied me and also competed as soloist. To my surprise, I came away with numerous gold and silver medals, and as a result Pierre gained a number of talented young pupils. Abramowitz, who had laid the foundation and taught me for seven long years, was bitter that Pierre, who had only been teaching me for a short while, was getting all the credit.

One of the bonuses of being a music student was making friends at last with like-minded people. Although Bedana Chertkow and I had been to the same school, we had never spoken to each other. Bedana was already well known in Johannesburg as a gifted piano student.

A week or two after the matric results had been published, my mother and I again spent a few days in Durban. As we were walking along the seafront, Bedana and her mother came hurtling down the steps of the Edward Hotel calling out "Eva, Eva!"

"Congratulations on your music results! When can we play together?" asked a breathless Bedana. Both she and her mother, a piano teacher who had taught Bedana in the early stages, before she went on to study with Isidore Epstein, were endlessly encouraging toward me. Through Bedana I met fellow piano students Philip Levy and Ivan Melman, students of Adolph Hallis. All three of them were remarkably individual, talented pianists and fine musicians, and I was never short of willing duo partners. I played with each of them in turn, and they introduced me to a wealth of music and musical ideas that were new to me. I had a so much to learn.

Ivan's performances of Beethoven's Sonatas Opus 110 and 111 were unforgettable in their intensity, and his *Emperor* Concerto, with the Johannesburg City Orchestra, convinced Pierre that Ivan was the most outstanding pianist in South Africa. "I don't understand why you two don't get married!" he said to me. But we were truly "just good friends."

Besides excelling at the piano, Ivan also tried his hand at composition, and on one occasion asked me to take part in a lunchtime performance at the University, of a piano trio he had written. We knew no cello students, so Ivan invited an elderly, slightly mad, amateur cellist to play with us. We had only one rehearsal before the performance, which perhaps accounted for the cellist losing his place in the music during the performance. When Ivan realized what had happened, he softly called out the bar number we'd arrived at, and our cellist, instead of jumping to the relevant bar, started playing at double speed in order to catch up with us. Reduced to hysterics, I laughed until the tears ran down my face—while continuing to play in front of a hall full of students.

I auditioned successfully for the Concerto Festivals, and the feeling of floating above the orchestra in the University Great Hall was bliss, even though I suffered agonies of stage fright. A year after I left school I performed Mozart's D major Violin Concerto, and despite my fear, it went well. Miss Starke, our school music teacher, came backstage excitedly to congratulate me. "My, you've come a long way!" she exclaimed. "Aren't you proud of her, Mrs. Schay?" she asked my mother. The following year I played Bruch's G minor Concerto as well as Bach's D Minor Concerto for Two Violins, with Margaret Tillett, a violinist of about my age. We were subsequently invited to play this at a lunchtime concert in the Johannesburg City Hall, and Pierre said, "I doubt whether many of my colleagues would play it as well as you two!"

However, my nervousness during the Bruch had disastrous results. My mind completely blanked out before the second introductory arpeggio passage. I stopped dead. Trauneck gestured to me to come and look at the music on his stand, which I stubbornly refused to do. We started anew. I stalled at exactly the same place. Mrs. Pirie, the elderly leader of the orchestra, played the beginning of the passage for me. This produced total panic in me, but again I was too proud to look at the music. When I stalled yet again I finally relented and went over to the conductor's podium, glanced at the music, and from then on I was away, too stunned for any further mishaps. When it was over, the audience applauded as if they had just heard the greatest performance of their lives, probably out of sheer relief that I'd got through without any further memory lapses. I felt wretched and ashamed, and hid backstage from all well wishers. My mother, together with Pierre and Joyce, eventually rooted me out. Pierre was in almost as bad a state as I. Joyce said he'd been squirming so much, he'd made holes in his socks.

The next morning I refused to get out of bed to face the world. The telephone rang. It was Bedana's mother. "How's Eva?" she asked my mother.

"She won't get up. I don't know what to do with her!" was the reply.

"Have you seen this morning's paper?" asked Mrs. Chertkow. "Well then, you'd better go out and get one. There's a rave review about Eva's playing. Listen to this: '…despite a lapse of memory in the first few bars the very vigorous applause of the audience was deserved acknowledgement of her mature handling of the violin. Very few young players succeed in drawing from the instrument such mellow tone…' and so on. She'll get up soon enough when she reads this."

When Trauneck told me that the eminent Johannesburg cellist, Betty Pack, was about to start giving chamber music lessons, I applied immediately. I wanted to play string quartets, but she had so many pianists to accommodate that all the groups consisted of strings with piano. I led several small groups—piano trios, quartets, and quintets—and we gave many chamber music recitals, as well as a radio broadcast of our trio, for a series entitled "Young South Africa."

Before one of our first concerts, I suffered from nervousness, and Betty said to me, "You must have faith!"

"Faith in what?" I asked.

"In God, of course!" she exclaimed.

"Oh Betty, don't give me that!" I begged.

She said, "*Now* I know what's wrong with you."

A few months later I asked Betty if I might come and play to her and she said "Of course you may, I'd be delighted to hear you. You know you're always welcome!" I played Beethoven's *Romance* in G, and Betty said, "Eva, hearing you play like this, I realize there is nothing you can't do musically, if you put your mind to it." I was never really convinced, but over the years I remembered those words, and they gave me courage. Apart from her faith in God, Betty had enormous faith in my ability, much more than I ever had, and she never stopped encouraging me.

Later she also founded a string orchestra, and although in principle we rotated, I led most of the time. "Eva is my rock!" she declared.

Betty had a larger-than-life personality, and an extra large figure to go with it. She shared a small house with three sisters. Only one of them had ever been married—and divorced— and she had a young daughter, Marian, who was her aunt's most gifted cello student. Marian became, and still is, an outstanding cellist in South Africa.

All four sisters used to dye their hair black as ink. They were all musicians, but Betty was the most distinguished. Her slanted eyes gave her an inscrutable expression. She was always heavily made-up, her face powdered white, her lips carmine, and she carried with her the intoxicating scent of Lanvin's "My Sin." She was warm-hearted and generous, charging a bare minimum for lessons despite her eminence as a cellist, and did not spare herself, either as teacher or performer. She never seemed to run out of energy. After every concert she would invite us all to a party, parents included. Her erstwhile-married sister Ethel did all the cooking, but Betty tended the garden, a mass of perfect dahlias, and took her several fierce Scotch collies for regular walks. She played the cello sublimely, and to me she seemed beautiful and mysterious.

Betty Pack, 1950.

I thoroughly enjoyed academic life at Wits. Like most students there, I was proud of the fact that Wits had the courage to make a stand against the apartheid laws of the country. Black students were welcomed and treated with respect, as equals. The pity was that owing to lack of adequate schooling, so few of them were able to make the grade. Professor Kirby, the distinguished head of the music department, was a font of fascinating information and always had an unusual and interesting angle, which stimulated us into thinking for ourselves. His knowledge of African speech patterns and music was enormous, and he had a large collection of indigenous musical instruments. His sub-

Betty Pack and friend crossing bridge, 1950.

jects were history of music, the structure of music, orchestration and instrumentation, and he also conducted the student orchestra, in which I played. He was a kindly man with curly gray hair, fine features, keenly searching eyes, and a bit of a corporation. He spoke with a Scottish accent in a slightly husky voice. One day he caught me gazing out of a window, lost in thought, and quoted the Welsh poet, W.H. Davies:

"What is this life if, full of care,
We have no time to stand and stare."

Dr. Paff taught harmony and counterpoint, and the physics students joined us for his lectures on acoustics. During the last year of our studies, he invited some of us to his home to play Mozart on his set of musical glasses, a rare experience. In addition to musical subjects, we studied English language and literature for two years, and had a choice of subjects for one year each, from which I chose French and the history of fine arts, all of which gave me enormous pleasure.

The Right Reverend Ambrose Reeves, Bishop of Johannesburg, was a firm anti-apartheid activist. He gave a lunchtime lecture on Existentialism, which I attended during my second year at university. There was little time for questions from the floor, so I approached him afterward and said that while I thought I had understood the concept of atheistic Existentialism, I was not able to reconcile this idea with Christian Existentialism. "Well now," he said, "that's very interesting. How about coming to see me at my home and we can discuss it at leisure?" I said I'd love to, and I went. He tried, of course, to open my mind to religion—not necessarily Christianity, just to the idea of God—and he lent me a book called *Reality*, which he wanted to discuss with me after I had read it. The book did nothing to convince me, but the man had such charisma that I was afraid of being converted, merely by the power of his personality. So I returned the book without arranging to see him again; yet the fascination with the idea of religion remained.

Pierre De Groote was my violin teacher throughout my years at university, except for a short while when he was away on tour, and his wife taught me in his place. Musically stimulating though Pierre was, he changed his mind about technical problems every week, which was confusing, and spent much of my lessons talking—thinking aloud—instead of letting me play. Joyce, having studied with Max Rostal in London, was more methodical and sensible, and I thrived under her tuition. She felt strongly that I should be sent to study with Rostal after finishing my degree, so she wrote, asking him to take me on as a student. While she encouraged me in my ambitions, she said only too truly of the violinist's life, "So much pain; so few moments of bliss!"

My mother and I became friends of the family and often had meals and stimulating conversation with them. They had three sons at the time, later four. The eldest, André, who still remembers playing Beethoven's C Minor Sonata with me, is a pianist now based in Brussels, and Philip is the gifted cellist in the Chilingirian Quartet. The other two sons, Oliver, a clarinettist, and Steven, a phenomenally gifted pianist who won the Van Cliburn competition, played at Carnegie Hall, and had a potentially great career ahead of him, died tragically young. I knew them all as delightful children, but Steven, the youngest, only after my return from London.

I obtained my degree with first class honors, and the University awarded me the Melanie Pollack Scholarship in Music for further study overseas. This did not cover all my living expenses, which meant my mother would have to continue to support me until I supplemented my scholarship with teaching. Despite this, and although she had come to depend on my companionship and would suffer appalling loneliness, she encouraged me to take it up.

I did not wait for graduation day the following year. On the morning of December 24, a large group of friends came to bid me farewell at Johannesburg railway station, including Joachim—"Achim"—who had come from Manila to visit his mother, our Tante Ilse. My mother traveled with me to Cape Town, where she stayed with Illa and Fred for a few days, and saw me off on the *SS Carnarvon Castle* on Friday, December 26, 1952.

Masses of colored streamers attached the ship's passengers to the friends we were leaving on the quayside, until we pulled away, and the streamers slipped out of their hands and dropped into the sea. How lonely my mother must have felt. As for me, I was filled with excitement, anticipation, and a sense of a new, different self about to emerge.

Chapter Thirteen

◈ LONDON, WINTER AND SPRING 1953—MUSIC ◈

My new self began to emerge on board the *Carnarvon Castle*, where I met two fellow music students who were about to become part of my London musical life. Neil Solomon had studied at the Cape Town College of Music with that marvelous pianist, Lilli Kraus, and was now studying with Harold Craxton at the Royal Academy of Music in London. He was returning to London after a visit home to Cape Town. Derek Osche, from Rustenburg, was on his way to study violin with Albert Sammons. I remembered Derek as leader of our children's orchestra at the Teachers' Training College and also as soloist in the Concerto Festivals. He had studied the violin with Harold Ketèlby. He introduced me to Neil, with whom I immediately found a very special musical rapport. Neil accompanied both Derek and me on the piano in the ship's saloon and rehearsed my audition pieces for Max Rostal with me. His renditions of Schubert piano sonatas and of the *Wanderer Fantasy* were a revelation and delight for me. He was kind, clever, and amusing, and there was always laughter and joy in his company. Neil taught me the rudiments of chess, and Derek and I danced in the evenings.

"By the way," Derek said to me on our first evening aboard, "I'm engaged to a girl back home, and I intend to remain faithful to her. I thought I should tell you." Overprotected and virginal as I was, I felt somewhat indignant that he should feel the need to warn me. All the same, he seemed to like my company, and we spent a lot of time together, as well as with Neil. I came to an agreement with the girl who shared my cabin that I could have the cabin to practice in for half the day—and she could have it the rest of the day to sleep in.

I never tired of watching the sea and sky, with the ever-changing play of light and the changing cloud formations. Many passengers said they were bored, with nothing but the sea to look at for an en-

Derek and Neil aboard the Carnarvon Castle, January 1953.

tire fortnight, but I found it an endless source of fascination, and in the moonlight it was quite magical. Of course there were deck quoits, a swimming pool, and all sorts of entertainment for bored passengers: dances, a fancy dress party, not to mention the Crossing the Equator ceremony on New Year's Day, with people being thrown into the pool, Father Neptune himself presiding. Except for Madeira we did not see land until we arrived at Southampton, a fortnight after our departure.

I wrote to my mother about Madeira:

> We saw it like a cloud in the distance a good hour before we were due to arrive there at 5.30 p.m. When we got as close to land as was safe for the ship, we anchored. Hundreds of little boats came rowing towards us: first the divers for coins—when it got really dark they dived by firelight which was lovely to see—then the merchants who climbed up the side of the ship with ropes. They transformed the deck into an Eastern-looking bazaar. Finally, ladders were lowered for the police to come on board, and after they left, a motor launch came to fetch those of us who were going ashore. The ship looked glorious in the dark night, its many lights reflected in the water, and Madeira looked very inviting.

A group of us spent an enjoyable evening there, exploring, eating, shopping, admiring the clean cobbled streets, the ox-drawn carriages, and everything that was so different from what we had been used to in South Africa.

Bedana Chertkow and Ivan Melman had preceded me to London, as well as Babette Botha, a piano student from Pretoria who had also played in a Concerto Festival. They came to meet us at Waterloo station, amidst great jubilation. They had booked tickets for us that very evening to hear Alan Loveday and Leonard Cassini in an all-Beethoven violin and piano sonata recital at the Wigmore Hall, and we arranged to meet there later.

My first day in London was unforgettable. From Waterloo I took a taxi to 24 Eastholm, in the Hampstead Garden Suburb, to stay with Mutti Kaufmann, now reunited with her husband. It was she who had come to the rescue and made room for us when my father had lost his job in Johannesburg at the beginning of World War II. They had invited me to stay with them in London for as long as I liked, or until I found suitable student accommodation. I was delighted to be with Mutti again, and they both made me feel welcome.

There was a magnificent bouquet of flowers awaiting me from Achim, with a greeting card and instructions to telephone him at his hotel as soon as I arrived. Having seen me off at Johannesburg railway station, he had managed to arrive in London ahead of me by air. He picked me up by taxi and bought me my first pair of snow boots and warm sheepskin gloves against the freezing cold. "I want to spoil you!" he said. Then he took me out for a meal, and reluctantly dropped me at the Wigmore Hall, to join my friends and experience my first concert in London. Everything was new and exciting.

Achim was due to fly to New York later that evening, but fog delayed the flight. The next morning I had a surprise phone call from him from the airport, on the verge of departure. "If only you hadn't been at that concert we could have spent the evening together. I really missed you!" he complained. "But never mind—I'll come back!" And he did, many times over the years, wherever in the world I happened to be, bearing gifts of jewelry and perfume.

Two days after my first Wigmore Hall concert, Bedana had arranged for us all to attend a string quartet recital there, the first of many we attended by the superb Amadeus Quartet. Norbert Brainin, their leader, Sigmund Nissel, the second violin, and the viola player, Peter Schidlof, had all come to England as young Austrian refugees from Hitler and were for a time interned as "enemy aliens" during the war. Martin Lovett, the cellist, was born in England. Both violinists and the violist had been pupils of Max Rostal, as he proudly told me when, after my initial interview with him, I mentioned I was going to hear them that evening. The cellist had studied with William Pleeth, who had also coached the quartet. They excelled in the works of the Viennese School, especially Mozart and Schubert, and played with tremendous vitality and lyricism.

And so we six continued, going to concerts singly, in twos or threes, or all together, mostly at the Royal Festival Hall or Wigmore Hall, occasionally at the Albert Hall, and occasionally to opera or ballet at the Royal Opera House. We made music together, listened to each other play, listened to recordings, talked about music, breathed, lived music together.

I made my way to Rostal's house at Brondesbury Park on a bitingly cold January morning. He was a short, round man, with a terrible squint, so that you never knew whether or not he was looking at you, and he had a huge personality. He was about to leave on a concert tour until the spring, and introduced me to one of his assistant teachers at the Guildhall School of Music and Drama, Miss Peggy Radmall. I played Lalo's *Symphonie Espagnole*—without accompaniment, which was scary enough—while he prowled around me, inspecting my stance, position of my violin, arm, fingers, bow hold; in short, to see how everything was working. Eventually he took a seat some distance away from me, much to my relief. Suddenly he rose from his chair, came up to me, and gently took the bow out of my hand. In my agitation I had unknowingly caught my thumb joint on the thin steel E string, and to my embarrassment, was bleeding profusely. There was blood on my violin, blood on my bow hair, blood all the way down my dress.

However, although my technique was insecure, Rostal said, "You have a natural approach to the violin, and you have temperament. Not all my pupils have temperament, and that is *not* something that can be taught! I believe you have the makings of a soloist."

Secretly I thought, "Just wait until you discover how awful I really am!" Despite all the encouragement I had since received, I remained haunted by Abramowitz's lack of belief in me. Seven years I had remained with him, seven years of having my self-confidence eroded, and of never really understanding what it was that I lacked, when what I needed to know was what I actually had. Much later, when I was already a professional musician working in London and had some lessons with Emanuel Hurwitz—the most generous-spirited violin teacher I ever had—he said to me, "There's nothing wrong with your violin playing, the trouble is with your mind!"

Apart from this damaging lack of self-confidence, which continued to haunt me, I was extremely happy in London. I enrolled at the Guildhall School of Music and Drama, not as a full-time student, having already obtained a Bachelor of Music degree and a teacher's diploma, but only for violin and chamber music lessons.

The London Underground system made a great impression on me. I had never experienced anything like it but learned to find my way around it quickly. The fact that all the different lines connected up somewhere or other was reassuring; one need never be completely lost. So I enjoyed traveling to Blackfriars station, watching people—I had never seen as many eccentric people as in London—or reading a book, in which case I invariably missed my station and had to take a train back to Blackfriars. From there it was just a short walk down to Victoria Embankment alongside the Thames, where the Guildhall School of Music was situated. (It has since moved away from the river, to more up-to-date premises at the Barbican.)

I felt enormously privileged to have string quartet lessons with that most inspiring teacher and cellist, William Pleeth, though I was not entirely happy with the players with whom I had been placed. The only one I enjoyed working with was Rose, our intelligent and pretty Irish viola player. The second violin complained, "I was brought up never to show emotion. Now I'm expected to express emotion, and I don't know how!" I felt sorry for her predicament but couldn't help wondering how she had managed to get this far in music without expressing emotion. Nor did I think much of the cellist. Even so, I treasure the memory of our lessons with William Pleeth from whom we learned a great deal.

Rostal made me go back to beginnings, to establish a sound technical foundation, under the tutelage of Peggy Radmall, and gave me periodic lessons himself to oversee my progress. He was not satisfied with my little Grancino violin, which, owing to certain weaknesses, prevented me from producing a big enough sound when necessary. At his suggestion, Peggy managed to persuade a friend in Scotland to lend me her splendid Gabrieli violin, which I treasured.

On the first Wednesday in April, after his return from his tour, I entered a classroom full of Rostal's students at the Guildhall, just as Leonard Friedman was about to start playing the Debussy Sonata. I held my breath and sat down quietly. He played beautifully, but Rostal had many suggestions to make. Then an Italian girl from Egypt, Gina Panunzio, played a Paganini Caprice and Ravel's *Habanera*. She had an abundance of vitality and talent, but was so anxious that Rostal kept telling her to calm down. "I won't shoot!" he promised. I heard Schubert's ravishing *Arpeggione* Sonata, composed for the now obsolete stringed instrument, the arpeggione, for the first time that day, superbly played on the viola. One after another, his students stood up to play the studies and pieces they had prepared. They came from many different countries: South America, the United States, Yugoslavia, Israel, as well as Great Britain. Most had attained high standards and were destined for fine careers. Throughout the day Rostal criticized, explained, made picturesque analogies to try to get his ideas across, and demonstrated, picking up his own wonderful Stradivarius, or one of his students' violins, a worryingly ash laden cigarette suspended from his lips, to play a passage. Those were the most inspiring moments of all.

This was my first experience of a master class, and thereafter I attended his classes every Wednesday.

I remember hearing Leonard Friedman play part of the Beethoven Violin Concerto, and Rostal asking him, "Are you studying this for the first time?"

"Yes," said Leonard.

"Oh how I envy you," exclaimed Rostal, his hand on his heart, "how wonderful to be studying the Beethoven Concerto for the first time!"

The varying qualities of the students fascinated me, and Rostal's musical demonstrations were a source of wonder and inspiration. I was on a perpetual "high."

And of course there were the concerts. The Royal Festival Hall had been built only two years before I arrived, for the 1951 Festival of Britain. The setting, for me, coming from a city without a river, was magical. During the intervals one could step out onto a wide balcony overlooking the Thames, and watch the evening lights reflected in the water and the people down below, walking along the riverbank. My group of South African student friends and I attended so many concerts there that we joked about putting up camp beds and spending our nights there. We would buy the cheapest tickets in the "orchestra stalls" behind the orchestra, where we could get close up views of all the instrumentalists and watch the gestures and facial expressions of the conductors. I particularly remember Joseph Krips—no beauty, but tremendously expressive—conducting the London Symphony Orchestra in the complete cycle of Beethoven symphonies; and later, the great Otto Klemperer's Beethoven interpretations, with the Philharmonia Orchestra, which had a depth and warmth unequalled by anyone in my experience. The young Herbert von Karajan came from Austria, where he had enjoyed adulation during the Third Reich, and appeared to be challenging the supremacy of Klemperer, conducting Beethoven himself with the Philharmonia Orchestra. I found him cold, with a superficial brilliance that was light years away from Klemperer's depth. Sometimes we sat in the Grand Tier, where we got a much more balanced orchestral sound. One of my outstanding memories is of a performance of Beethoven's *Missa Solemnis*, when it seemed to me that the entire audience listened with deep emotion and responded as one soul. It was here that I heard Mahler and Richard Strauss for the first time. I made it my business to listen to music by all the great classical, romantic, and modern composers, and to the great contemporary performers.

Shocked, I could hardly believe my ears when the sweet toned virtuoso and legendary violinist, Mischa Elman, during his farewell London recital, loudly and obtrusively tuned his violin over a solo passage by his pianist. I was just in time to hear farewell piano recitals by Edwin Fischer and Alfred Cortot; I thrilled to the playing of violinists Nathan Milstein and Isaac Stern; and I was awestruck by David Oistrakh's violinistic perfection and richness of sound.

On more than one occasion, Yehudi Menuhin performed embarrassingly badly in the first half of a concert, then swept one away in the second half by his sublime playing of the Beethoven Violin Concerto. He seemed like a god then, unsurpassed by anyone else. And there was a wonderful occasion when he played unaccompanied Bach in the richly resonant St Paul's Cathedral.

Sometimes I could hardly believe it was not all merely a dream. Dietrich Fischer-Dieskau gave a deeply moving rendition of Schubert's *Winterreise* together with that peerless accompanist, Gerald Moore, at the piano, and gave delightful duet recitals with Elisabeth Schwarzkopf and with Irmgard Seefried.

And so it went on: Pierre Fournier with his deliciously warm cello tone, Dennis Brain, the superb French horn player who died so tragically young, and more and yet more wonderful musicians that we had the good fortune to hear. And at the Mermaid Theatre, we heard Kirsten Flagstad sing in one of her last performances, the role of Dido in Purcell's opera, *Dido and Aeneas.*

Various acquaintances that I have forgotten tried to pair me off with eligible bachelor millionaires. I think there were three in all over the years. Where did they find them? It never worked, because I had a prejudice against very rich, business-oriented people. Achim was the only businessperson to succeed in breaking down that prejudice, to make me appreciate his humanity and humor.

However, in my first year in London, a young American millionaire (according to whomever it was who sent him to me) invited me to a magnificent evening out. First, dinner at the Ivy restaurant, famous for its superb, expensive cuisine, and for being much frequented by well-known actors and actresses; then to a performance at the Festival Hall of Mozart and Tchaikovsky violin concertos by the great Jascha Heifetz.

At the Ivy, it happened that the actress, Martita Hunt, who had played the role of Miss Havisham in the classic film of Dickens' *Great Expectations*, was sitting at a table near us. My escort was thrilled and decided to go over to her table to compliment her on her performance as Miss Havisham. I mistakenly thought this a very crass thing to do, feeling that celebrities ought to be left in peace, and begged him not to, but he insisted. I cringed. Then to my surprise, I saw her face break into a smile of pleasure, and I realized that no matter how famous, everyone needs a pat on the back, a sign of appreciation for a job well done.

We had lobster thermidor as our main course, neither of us following Jewish dietary laws, and I at the time ignorant of the gruesome end that lobsters meet in the cooking pot. It was the most superb meal I had ever eaten. To my shame, throughout the concert that I had been looking forward to so much, my mind was still on that lobster thermidor.

But perhaps it had more to do with my disappointment at the charmless Mozart and the invigorating but cold Tchaikovsky from a violinist whose glorious recordings had so thrilled me as a schoolgirl.

Chapter Fourteen

⌐ LONDON, WINTER AND SPRING 1953—PEOPLE AND PLACES ⌐

When I first came to London, Bedana and Babette were living in a boarding house in Bayswater. Their landlady provided dinner, and all her lodgers sat at one long dining room table. Soon after I arrived I was invited to a meal there. We were halfway through dinner when we heard a low, unearthly moaning coming from the far end of the table. We all turned, bewildered, in its direction.

A young Uruguayan guest was swaying forward and backward, in obvious distress. Suddenly he burst out: "Oh my God, Oh my God! I have sinned against you. There is no salvation. I am damned forever!" We could not imagine what dreadful sin he had committed and tried to reassure him. But he said, "I cannot be forgiven. It happened some time ago, but I kept it secret. Secret! Such a secret cannot be kept from God. I spent one night with a woman. She was beautiful, *but she was not my wife*! *I have betrayed my wife*!" He was beyond solace, and we were filled with distress and a sense of helplessness. He became increasingly upset, banging on the table, rocking to and fro, and shouting, until he had to be taken to hospital. We kept in touch for a while and learned that at first his condition had deteriorated further, but later, to our relief, improved considerably.

A month or two later, Bedana and Babette were given notice to quit. They were upset, but I imagine having two pianists practicing in one boarding house was rather too much for the other guests. After much unsuccessful searching they moved into digs in West Hampstead.

London in winter meant fog, or rather "smog," a dense combination of smoke particles and fog, before the era of smokeless fuel. My worst experience of it occurred early in March 1953. I had been invited to dine at Southgate with friends of friends in Johannesburg, and I still have the letter I wrote to my mother, who kept all my letters from London, describing it:

> When I was about to leave, Gerda opened the door and said, "Goodness, look at the fog." Norman laughed at her. "Fog? That's just a thin mist. Look, you can see the streetlights—you can even see the outline of that tree…"

85

But he walked with me to the Chase Side Tavern, where I had to catch the bus to Muswell Hill. From there I was supposed to get a bus heading for Golders Green, alight along the way at the Market Place in Hampstead Garden Suburb, and then make my way on foot to number 24 Eastholm. The fog seemed to be getting thicker all the time; I had never experienced anything like it. When we arrived at the bus stop we almost turned back, thinking no bus would appear in such bad visibility, and Norman said I'd have to spend the night with them. We waited for a bit and were just about to give up when a bus suddenly loomed into view. My letter continues:

> I asked the rather vague conductor if the 102 bus was still running and he said, "Well, if we are, I don't see why they shouldn't be able to manage." So I got in. When the bus was well on its way, the man I sat next to said, "Did you want to go to Golders Green? You'll never catch that bus!" and the vague conductor began to agree with him. I said, "Well if there is no bus, what on earth am I going to do when we arrive at Muswell Hill? Is there a bus station where I could spend the night?" "Ask the bus inspector when you get there," was the conductor's less than helpful reply.

> As it turned out there was no shelter where I could have spent the night, and I had simply no idea of what lay ahead of me. The bus crawled along more and more slowly, sometimes coming to a complete stop. The driver could hardly see, and it seemed unlikely that a 102 bus would still be running when—if—we ever arrived at Muswell Hill. And even if it did, I didn't relish the thought of walking home from the bus stop in the ever-thickening fog. Suddenly I remembered that Neil Solomon lived in Muswell Hill, though I had no idea of just where. By great good fortune I had that very morning put my address book into my handbag. I did not know how I was going to find the house where he lived but the man sitting next to me offered to help me. He happened to have a torch on him—without it we would both have been lost. I had no choice but to put my trust in him. Slowly, almost blindly, we crept along through the thick blanket of fog, and it seemed a miracle to me when at last we actually found the house. I felt enormous relief and gratitude that my trust had not been misplaced. Neil had mentioned that his landlady went to bed early, also that she was sometimes quite cross, and I felt a little scared. But to my relief the light was on; she had been held up in the fog herself and had just got in. She knew who I was as we'd spoken on the phone and discovered we were both called Eva, and she cordially invited me in. Although she thought Neil was asleep she went up to his room to scrounge a blanket for me, brought me one from her bed too, and made a bed for me on the living room sofa.

> The first thing I did was phone the Kaufmanns to let them know I was safe, even though it meant waking them. Then Neil came down in his pyjamas and dressing gown, and we burst out laughing when we saw each other. Eva made tea for all three of us, and we chatted cosily for over an hour. Neil brought down his raincoat and overcoat, and I put my own coat on top of all that, and Eva brought me a pair of her pyjamas to wear. In spite of it all I lay freezing and shivering all night in that cold, cold room, but my only feeling was one of gratitude to have a roof over my head at all. I fell asleep in the early hours, and later in the morning Neil woke me up for breakfast, and we played chess until lunchtime. He and Eva tried to per-

suade me to stay longer, and I felt tempted because it had all been such fun, but I decided it was time to be off.

Before I had left Johannesburg a former classmate had said to me, "When you're in London, make sure you get in touch with Wanda Simson. I stayed with her for a year in her flat at St John's Wood. She's a wonderful person." Wanda was studying piano with Ilona Kabos, and she was more worldly-wise and sophisticated than anyone else I knew. She was dressed in red when I met her, in a clinging woolen dress that showed her slightly fuller figure to good advantage. Her hair was smoothed back in a ponytail, and she had a knowing smile. She took my arm in hers and led me down to the restaurant beneath the flats where she lived. There she introduced me to an habitué, Karl Haas, conductor of the London Baroque Ensemble, who annoyed me when he declared that he would never allow women in his orchestra because, according to him, we had no sense of rhythm.

Wanda's childhood experiences had run somewhat parallel to mine. Born in Milan, she had left Italy with her parents and brother in 1937 to escape Mussolini and the race laws, and she had grown up in Rhodesia, now Zimbabwe. Wanda now writes poetry under her married name of Barford and movingly expresses the horrors and grief of the Nazi and Fascist persecutions.

It was Wanda who first introduced me to Hampstead. Its old-world atmosphere enchanted me, with its narrow lanes and marvelous old shops, many of which have long since gone, its beautiful Georgian and Regency cottages and villas, and its pretty churches.

I particularly remember Knowles Brown the jeweler, in Hampstead High Street, whose honor and integrity one would be hard pushed to find today. I once took a silver ring with malachite stone, which had come out of its setting, to be repaired there. Because the setting itself was uneven, they were unable to do the job to their complete satisfaction, so they refused to charge me.

There was an "olde worlde" Barclays Bank next door where, too, the service was gentlemanly, kind, and not at all daunting to a somewhat impoverished student. In Heath Street, facing the top of the High Street, there was an old fashioned style Sainsbury's, where you could buy two ounces of butter, cut with a butter cutter on a marble slab and wrapped in greaseproof paper. Picturesque Flask Walk, named after its public house, The Flask, had ancient flagstones, charming old shops, and a Public Baths where people still went once a week, because many homes in the vicinity did not have a bath. A chimney sweep still lived there. Flask Walk led to Well Walk, which had a pottery where I liked to browse. Lower down the High Street there was a greengrocer, a butcher, and a fishmonger. Further down still, the High Hill Bookshop was a treasure house of books and art materials. On the corner beyond, an apple cheeked Cockney flower lady sold flowers on the pavement.

There was a surprise around every corner: hilly tree-lined back streets with small architectural gems, not all as well-preserved as they are now, and also grand historic houses, and historic inns. Dickens had written about it, Keats had lived there, Constable had painted there. Famous artists, writers, and politicians still lived there now. Downshire Hill, with its beautiful Regency villas, its cheerful Freemasons Arms pub, and lovely St. John's Church at the point of the V junction it made with Keats Grove, enchanted me. Keats Grove contained the house where Keats once lived, in the garden of which he wrote "Ode to a Nightingale." Next door was a public library.

Wanda took me to see a film by Jean Cocteau at the Everyman Cinema, a tiny cinema with a lot of atmosphere that specialized in showing foreign films. It was a new and astonishing experience for me. We had a meal in one of the many small cozy restaurants. Hampstead was at the same time cosmopolitan yet very English, impregnated with history and past literary associations. This, I decided, was where I wanted to live.

And so I searched for accommodation in Hampstead, and found an advertisement offering a room to let in an art student's ground floor flat with garden. It sounded ideal, and I went to see it and met the painter, Edwina Leapman, who was at the time a student at the Slade. She was softly spoken, slim, short-sighted, and had a mop of curly red hair. The flat was too cold for me—at the Kaufmanns we had central heating, which was rare in those days—and I was used to South African sunshine. Edwina and I discovered that on that very evening we were both going to the same talk by pacifist Tom Wardle on South Africa and the passive resistance movement inspired by Mahatma Ghandi. We spent hours discussing apartheid, exchanging ideas about pacifism, and talking about our lives. Although we did not necessarily agree on every issue, we found we were in many ways kindred spirits, and a lasting friendship ensued.

She always showed me her latest paintings when I visited her, told me about recent trends in art and her views on them, and we would talk about Life with a capital L. We took it all—and ourselves—very seriously! She was going through an emotionally difficult time, but she was always sure of the path she was following. In those days, she did still life paintings and portraits, and loved above all painting musicians at work. Music was supremely important to her. She met my friends, attended our chamber music rehearsals, and sketched groups of musicians playing, which she later painted. I loved those paintings, but they always left her dissatisfied, until she realized that what she really wanted to do was "paint the music."

"That's how I eventually came to paint abstracts," she told me years later, "but I had to find my own way. I had no examples to follow in this country. It was very difficult. When you came back to London you had no idea at all what I was about."

But she found her way, has had many one-man exhibitions, is written about in various books about artists, and is admired by other artists. Edwina's paintings have a contemplative quality, a feeling of space, stillness, and luminosity, the result of painstaking labor, sincerity, and inwardness.

We sometimes went for long walks on Hampstead Heath. It seemed to extend for miles in every direction, and from a grassy hilltop you could get a clear view of London, far into the distance. It was easy to get lost in the woodlands or take a wrong turning on a footpath, but each turning would take you to something new, and the changing light gave infinite variety to the ever-changing landscape.

Queenie Tobacoff had been a year ahead of me at Barnato Park School. She had large, dark-brown eyes, a face full of freckles, and a huge smile. We met by chance in London, went to see some plays together, and found we enjoyed each other's company. She was living at a hostel on Primrose Hill and was longing for independence. We discovered that we were both looking for accommodation in Hampstead and decided to try to find a flat to share. It was a disheartening experience. Most landladies wouldn't consider a violin student, and the only one who didn't see me as a social menace showed us a flat that was so ugly and dirty that we turned it down. We couldn't afford a nicer one, so after a long and fruitless search we eventually gave up the idea of a flat. Instead, we took a large double room with use of bathroom and kitchen, shared only with the housekeeper who hardly used it, between Hampstead and Belsize Park tube stations, not far from the Heath. The absentee landlord had left the house in charge of the housekeeper, who assured me that my violin practice would disturb no one. The other tenants were all young business girls who were out all day and most evenings as well. Queenie, too, was out at work during the day, when I could practice in our room; evenings and weekends I could practice in the kitchen. Most of my friends lived nearby: Ivan and Edwina in Hampstead, Bedana and Babette by now in West Hampstead, Wanda in St John's Wood. It seemed ideal.

On Saturday May 2, Queenie and I moved into our new home. It had creaking floorboards, unmanageable sash windows that let the draft in, and a gas meter you had to feed with shillings or the heating would run out. We didn't care; it was such an adventure to have a place of our own, in the very area where we wanted to be.

Mrs. Mutch, the housekeeper, couldn't have been kinder. She went to great trouble, the evening we moved in, to instruct me how to light the gas geyser over the bath. I had never experienced gas fires before, and had never ever confronted a geyser. By the next morning I had forgotten that I had to light the little pilot light before turning the gas on fully, in order to run a hot bath. There was a tremendous explosion. Mrs. Mutch came rushing upstairs, fully expecting to find me dead on the bathroom floor. I was lucky: the only harm I'd come to, apart from the shock, was the singeing off of all my eyelashes. I looked a sight.

The worst of it was that I had been invited to spend the day in Cambridge with a professor at St. John's College and his wife, a cousin of Joyce De Groote. I was awe-struck to be in such grand company, wanted to make a good impression, and felt mortified to be meeting them without eyelashes. Despite everything, the day went well. My hosts were kind and welcoming, eager to hear

Mutti Kaufmann.

all I could tell them about the De Grootes in Johannesburg. They showed me around Cambridge; its beauty and serenity filled me with amazement and delight. They fed me like a princess and invited me to come and stay any time I liked.

Our "gang of six" continued to go to fabulous concerts and to play music with and to each other. Ivan often rang and persuaded me to go for long walks across Hampstead Heath with him after he had been working hard at the piano and wanted to clear his mind and talk of other things. I enjoyed visits to the National Gallery and to the Tate, thrilled at last to see paintings of which I had only been able to see reproductions in the past, and to experience so many more paintings and sculptures that were entirely new to me. Mutti remained a constant in my life, for I was not only fond of her, but revered her. I loved hearing about her philosophy of life when chatting with her in her living room or going for walks with her in Bigwood, in the Garden Suburb.

Chapter Fifteen
⪼ ENGLAND—SUMMER 1953 ⪻

On June 2, 1953, the day of Queen Elizabeth II's coronation, I wrote to my mother:

The weather is dark, rainy and miserable. Thousands of people have spent the night exposed to it, and have stood in the streets today, crushed by the millions more who joined them this morning, in order to catch a glimpse of the Coronation Procession as it passed by. Thousands have come to London from all over the world to see this event—and here am I in my Hampstead room, sitting cosily by the fire as I write, glad that my day's practising has not been interfered with. Queenie was going to meet a friend in the West End at 2 a.m., but she was tired after our little dinner party last night, so she went to bed instead. But this morning she was like a caged bird, dying to be outside, to get the feel of the holiday spirit, to see something at least of what everybody has been discussing for the past few months with such anticipation. Finally, determined not to let it slip by while she was missing it all, she took a chance and went to the West End—and left me in peace. I have the whole house to myself. It has been full of visitors from outside London, friends and relatives of some of the girls living here, excitedly making arrangements for this day. Now the house is wonderfully quiet, except for my playing.

In the evening I wrote:

Now that it's all over, and people have come back telling of the wonderful two-mile procession and how beautiful it all was, I am dreadfully sorry I did not go. I couldn't imagine what all the fuss was about, how grand it was going to be, and now it's all over, and I've missed it! Queenie's not back yet, so I've just rung Babette, who also stayed at home to practise (though she did listen to the broadcast) and she, too, could kick herself for not having gone. I said, "Why don't we go and see the fireworks on the Thames tonight, so we won't feel we've missed everything?" and that's what we decided to do.

Next day I wrote:

Babette and I strolled up the Mall towards Buckingham Palace in a leisurely fashion merely to see the floodlighting and decorations, ignorant of the fact that the Queen was expected to appear at a definite time. When we looked back we found ourselves locked in by a crowd of ever more densely packed people. It was a solid mass, and yet it moved! There was a constant writhing and pushing that made one feel all one's innards were getting thoroughly mushed up.

I didn't mention that the man behind me was taking advantage of the situation, pinching my bottom. I complained about him to Babette in Afrikaans, the language we used when we didn't want to be understood, and he joined in, in Dutch: he had understood every word. I continued:

> At last the Queen emerged onto the floodlit balcony in shimmering white, looking like a fairy-tale queen. This contrasted with the austere aspect of the Palace and made a dramatic picture. A great roar of appreciation came up from the crowd. They would not go until she had returned again and again, with Prince Philip and little Prince Charles and Princess Anne. There was no way of getting out of that crowd until the Queen and Prince Philip finally waved goodbye and withdrew. That was the worst moment, the whole mass turning and trying to get out all at once, like a herd of elephants.

> Finally we managed to get away from the main part of the crowd through St. James's Park. The air was fresh and cool and if one could ignore the picnic papers lying around and the blare of cheap, piped music, one could enjoy the freshness of the grass after the rain, the gorgeous rhododendrons and the fairyland appearance of floodlit Whitehall. Suddenly we heard a tremendous cheer—we had walked right round to the side of Buckingham Palace and there the Queen had emerged again with her consort, waving to the crowd we had escaped from, and yet we had a better view than if we had been among them. Although we walked in the opposite direction from everybody else, we somehow worked our way to the firework display.

> We must have become extremely disoriented for we found ourselves walking around in circles, and it was well after midnight when we finally managed to find a tube station and make our way home, together with thousands of others.

Later in the week the royal couple rode through Hampstead, and watching them it struck me that their lives were now public property.

Queenie Tobacoff and I got on remarkably well. I learned much about how to enjoy life from her, but for all the fun of our life together, the time came when I realized I had to find a room to myself. The problem was that I had developed insomnia as a result of the different hours we kept; Queenie often arriving home long after I'd gone to bed. I would wake up and be unable to fall asleep again, eventually becoming unable to go to sleep in the first place, for fear of being woken up when she arrived. I needed a lot of sleep, and almost every day was like a hangover, so that I couldn't concentrate properly on my practicing, felt I was making no progress at all, and that I was becoming a nervous wreck. Queenie was such a relaxed person that she found it difficult to understand my problem and was upset at my decision because, she told me, she'd never felt so happy living anywhere in her life. She decided to keep the room on her own for the time being. I hated hurting her, but my mind was made up. In August I moved to Maresfield Gardens, Hampstead, and we continued to see each other until she left for Rome to study art some months later. She kept in touch by writing to me, and I learned that she had met a handsome young Italian and married him, throwing her Jewish family in Johannesburg into despair. Her father was eventually reconciled when he became a grandfather.

I had found a pleasant semi-basement room in a large, comfortable house in Maresfield Gardens. The great violinist and pedagogue Carl Flesch, teacher of my teacher Max Rostal, had lived in Maresfield Gardens, as had Sigmund Freud, both refugees from Nazism. Bedana and Babette soon also decided the time had come to part while remaining fast friends, and in October, Bedana moved into the house where I was staying, into a room two doors away from mine. During our time there, I came to know every note of Beethoven's Piano Sonata Opus 109, a struggle for her small hands. It is only after having heard many well-established pianists play it since that I realize how well she finally played it.

Our landlady lived upstairs. She was a neurotic, weepy person who handed over the charge of her whole house, her finances, in fact it seemed her very life, to her housekeeper. We had no doubt that the housekeeper was roundly cheating her. She regularly stole from us. I particularly remember my only pair of gold earrings missing from the drawer in which I had left them. When we warned her that we were expecting Christmas parcels from our mothers, she had the effrontery to tell us that we were unlikely to receive them, because "Parcels always get stolen around Christmas." We did not receive them.

Queenie had introduced Bedana and me to the "Dominions' Fellowship Trust," an organization run by a group of aristocratic ladies, in gratitude for the help the Dominions had given Britain during the war. "It's a good place to go to if you're feeling hungry or lonely," she said. "They're in South Kensington, and every Sunday they have 'open house.' There's always plenty of food, and there's a separate room set up for table tennis. It can be quite fun." Miss Woodruff—the only untitled lady there—had a steady supply of concert tickets for the Royal Box in the Albert Hall, as well as occasional tickets for a certain Duke's box in the Royal Opera House. She was a dear lady who took Bedana and me under her wing because we were music students, and she always gave us first choice of tickets. We were so spoiled that we would only attend concerts at the Albert Hall if we had seats in the Royal Box, where we'd found the acoustics—which were to be drastically improved years later—to be so much better than elsewhere in the hall.

Bedana and I were invited one year to attend a huge gathering of members of the Trust at one of the guildhalls in the City to meet the Queen Mother. To my amazement, thousands came from all over Britain: black, brown, and white members of the Commonwealth. We stood in rows literally for hours waiting for the Queen Mother to arrive, and were not allowed to touch any refreshments until after she had left. Miss Woodruff led the Queen Mother between these rows of young people, stopping here and there to chat, and to my astonishment stopped to introduce me, explaining that I was a violin student from South Africa. The Queen Mother, smiling, asked me a few polite questions, then moved on.

In Johannesburg, Bedana's mother telephoned my mother after Bedana had described the scene to her. "Guess who the Queen Mother stopped to talk to," she said.

"Bedana, of course," replied my mother.

"No—Eva!" said Bedana's mother, to my mother's delight.

The following year we were invited again, this time to meet the Queen herself, but we agreed once was enough. We had done our duty by our mothers.

In August 1953, soon after moving into my new room, I attended my first summer music school, staying for a fortnight at Dartington Hall, in South Devon. The gardens were so extensive and beautiful that I thought I had arrived in Paradise. There was a large abstract sculpture of a "Reclining Figure" by Henry Moore, situated on a grassy hilltop overlooking the gardens. It took my breath away. At Dartington, I met other music students, played chamber music, attended lectures, and heard an amazing harpsichord recital of Bach's *Goldberg Variations* given by George Malcolm. There was a concert every evening, and I soon learned to arrive early in order to find a seat in the front row and worship at the feet, especially, of the glorious baritone, Dietrich Fischer-Dieskau, and of the peerless Vegh Quartet. I was in a constant state of ecstasy.

Several years earlier Joyce De Groote had played second violin in the Robert Masters String Quartet, the then resident string quartet at Dartington Hall School of Music. Robert Masters, a past student of Max Rostal, had led the quartet, and the violist and cellist were Nannie Jamieson and Muriel Taylor. "They're great company," Joyce had said, "You must go and see them. I'll write and tell them you are coming to London."

Nannie and Muriel duly invited me to have a meal with them in their flat. They welcomed me warmly and were full of enthusiasm and humor. When I told them I was going to Dartington Hall, they said, "But you must come to *our* summer school too! The Robert Masters Summer School. When Joyce was with us we were a string quartet but we're a *piano* quartet now."

"Who's your pianist?" I asked.

"His name's Kinloch Anderson. He's a very sensitive chamber music player. We'll be in a beautiful old stately home near Wokingham. That's not far from London and it's easy to get to. And you can apply for a grant if you're short of cash. You'll have a week of intensive chamber music coaching, by all four of us. In the evenings you'll hear us play. We've got some lovely programs lined up."

And so, at the beginning of September, I was on my way to their summer school. We were all allocated partners, and I led a string quartet. We had lessons with each member of the Robert Masters Quartet in turn, and each one had something unique to give. I found Robert Masters himself particularly stimulating, but perhaps that was because as a violinist he paid me the most attention.

It was at the Robert Masters Summer School that I became acquainted with Jenny Welton, who studied viola with Nannie Jamieson and string quartets with William Pleeth at the Guildhall. Jenny's quartet lessons there took place immediately after ours, and she had several times come running after me down the corridor when our quartet lesson was over, to ask me to stand in for a violinist in her quartet who happened to be off sick. Now for the first time she and I had the opportunity to talk and get to know each other. Little did I guess then what a large part she was to play in my life less than one year later.

Chapter Sixteen
⌒ New Perspectives—1954 ⌒

In January 1954 I received a letter from Joseph Trauneck, telling me to look out for an African tenor at the Guildhall, for whom he had given benefit concerts to enable him to study in London. Ignatius Temba was a large, attractive man with a glorious voice and a great personality. Despite having lived in South Africa for most of my life, this was my first opportunity to get to know a black South African socially and make friends with him. This was a freedom unheard of, except in certain political circles that were being driven underground, back in South Africa.

I wrote to my mother regularly, telling her of my studies and friendships, eventually begging her to leave South Africa, with all its racism, and to come and join me in London.

"Don't forget we owe a debt of gratitude to this country," she admonished me. "It gave us a home when we were refugees, when no other country would accept us. Besides, I'm tired. I can't face uprooting myself yet again."

I realized I also owed a debt of gratitude to her, for all her hard work and the support she had given me, as well as to the University of the Witwatersrand, which had awarded me the scholarship to enable me to study in London. And so I knew I would inevitably, if unwillingly, return.

Early in 1954, Mrs. Rostal telephoned me: "A young German girl is coming to have lessons with my husband and she'll be staying with us," she said. "She's highly talented, but she's only sixteen years old, and she'll be a complete stranger here. I wonder—as you can speak German—would you befriend her?" "Sorry, no," was my implacable answer. It was less than nine years after the war, and I was not prepared to make friends with any Germans. Mrs. Rostal, herself an Austrian, said, "It's okay. I understand."

Then I came to Rostal's master class, and there was this young girl with a strikingly strong and interesting face. Exceptionally, for he was usually punctual, Rostal was delayed for over an hour that day. To while away the time, I found a soft pencil and blank paper and sketched a portrait of the newcomer. She was overcome with admiration and begged me to give it to her. She subsequently had it framed and hung it on her bedroom wall. Her name was Edith Peinemann, and she became Rostal's star student, out of many brilliant students.

She had enormous talent, and after all, we became good friends. There was no subject we could not talk about—including my initial refusal to befriend her. "Schneiderhahn had already accepted me as a student," she told me, "but then I heard Igor Ozim and other Rostal students at the international violin competition in Munich. I told my father I wanted to go to London and study with Rostal instead. My father said it was impossible. Rostal is Jewish. My father was a soldier in the German army during the war, so he was sure Rostal would never accept me. Well, I played to him anyway, and not only did he accept me, but I am living in his house, and he is giving me free lessons!"

Edith later became well known on the Continent and America as a soloist, but she never really carved out a career for herself in Britain. Yet I heard her give outstanding performances in London, of the violin concertos by Dvořák and Bartók, as well as stunning, unforgettable broadcasts of Bach's Solo Sonatas and Partitas.

That spring I went on an inexpensive National Union of Students' tour of Paris. It was a time when nearly all the students in Paris called themselves "Existentialists" and followers of Jean-Paul Sartre. The girls all seemed to wear black sweaters and flared floral skirts, and that became my "uniform" too. Apart from the seedy hotel we stayed at, in the Latin Quarter, Paris was a long-cherished dream come true: soaking up the bohemian atmosphere while sitting drinking coffee on pavement cafés; the romance of Montmartre, once home to so many great artists; the breathtaking spectacle of the chestnut trees in bloom along the Seine and the bookstalls along the Left Bank; Notre Dame Cathedral and the glorious Sainte-Chapelle; Rodin sculptures, Impressionist paintings, Gobelin Tapestries; the Bois de Boulogne and the Palace of Versailles.

My pianist friend Philip Levy, who studied first with Marguerite Long, then with Nadia Boulanger in Paris, was living at the Cité Universitaire, where I visited him and was fascinated by the medley of international students there. I was impressed with the quality of the canteen food, compared to what was available to us in post-war London. Philip showed me many haunts unknown to tourists and was a lot more fun than my NUS group. We spent an evening at a café mostly frequented by artists, where a guitarist played flamenco music, and where I met a girl who was studying painting with none other than Joan Miró himself. We had picnics of wonderful French bread and cheese in the woods of Fontainebleau and in the lovely countryside outside Paris, walking, climbing, and admiring the views. Philip made no demands on me, we were always laughing, and I felt understood, relaxed, and happy in his company.

In the summer of 1954, Max Rostal held his first International Summer School for violinists at Strobl am Wolfgangsee, near Salzburg, in Austria. I was longing to go there, but I could not afford to retain my room in Hampstead and yet be away for a whole month. I mentioned this to Jenny Welton, the attractive viola student at the Guildhall with whom I'd made friends at the Robert Masters Summer School the previous summer, and who was going to Strobl.

"Come and live at my digs," Jenny said. "It just happens that there's a vacancy. I know it would suit you!"

"But I don't want to leave Hampstead, I love it there!" I said.

"Hampstead is much too *chi-chi*," declared Jenny. "Hammersmith is real. You'd love it where we live," she said persuasively. "It's a Georgian house in a beautiful Georgian square with a little green park in the middle. All sorts of interesting people live there. Alec Guinness is in the house next door to us. Mind you, I've only caught sight of him once. And Michael Redgrave and his family live just around the back of the square on Chiswick Mall, along the Thames. My barge is moored there, and my nearest neighbor is A. P. Herbert. We've had lots of discussions about the difficult divorce laws."

"You own a barge?"

"Yes, it was a wedding present from my parents," she replied. "Well, we were *meant* to buy a house with the money but we bought a barge instead."

"You're married!" I exclaimed.

"Divorced. Wilf, my ex-husband, still lives on the barge."

"Wilf?" I asked.

"Dr. Wilfred Wren."

"So you were called Jenny Wren! Amazing—and how sweet!"

Jenny and Wilf had been childhood friends and had made a pact to marry by a certain date if no one else had turned up in their lives. Unsurprisingly, the marriage lasted no longer than a year. Now Wilf had become her lodger—as well as a shoulder to cry on when a love affair went wrong.

It seemed I had no choice if I was going to attend the summer school, and I did move out of my Hampstead digs and left Bedana, who generously forgave me, before going to Strobl. On my return I moved into Number 8 St. Peter's Square and never regretted it. Jenny Welton and Margaret Hayhurst, a co-lodger who was studying textile design at the Hammersmith College of Art—she was later to become a remedial teacher—became my closest friends. Until then I had been convinced that practically all Gentiles were basically anti-Semites, and at first I was suspicious of their friendship, but eventually, after honest and open discussion, they succeeded in ridding me of my suspicion. They also talked me out of my fear of sex. They cared and helped me grow up; they were fun, and life with them was a great adventure.

Our three rooms were on the top floor of the house. There was a bathroom and a tiny kitchen on the landing; we were quite self-contained. We had a delightful landlady, who lived on the ground floor. She was full of contradictions: a titled lady who was a Communist, who took us for drives to Richmond Park in her Rolls Royce shooting brake—an estate car with plenty of space for passengers and luggage, which I imagined full of guns and other equipment for game-hunting—and gave us lettuces from her garden and much homely advice. One evening I met her going home from Stamford Brook Underground Station, in a state of great distress. As we walked through the park in St. Peter's Square, she told me she had been to a Party meeting where it was officially announced that Khrushchev's denunciation of Stalin was true, not American propaganda. Everything she'd believed in had collapsed around her. It appeared that good, kind "Uncle Joe" had actually been a monstrous tyrant, ruthlessly executing any party officials who disagreed with him in the slightest, creating a regime of suspicion, treachery, and terror, and responsible for the deaths of thousands of innocent Soviet citizens. The Party faithful had never previously countenanced criticism of their beloved Joseph Stalin. It was more than she could bear. Stalin had been our much needed ally in the latter part of World War II, and I, too, felt a shock of horror and disillusionment after the revelations about the mistakes and excesses of his regime.

Margaret, who soon became Maggie, and I were both great readers and loved discussing books. I found her company relaxing and reassuring, for she had a way of simply accepting one as one was. Early in our friendship she asked me what was the most important thing in my life. "Music," I said, without hesitation.

"For me it's people," she said. "Surely there can't be anything more important than people!"

This was a novel idea for me. Betty Pack, my chamber music teacher in Johannesburg, had always told us to put music first: "You can't rely on people. You never know when they'll let you down. Music will never let you down," she had said. "Always put music first." And I had.

Now here was Maggie, suggesting an even higher value: humanity. Of course, I realized she was right, but it hit me like a bombshell. It didn't strike me at the time that there might be a value beyond that, of which both music and humanity were manifestations… Unfortunately, it led to my spending many hours, when I should have been practicing, having cups of coffee and chatting with her. Yet it cemented a friendship that has enriched my life.

I don't know how Maggie managed to put up with Jenny and my practicing when she was at home: I on the violin in one room, Jenny on the viola in another. Jenny was studying viola with Nannie Jamieson. She used to beg me to wake her up early in the morning so that she could get enough work done. "Don't take any notice if I tell you to go away," she said. "Just keep on shaking me, tear the bedding off me, *make* me get up!" It was a regular battle. Once we were both up and dressed, we would go for a quick walk around the square, to wake ourselves up further—I don't know why we were always so sleepy—ending with a cup of coffee at a café nearby, before starting our morning's practice.

Jenny and I spent a large part of our lives together. We studied for the Royal College of Music Teacher's Licentiate together: my previous teaching diploma, taken in Johannesburg, was from Trinity College, London. We went to student orchestra rehearsals at Morley College, conducted by Norman del Mar and Lawrence Leonard, where the delightful cartoonist Gerard Hoffnung (another former child refugee from Nazi Germany) played tuba and regaled us with hilarious stories during the breaks. We played chamber music, sometimes string quartets, and sometimes with the flautist William Bennet who lived just a few doors away in St. Peter's Square, and we spent much of our leisure time together, as well as with Maggie. We heard the entire series of Beethoven violin and piano sonatas together at the Victoria and Albert Museum, played superbly by Schneiderhahn and Kempff. With Edwina Leapman I went to hear Bertrand Russell speak on "History as Art." With Bedana Chertkow I went to Covent Garden and saw the miracle of Margot Fonteyn dancing in Ravel's *Daphnis and Chloé*. Until that moment I had thought ballet was not for me; Fonteyn opened my eyes and heart.

Derek Osche was the first of our group of South African students to marry. In September 1954, Anne, Derek's fiancée, about whom he had told me on our voyage from South

Africa, arrived in London. On the 30th of that month they were married at the church of St. Lawrence of Little Stanmore, Whitchurch. Bedana, Babette, Neil, Ivan, and I, all of our gang of January 1953, plus several more musicians from South Africa, attended the wedding.

Bedana next to the bride; Babette's head between Anne and Bedana; Eva's head between Derek and Anne; Neil's head on the other side of Derek; Ivan to the left in the back row, head tilted back, wearing glasses; Peggy Haddon, who occurs later in my story, is in the front row next to Bedana; Peggy's husband Neville Richardson beside her.

Life with Jenny and Maggie was a joyful affair. They were both slim and pretty, and they had great style, charm, and wit. I was never much of a partygoer, but the parties they gave were sheer delight. They had a gift for setting an atmosphere with special lighting effects, music and incense, delicious food and drink, and everybody would have a marvelous time. Ignatius was always present at our parties and always the center of attention. He would be seated like royalty on a throne, surrounded by spellbound girls on cushions on the floor, listening attentively to his every word.

The Oxford and Cambridge boat race passed our section of the river, and we invited friends to a party, before we all went down to the river to see the Eights pass by and to cheer them along. The most memorable occasion of all was when Wilfred finally moved out of the barge, and we had an amazing party there before Jenny sold it. Not that she ever had any money; even after selling the barge she managed to fritter it all away. Jenny was the quintessential femme fatale. She had only to look at a man through partly lowered eyes, with that half-challenging, slightly mocking way she had, and he would be at her feet. Forever. Well, almost.

Every morning, on awakening, I would look out of the window at the square below. Never before had I enjoyed the luxury of living with such a lovely view. Sometimes I would go downstairs and relax in the garden there, enjoying the shade of the trees, the scent of the flowers. One day, sitting alone on the grass, suddenly aware of the ground beneath me, the texture of the grass, the sights, smells, and sounds around me, I was overwhelmed by a sense of oneness, a realization that every living thing was part of a unity, and that I was part of that unity too. I, who from the moment of being torn away from my unselfconscious childhood in Mallorca had always had a sense of isolation, of being an outsider, despite my student friendships, suddenly knew that I belonged. I was part of this universe, and the universe was mine. Momentarily, I was lifted above my everyday self into a state of ecstasy. It was my first intimation that reason is not the only way with which to perceive the world, that there is another way, arising unbidden, when the mind is still, which is more direct but beyond the power of words to convey.

Chapter Seventeen

☽ STROBL AM WOLFGANGSEE—AUGUST 1954 ☽

Max Rostal held his first month-long international summer school at Strobl am Wolfgang-see in August 1954.

Strobl was a small village in the Salzkammergut, situated on the shore of Lake Wolfgang, surrounded by blue and purple mountains. I could imagine no prettier place. To the right it faced the village of St. Wolfgang, with its famous White Horse Inn. At the far-left end of the lake lay the village of St. Gilgen, where Wolfgang Amadeus Mozart's mother was born.

My journey there was dramatic. I had a South African passport and required an Austrian visa. When I applied for a visa at the Austrian Legation, I asked whether I would need a German transit visa for the train journey. I was told it wouldn't be necessary, and foolishly, I did not check with the German Embassy.

On Friday, July 30, I traveled with a small international group of students, crossing the Channel from Dover to Ostend. At the station platform we left our luggage to the porter, except for our violins, which we ourselves carried. As the train drew off we noticed to our dismay that our luggage was still standing on the platform. We rushed off the train at Brussels and telephoned Ostend to make sure that the luggage would be sent after us. By the time we returned to the platform, our train, with our reserved third class compartment, had departed. The next train was crowded, and we had to make do with hard slatted wooden seats in the fourth class, though we were lucky to get a compartment to ourselves.

At Aachen, German passport officials boarded the train. A stern faced, middle-aged official entered our compartment. He returned all the passports except mine, which he examined with a puzzled frown.

"*Warum haben sie kein Deutsches Durchreisevisum*? Why do you not have a German transit visa?" he demanded. It was my first return to Germany since before the war, and I could only too well imagine this man as a Gestapo officer. In my terror, my usually halting German became perfectly fluent, and I explained that I had apparently been incorrectly advised. He stood over me threateningly, and I became angry.

"Well, are you going to throw me off the train?" I challenged.

"I shall come back for you later," he said, ominously.

And so he did, several stations further on, saying, "Follow me!"

He led me, quaking, to a plush first class compartment, where no fewer than five more officials were discussing what to do with me. I turned on as much charm as I could muster. They decided to issue a temporary visa, on the understanding that once in Austria I would send my passport to West Berlin, to obtain a regular German transit visa for the return journey. I was none too happy at the thought of having to part with my passport, but I had no choice. Then they pondered at length how much to charge me, and after much flirtatious deliberation, they decided not to charge me anything at all.

One young official, on examining my passport, noticed that my birthplace was Cologne. "But that's where I live!" he exclaimed, "and it's on our route. In fact, I'm getting off there. Please allow me to show you our home town!"

"I have to get to Salzburg," I said.

"That's no problem! You can easily come with me and continue your journey later," he said.

I didn't think it occurred to him that I was Jewish and had left Germany as a refugee, and I marveled at his lack of imagination. They all wanted to flirt with me. "*Bleiben sie doch hier mit uns*, do stay here with us, *Fraulein Eva*," they invited me. "It is so much more comfortable in our first class compartment!" Politely, I turned down both invitations and returned to my friends in fourth class.

"What happened?" they asked. "Was he nasty to you? Did you get your visa?" and I recounted the whole story.

Eventually we arrived at Salzburg, where we first telephoned Mrs. Rostal to explain our delay. We transferred to a small local train and found her waiting to meet us at the station at Strobl, dressed in an Austrian dirndl. I never quite understood how the Jewish refugee Max Rostal could have married someone so ostentatiously Austrian, so soon after the war, though she was undoubtedly charming, good-looking—which he decidedly was not—efficient, and in great admiration of her husband.

We had been given a choice of accommodation, from the one smart hotel in Strobl to various grades of bed and breakfast accommodation, and she kindly accompanied us to each place of our choice. I had opted for the simplest and cheapest, in the home of an elderly peasant couple. My bedroom was an extension at the front of the house, with a corrugated iron roof. The only washing facilities were the kitchen sink, when available, and a cold water tap in the courtyard, where I used to strip and wash in the dark, after everybody had gone to bed.

When she realized I could not afford to eat out twice a day, my hostess said to me in German, "You know I always have a pot of soup on the hob. I could let you have a bowl of soup for lunch every day at very little cost to you, and no extra trouble for me. And you could have some strawberries for dessert. They're in season now. Would you like that?"

"How kind of you!" I exclaimed. "Yes, please, I'd like that very much."

Every morning I saw local children deliver baskets of tiny, red, wild strawberries, which they had picked in the woods. They were fragrant and sweet, delicious served with *Schlagobers*, whipped cream.

My host and hostess appeared to be good, warm-hearted people who made me feel at home, and I settled down contentedly.

The summer school took place in the village school building, the regular pupils being away on vacation. Violin lessons, in the form of master classes, took place in the mornings, and all those attending the summer school were allowed to listen and observe. Lectures on violin technique and musical interpretation, which I found endlessly stimulating, took place in the evenings. One evening Rostal sang us a little folk song, which he had overheard local children sing. We all recognized the tune, an episode in the Rondo movement of Mozart's G major Violin Concerto, proof of his strong connection with the area two centuries earlier.

Yfrah Neaman first row standing; Max Rostal next to him; Eva seated far left in front row; Peggy Radmall seated to the right of second row; Edith Peinemann's father looming tall behind Rostal at entrance to school building.

Afternoons were set aside for individual practice, rehearsals with pianist Paul Hamburger—an excellent musician who was the official accompanist—and outings. Sometimes we would congregate for dinner at a restaurant before the evening lecture, and there was a great feeling of camaraderie.

Back in Johannesburg, Melanie Pollack, the donor of the scholarship I had won at Wits University to enable me to study abroad, had learned that I was going to be in

Strobl summer school signed beer mat, 1954.

the vicinity of Salzburg when she was attending the Salzburg Festival. Although we had never met, she regarded me as her protégée. She had befriended the young violinist, Yfrah Neaman, when he had come to Johannesburg on a concert tour, shortly after the war. Now she wrote to me:

> I know that my great friend Yfrah Neaman is also going to be at Strobl. It will be a refresher course for him as he was a student of Max Rostal. I want you to arrange to come with him to visit me in Salzburg. I am very much looking forward to meeting you at last.

This was a pretty tall order for me. I remembered Yfrah performing in Johannesburg when I was still a schoolgirl. He was famous, and I was shy, but I found him approachable and friendly. And so, on a Saturday afternoon, Yfrah and I hitchhiked to Salzburg to visit Mrs. Pollack, a wealthy, attractive woman in her eighties. She entertained us with coffee and cakes and lively conversation.

Suddenly, she turned to me and announced: "Now I would like you to go for a walk. Salzburg is a beautiful city, and you will find much to interest you. I wish to be alone with Yfrah for an hour or so." I was taken aback, but when Melanie Pollack commanded, you obeyed. Inwardly I seethed at my peremptory dismissal, and I never quite forgave her, but Yfrah and I laughed about it on the way back to Strobl.

Rehearsals with Paul Hamburger went well. I was focused, and he was encouraging but puzzled as to why I should go to pieces in front of an audience. Yfrah came to listen and expressed an interest in taking me on as a pupil.

There were a number of non-participating Yugoslav and German violin teachers who had come only to observe and listen. Remembering my early piano and violin teachers, I expected the Germans all to be perfectionists with standards far beyond my reach. I was terrified. On one occasion I broke down completely.

Rostal said to me: "Vanity can be a very good thing: it can spur you on to greater and greater achievements. But in your case it has gone beyond all reasonable bounds!"

Vanity? But my overriding feeling had been one of inadequacy. He urged me to read Eugen Herrigel's *Zen in the Art of Archery*, which at the time had not yet been translated from the original German into English. When eventually I did read it, I realized at last what he had meant: that what was required was sincere, one-pointed attention to the music, with no thought of self or of the impression one was making on the audience. But at the time I wept inconsolably, and the other students crowded around me, reassuring me that Rostal's cruel words—as they seemed then—were undeserved. As I left by the school entrance one of the German teachers I had so feared said, *"Aber warum weinen sie? Sie spielen so gut!* But why are you crying? You play so well!"

That afternoon, Henry Werro, the internationally renowned violin dealer from Switzerland who had come to talk to us about violin maintenance, invited me to join a group of students he was taking to coffee and delectable cakes at the famous Café Zauner, at nearby Bad Ischl. We took a local train, and on our walk from the station, we passed a gift shop. One of the students stopped in front of the window and rhapsodised over a porcelain elephant. It was embarrassingly plain that she intended him to buy it for her. Henry Werro said,

Henry Werro with Peggy Radmall, Edith Peinemann and Eva (back row right).

"Okay, I shall go in and buy it, but you are going to draw lots for it, and I shall give it to the winner." Seated around a table at Zauner's, we drew lots, and I knew in my bones that he would somehow make sure I would win the elephant, because he wanted to comfort me. I was touched, but I didn't even like the ornament; to me it was *kitsch*. Many months later, when I thought the danger of his discovering it was over, I gave the elephant to Elizabeth, the girl who had so coveted it in the first place.

I was much in need of Henry's advice. As soon as I had asked the owner of the Gabrieli violin, which I had become so used to playing, for permission to take it out of the country, she had insisted that I return it to her at once. So I had to resort to my

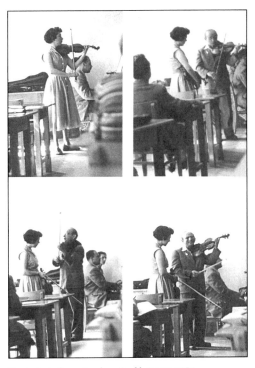

Eva in Rostal's master class, Strobl, August 1954.

little Grancino. Its many cracks soaked up the dampness in the air at Strobl to the detriment of its sound, at times driving me to despair. He recommended that I leave it out of its case to air as much as possible, and this helped to some extent. Henry was also a keen photographer. He used up a whole roll of film photographing my next lesson with Rostal, and presented me with a set of the prints, which are still in my possession.

Early on the Sunday morning after my arrival at Strobl, I was still in bed when the front door opened, and a young man entered, calling: "Heil Hitler!"

I froze with shock. Who was this monstrous person? How was he related to the old couple in whose house I was staying, who, until that moment, I had taken to be such kind people? What, after all, were they? I was filled with suspicion and horror.

He turned out to be their nephew. His name was Walter, and he had come to stay. He was young enough to have just missed being a soldier in the war.

Walter took a fancy to me and kept trying to persuade me to go up the *Schafberg*, a mountain looming 1783 metres above the *Wolfgangsee*, with him early one morning to watch the sunrise over the lake. "I promise you, you have never seen anything to equal it!" he said.

"Don't you realize I'm Jewish?" I asked.

"That makes no difference to me. We don't think about such things," he replied.

"Well perhaps you *should*, after all that's happened!" was my retort. "How could you have said, 'Heil Hitler' when you arrived, if it meant nothing to you?"

"It was just a joke. My aunt and uncle knew I meant it as a joke," he said.

"Have you really no idea what my people suffered under your Herr Hitler?" I asked. "Can't you see how your joke offends me?"

Undeterred, he went on begging me to go up the mountain and watch the breaking of the dawn with him. Looking back, I am still surprised that I gave in. Instinctively, I must have trusted him, and I came to no harm. As the sun gradually filled the sky with pink, orange, and gold, edging the mountains with fire, the shimmering silver lake turning pink and golden, his mood became romantic, but he did not make a pass at me.

He later wrote to me in London: "You and I are meant for each other, like Walter and Eva in *Die Meistersinger von Nürnberg*," but I dismissed this as a bit of nonsense.

A middle-aged German couple arrived on holiday two days after me and were given a double room upstairs. They never spoke to me, not even a "Good morning," but the way they looked at me spoke volumes. I still remember the woman's lined, hard-bitten, thin-lipped face and blond peroxided hair. I had no doubt they wished me dead.

On the evening of August 4, a terrific thunderstorm broke out. It was similar to the worst electric storms I had experienced in Johannesburg, when I had feared for the Africans in their mud huts or tin shanties. Now I was directly under a corrugated iron roof myself, with enormous hailstones clattering down on it. I told myself that I was safely indoors, that nothing would happen to me, but I was terrified.

Walter came to my door. "Fraulein Eva, we are keeping warm in the kitchen. Please come and join us!"

"No thanks, I'm alright here, really!" I said. I just couldn't face that German couple. The storm intensified, and I began to weigh my fear of it against my fear of the couple. Walter came back several times and begged me to join them, until at last I relented.

It was a horrible experience. I sat on my own, while my Austrian hosts and Walter sat around the stove, chatting with the Germans, from whom I felt palpable waves of hatred emanating in my direction. Astonishingly, after all Walter's cajoling, he did not ask me to come and sit with them. Perhaps even he had been intimidated. However, there was a young Belgian, whom I had not even noticed, who was on a walking tour and had found a room there for a couple of nights. He suddenly came over and seated himself beside me.

"Do you play chess?" he asked. He brought out a small travel chess set, and we started playing. Under his breath he said, "I know exactly how you feel. It's awful!"

I felt flooded with gratitude. We went for a walk together before he left Strobl, and he surprised me by saying, "*Partir, c'est un peu mourir*," parting is to die a little. I've never forgotten the humanity he showed me in the midst of the insensitivity of our hosts and their guests.

As the summer school drew to a close, I made up my mind not to continue working with an "assistant teacher," but only with a performing musician in his or her own right. Peggy Radmall had been invaluable in teaching me Rostal's basic technique, but I had gone as far as I could with her. I appealed to Rostal to accept me in his class.

"I can see that I've been able to help you," he said. "You've really made a lot of progress this month. Unfortunately, I'm going on a worldwide concert tour for the next ten months, so for the time being it's not possible."

I was dismayed, but then suggested working with Yfrah Neaman in the interim. After some initial resistance to the idea, Rostal agreed. He presided over my first lesson with Yfrah. The air was stiff with the tension and rivalry between them.

On our return to London, I arranged to leave the Guildhall School of Music and Drama and began to study privately with Yfrah, never thinking that in later years Rostal would make Switzerland his home and teaching headquarters, and that Yfrah would take his place at the Guildhall. I got on well with Yfrah, until I had so much teaching of my own to do that I found it hard to keep up with all the work he set me. "Couldn't you get married and let your husband support you?" asked Yfrah, but the idea of marrying for such a reason was completely foreign to me.

Whenever a pianist was required, Bedana Chertkow, who was a superb accompanist, would come with me to my lessons. Afterward, we would treat ourselves to coffee at the Dorice in Finchley Road and share an *Indianer*, a delicious spherical confection with a biscuit base and sponge top, filled with whipped cream and covered in chocolate.

Paul Hamburger's solution to my problem of uncontrollable stage fright was to send me to a psychoanalyst friend of his on our return to London. After an hour's interview, the psychoanalyst told me that my problem was that I had been in love with my father and hated my mother. I said this was preposterous, and that I adored my mother, which only seemed to confirm him more strongly in his view. Fortunately, Paul had warned him that I could not afford a whole course of psychoanalysis, so that was the end of a blind alley.

Henry Werro used to look Jenny and me up whenever he came to London on business, treated us with great kindness, and always invited us to a meal at an expensive restaurant.

Eventually, Rostal returned to London. Thereafter I worked exclusively with him until my departure from London in September 1956. I both feared and admired him, and felt there was no limit to what I could learn from him. For the last few months, I stopped giving lessons and handed over my teaching to someone else in order to have more time to prepare for my lessons with him. Shortly before I left, I had the joy of hearing Rostal say that I had "magic."

Chapter Eighteen

⌒ INTERLUDE WITH MY MOTHER—SPRING 1955 ⌒

In the spring of 1955 my mother came to London to see me and to pursue her German restitution claim.

I noticed quite a change in her. Success in her work had given her confidence, and she was more smartly dressed. She had lost a little weight, and her iron-gray, naturally wavy hair was well cut. She never wore make-up, but she looked altogether more soignée. She berated me for slopping about in the same old slacks and sweaters, and treated me to some new clothes. My mother's best features had always been her expressive gray-green eyes, and they were reassuringly as I remembered them, though the two frown lines between her eyebrows were deeper than before. It was a face full of kindness and character.

Together we flew to Düsseldorf, where my mother's restitution lawyer, a Dr. Karl Schultes, lived and worked. I had never traveled other than by sea and rail, and I felt a little scared to be flying, but also excited.

Dr. Schultes was one of the non-Jewish Germans who had been so disgusted with the Nazis that he had left Germany during the Nazi era, and was now doing all he could to make reparations. We were, of course, sadly aware that it was too late for those who had not survived the persecutions. He was kind to us, and he did his best for my mother. He even invited us to his flat in the evening and talked to us about his life and loves.

Matters progressed slowly, and I paid him another visit, on behalf of my mother, on my way back to Johannesburg in September the following year. Finally her life was made considerably easier, with a relatively small pension of her own and a larger widow's pension for my father's loss of professional earnings. Even I, who had been only eighteen months old when my parents first emigrated, was granted a lump sum in compensation for loss of educational opportunities in Germany. This went a good way toward helping to extend my studies in London after my scholarship came to an end.

While we were in the area, my mother and I visited Beethoven's birthplace in Bonn, and I was filled with wonder and reverence, standing in the very room where he had been an infant, this god among composers, this noble soul. At last I also visited the city of my birth, Cologne. Some emotional barrier prevented me from taking it in, even the famous cathedral, though we only saw it from the outside. It was too soon—memories were too raw.

However, one impression remains: a visit to the publishers who had published my father's book on income tax. According to my mother it had been the standard textbook on income tax in Germany until the Nazis banned it in 1933, and there were still some royalties owing.

We climbed up the steep stairs of this old publishing house to speak to the owners. Needless to say they denied all liability, but what really annoyed my mother was their avowal of having suffered greatly under the Nazis, when it was clear to her that they had, on the contrary, profited considerably.

She had been speaking to them in German and making asides to me in English. At one point, confusing the two languages, she turned to me and said, *"Glaub denen nichts—die lügen alle,* don't believe a word they say—they're all lying!" Not surprisingly, we left empty-handed, but my mother at least had the satisfaction of having made them squirm.

I wonder now that, ready as she was to take anybody on, she did not also confront the people who lived in, and presumably "owned," the large and comfortable house in Cologne that my paternal grandparents had been forced to abandon when they left for the Philippines.

We returned to London, where I had found bed and breakfast accommodation for my mother near St. Peter's Square. We went for walks along the river and talked about my father for the first time since his death. Only then did I realize how hard I had made it for my mother by refusing to speak of him. For ten years she had been living with the burden of thinking that I blamed her for his death. How unkind and self-centered I had been in my grief: I had not understood how important it was to go on talking to each other about the person we had both loved and lost and so cruelly missed. Nevertheless, we found great pleasure in each other's company, and my mother took a lively interest in all my activities, studies, and friendships.

I had an admirer, a violin student at the Royal Academy who was already making his way in the musical profession, playing in several chamber orchestras. I had met him through Bedana who was his accompanist at the Academy, and who had taken me to an orchestral concert in which he'd played, at the Victoria and Albert Museum. He telephoned me the next day.

Meyer was an attractive man and was, I think, used to women making advances to him, with no risk to himself of being rejected. I enjoyed his company: he was intelligent, interesting, and I found him attractive, but there was no way I would be making advances to him. I was far too sexually inhibited, unable even to meet him halfway, and his diffidence irritated me. I wanted to be swept off my feet, and he was not the one to do it. He played the violin beautifully, but I missed the fire and passion in the music. When I complained of this—for we sometimes played to each other and asked for comments—he explained to me that, just as I tended to lose control when I was nervous, his playing would become more and more careful. "I assure you I *do* have feelings," he said meaningfully, "it's just that I can't show them when I'm nervous."

In many ways it would have been a perfect match. He was a good person, we had much in common, and he was Jewish to boot. My mother was very taken with him and saw to her regret how I was holding him at bay. Her parting words to him were, "Go on being nice to Eva!"

Soon after she left, he took me rowing on the Serpentine in Hyde Park. "Did you feel embarrassed by what your mother said to me?" he asked.

I looked down, embarrassed still. "Yes," I answered simply, and looked up again.

He smiled. "You needn't be," he said, "my mother would have said exactly the same sort of thing!"

What a nice, sensitive person, I thought, but I went on giving him mixed messages, and eventually he gave up on me. He never did discover how attracted I felt toward him, but after all, my emotions were not really engaged.

My mother enjoyed meeting all my friends—Ignatius the tenor, Wanda the pianist, Edwina the painter. She found Jenny and Maggie, with whom I shared digs in Hammersmith, charming and beautiful, and had long, friendly conversations with Barbara, our landlady, who was astounded to hear for the first time of our refugee background. Of course she visited the Kaufmanns, and she visited art galleries with her old friend Mutti. We attended concerts together. I remember a meal we had with Bedana, Babette, Ivan, and Neil—all those of my South African student friends who now lived in Hampstead—at the Cresta, a Hungarian restaurant we used to frequent in Heath Street. It no longer exists, and I still miss it for its delicious, reasonably priced food and unique atmosphere. In my mind's eye I see my mother with Neil, who having accompanied so many Schubert lieder, knew many poems by Möricke and Goethe by heart. She had learned these poems as a schoolgirl, and they recited them together. I can still inwardly hear, "*Kennst du das Land wo die Zitronen blühen,*" and it makes my heart contract.

Chapter Nineteen
⪧ LOVE STORY—SUMMER 1955 TO SEPTEMBER 1956 ⪦

Later that year, in the early summer of 1955, I met the first great love of my life. I'd had suitable suitors before, and I'd had unsuitable infatuations, but Dušan Trbojević was the prince who awakened me from my slumber.

Two years previously I had met his then countryman (long before the break-up of Yugoslavia into its constituent states), the violinist Igor Ozim, past pupil of Max Rostal, the same age as I, but already a well-traveled international soloist. He was more suave and sophisticated than any of my friends. I met him at Ivan Melman's; they were playing Mozart sonatas together as I entered, and I was enchanted. I developed a crush on Igor, but he hardly noticed me. We met occasionally on his visits to London. He even took me out for a meal once. I was so nervous that I tore my paper napkin into shreds. He said, "Is it that bad?" and I was mortified.

Now here was I, playing the Brahms D minor Sonata with Ivan's girlfriend Pat Bishop—who had recently tied with Ivan in winning the prestigious Queen's Prize at the Royal College of Music—when in walked Dušan. He, too, was studying at the Royal College, a "mature student" six or more years older than we were. He was not at all what I considered to be "my type": not elegant and worldly-wise like Igor, but at once earthy and idealistic, spiritual and strongly masculine. I had always thought I preferred a pronounced feminine streak in my men. I set out to impress him, hoping he would mention how dazzling I was to Igor, whom he was bound to know. It didn't work out as I intended. He was indeed impressed, but eventually I was hoist with my own petard, and Igor was forgotten.

Dušan was tall and well built. He had a high forehead and a shock of brown hair, but he was very shortsighted and wore thick lenses, hiding his deep-brown eyes. He was not my idea of "good looking" despite his well-formed mouth and cleft chin. Those eyes and that cleft chin would later turn me to water, but not for several months. Meanwhile he pursued me relentlessly.

He went home to Yugoslavia to spend the summer there, during which time he bombarded me with letters though we hardly knew each other, and returned to London for the new academic year in September, laden with presents for me, of Yugoslav handiwork. I tried to ward him off with coolness, but he was not easily discouraged.

He sent me poetry and wrote me letters, one with a musical quotation: the gorgeous, romantic theme from the first movement of Tchaikovsky's *Pathétique* Symphony. On New Year's Day 1956, for lack of cash, he walked all the way from Hampstead to St. Peter's Square, Hammersmith, to deliver a book, *My Life and Thought* by Albert Schweitzer. Heartlessly, I pretended to be out, and he had to walk back without having seen me.

"I want you to understand Slavic soul," he said, when at last he managed to persuade me to meet him. "Best way is to read Dostoevsky"—which I had done—"and to listen to Musorgsky's opera, *Boris Godunov.*" Despite his Slavic soul he feared a Soviet takeover of Yugoslavia, treasuring freedom above all. (This worry intensified when later that year Russian tanks invaded Hungary and suppressed the Hungarian uprising.)

He wooed me with *Boris.* He invited me to visit him at his Hampstead lodgings, which had a piano in the living room. I sat beside him at the piano while he played and sang, and explained the entire opera, sweeping me along with him. His ardor set me on fire, and by the time I left him I felt dizzy and faint. "I don't know, but were you excited then?" he later asked me.

"Yes, tremendously. The music and the drama almost swept me away," I replied.

"Well, I looked at you, and there were tears in your eyes," he said. "Then I knew you could not be cold." And he began to talk to me about how he saw me, and he drew me out, making me feel warm and understood. He told me about his own life and the people in it, and I was deeply moved. Soon we became good friends, trusting each other and enjoying each other's company.

On January 28 we went for a walk on Hampstead Heath, and he told me how he had been suffering, how lost and lonely he had been, because the one person he felt close to in London—meaning me—had shut him out. I felt terrible and tried to explain that it was precisely because I cared and didn't want to hurt him that I had answered his letters so coolly, that I hadn't wanted to lead him on, and so on and so forth in the same vein. The more I said, the lower his spirits sank; the more depressed he became, the worse I felt. Until a strange thought struck me: Why was I so intent on putting him off? I had genuinely wanted to earlier, I had believed it only a few hours ago, but was it still true now?

According to my diary for February 4, 1956:

> And as I wondered, I started talking double-talk—heaven only knows what I said. I think I went on meaning to discourage him, but nothing I said sounded quite how I intended. All I know is that soon his spirits were up again. We went to the Cosmo for tea and sat at a table for two by the window, and I looked out of the window not daring to look into his eyes, wondering what had come over me. Dušan was pressing my hand emotionally and saying, "I am so happy now. I am so happy now!" I tried to think what I had said that could have caused him to be so overcome with emotion, but none of it made any sense to me. I only knew that I was wildly, irrationally happy, too. It didn't matter what either of us said, we were in a kind of ecstatic trance.

To my astonishment I realized I had fallen in love.

This was such a new feeling that I didn't trust myself and remained outwardly cool and distant. On the evening of February 8, he came to visit me, bringing the complete set of long-playing records of *Boris Godunov*, with Boris Christoff in the title role. It was tremendous. We sat side by side on the divan in my tiny room, and toward the end I laid my head on his shoulder. Until that moment I had held all men at arm's length. We remained motionless. When the opera came to an end, he kissed me. And covered me with kisses. Such kisses, so many kisses…

Next morning he telephoned. "I only want to know," he said tentatively, "did last night really happen, or was it a dream?"

"I feel as if I am newly born," I answered.

There followed seven months of intense happiness. I remember a walk at night along Hampstead Heath, Dušan reciting a Russian love poem to me. The sounds were intoxicating, though I didn't understand the words. We attended a students' concert at the Royal Academy, to hear Bedana play. As we left the artists' room afterward, he surprised me by turning around suddenly, sweeping me into his arms, and kissing me passionately. At other times he would be gentle and tender. His merest touch filled me with delight. I longed for him incessantly. The sound of his voice thrilled me. My love for him sometimes overflowed into tears. He understood and accepted everything about me. He asked me to call him Duško—Dushko—his more intimate diminutive. When he played in recitals he wanted me there, and I knew he was playing for me.

We told each other about our backgrounds, our lives up to then, our ideas on religion and on music. I had more than once been overwhelmed by a sense of the oneness of the universe, of the interconnectedness of everything, and myself as part of it. Such moments had filled me with wonder and joy. I could not conceive of a personal deity, but had become aware of a unifying force, which was the closest I had ever come to religion. Dušan said it was similar to the religious views expressed by Albert Einstein, so I felt I was in good company.

We regularly went to concerts together. I remember sitting beside him in the grand tier of the Festival Hall, listening to Gina Bachauer playing Rachmaninov's Third Piano Concerto. At the same moment in the music we were both lit up, and we looked into each other's eyes in sheer ecstasy. When we traveled together on the Underground people smiled at us, sensing the happiness we radiated.

Vati Kaufmann was dying, and I was summoned to his bedside. He asked me about my studies, whether I was taking care of myself and whether I was happy. "I'm happier than I have been in my whole life," I answered. As we left the bedroom Mutti asked, "Is it really true, what you told Vati?" and I replied, "Yes, it is really true."

Yet all this time we knew that we would inevitably have to part. Dušan's father was an Orthodox priest; his grandfather had been high priest of all Serbia. He himself had been meant for the priesthood, and when he had chosen the path of music, had overheard someone ask his father whether he was not disappointed. "My son will be a priest in his own way," was his father's reply. It was, for me, an impossible scenario. We both knew it and did not even discuss the possibility of marriage, to the perplexity of all our friends. The nearest Dušan came to it, as the time of our parting drew near, was softly humming the wedding march from *Lohengrin* and saying wistfully, "I wish…" And then, "You are so dear."

He felt deeply that his mission was to return home and give his people everything he had learned in London. I felt I owed it to my mother to return to South Africa, and I also felt obliged to give something back to that country in return for the scholarship that had enabled me to study in London.

In March I had written to him:

> It is a great weight off my mind that I have at last come to a positive decision to go home this year, of my own free will, and that my mother need not go on suffering her loneliness indefinitely.

> Meanwhile, I want you to know that this is the happiest period of my life. I love you, I love you, I love you endlessly and with all my being. I am flooded with joy and gratitude and tenderness—and anguish, too—but the anguish heightens my joy.

> There is a sense of tragedy I carry about with me ever since that evening when I first discovered that I loved you—that evening when for the first time, you told me last night, you felt the ecstasy that we share when we are together.

As the time drew near and our parting loomed darkly, my anguish was intensified by the feeling that he had withdrawn from me a little, that I was suffering alone. It was the time of his final piano examination at the Royal College, in addition to several recitals, and he was fully focused on his work. He was playing superbly. Before his examination I sent him a note saying: "Play well, my love. My thoughts will be with you."

He was told he had received the highest marks ever to be awarded for that examination. "It was thanks to your letter that I played so well," he said. I laughed in disbelief, and he said, "Truly! I kissed it twice before I left for the exam and I said to myself, after this I would play like a god!"

With his exam over, he suddenly became aware of how short a time we still had together and was overcome by sadness. We did not know how to cope with our feelings. My diary entry for September 18 reads:

> We were rather superficial and hard together this evening. We were sipping cool drinks at the Cosmo when I suddenly murmured softly, almost involuntarily, "Duško!" He looked at me as though electrified, and all our sham brightness and light-heartedness were shed in that moment. We were our essential selves, apart from the entire world, held in enchantment. Heavy-hearted and yet buoyed with ecstasy. Passionate, and yet with a love transcending passion.

He wanted to be alone with me, and I wanted him to see me off at the airport alone, so I asked all my friends to stay away. Jenny pleaded to be allowed to come; Maggie, now living and teaching at a Rudolf Steiner school in Surrey, was no longer at St. Peters Square. Barbara, our landlady, kind as ever, insisted on giving us a lift in her shooting brake. So there were, after all, four of us: Barbara, Jenny, Dušan, and I. However, Dušan and I had the whole morning and lunch alone together before it was time to leave. Again, my diary:

> Somehow we got on to the subject of his composition, which he had been neglecting lately for the sake of his piano playing. "It didn't last long, the inspiration I gave you," I said.

"Why, what do you mean?" asked Dušan.

He had told me in the beginning how he had been composing music in Yugoslavia and had suddenly run dry, unable to write music again until he met me.

The diary continues:

"Well, you stopped composing so soon after starting again."

"And what about my piano playing?" he asked. "Don't you know it was you who has inspired me all the time?"

"Your piano playing, too? Really, Duško?"

"Yes of course! I thought you realised that."

There was nothing dramatic in our parting—no tears, no scenes, just quietness and love. Neither of us could really register the fact that this was our last moment together.

The full impact only came later.

Our hearts were full, and I felt none of the despair I had felt earlier. When I had said goodbye to Bedana a few days previously, I had said to her, "I see only blackness ahead of me. I feel as if I am going to die."

And she had answered beautifully, "You will rise like a phoenix out of its ashes."

Jenny, Dušan, Eva, 8 St. Peter's Square, September 1956, about to depart for the airport. Barbara took the photograph.

Chapter Twenty

⌐ RETURN JOURNEY—SEPTEMBER 1956 ⌐

A few months after my departure for South Africa in September 1956, Dušan returned home to Yugoslavia.

Dušan, standing near the center, wearing spectacles, surrounded by his students in Serbia.

Before leaving London I tried to find a replacement violin for my little Grancino, within the very limited price range at my disposal. I spent many frustrating hours at dealers and in private homes, trying out unsatisfactory instruments. Eventually I gave up, and it was in Johannesburg, at the violin dealer J. J. van de Geest and Son, that I subsequently found the wonderful Vuillaume violin, which was to become my lifelong companion. Yfrah Neaman had sold me a Gand and Bernadel bow at a reasonable price, and my mother had bought me a less renowned but workmanlike German bow, on our visit to Cologne the previous year, so I was well set up to start on my career. Much later I bought a Hill bow, which suited me best of all.

I was desperately unhappy at having to part from Dušan, and I feared that prolonging the journey back to South Africa would be sheer purgatory. I had intended to fly straight home and get it over with, but at that time it was possible to make any number of stopovers at no extra cost, and my mother prevailed on me to take advantage of this. "It's the chance of a lifetime," she insisted.

Reluctantly, I worked out an itinerary with the travel agent whose services my mother had used on her visit the previous year, and I spent three weeks in limbo, not yet having to come to terms with my parting from Duško, and unexpectedly enjoying myself hugely.

First Cologne, where Dr. Schultes now lived and worked, to try to expedite my mother's restitution claim. I was a bit frightened of the responsibility, but Dr. Schultes put me at ease, gave me all the time needed to push things forward, and took me out for a meal in an expensive restaurant in the evening. Soon after my arrival in Johannesburg, my mother at last began to receive her German pension.

I telephoned Duško from my hotel room, feeling recklessly extravagant. At the time long-distance calls were prohibitively expensive. "Eva! I thought I'd never hear your voice again," he said, overcome with emotion.

After Cologne, I paid a brief visit to Zürich, to meet my mother's best friend, Gretl Gideon—she who had managed to keep in touch with my grandparents and Aunt Selma in Theresienstadt via the Red Cross, and had sent my mother the letters after the war. I had heard so many anecdotes of their childhood and youth together that I was intrigued to be meeting her at last, and from the start we had an excellent rapport. She was a beautiful woman, had never married, and was now, at the age of fifty-six, still living with a somewhat dominating, blind mother to whom she was devoted and an aunt whose husband had been instrumental in helping her and her mother escape to Switzerland from Nazi Germany.

I took the train from Zürich to Biel/Bienne, where a fellow Rostal pupil, Marianne Egli, had invited me to come and stay at her parents' grand old eighteenth century house. It was beautifully situated, overlooking the old town, and she had her own studio in the garden for practicing the violin. "How I envy you," I said.

We visited Berne. I was enchanted by the old city, with its bear pit and real live bears in the center of the town; the ancient clock tower, *Zytgloggeturm,* its many painted figures all springing into action when bells pealed on the hour; the many fountains and character-filled old streets. We went to a Paul Klee exhibition, which I loved, at the Kunstmuseum, and attended part of a parliamentary sitting in the Bundeshaus.

In the evening we ate in the balmy open air, at a posh restaurant, where Marianne introduced me to cheese fondue. There was a group of men at an adjoining table, possibly the worse for drink, who had overheard us speaking in English. One of them leaned over and said contemptuously, "A fine country you live in, ruled by a woman!" meaning Queen Elizabeth II. They teased me mercilessly.

"Is this the usual attitude toward women in Switzerland?" I asked Marianne.

"Well, we don't even have the vote. That must tell you something," she said.

"But I thought Switzerland was so advanced and democratic. I really am astonished!" I exclaimed.

In fact, women's suffrage was only introduced there in 1973.

My friend Philip Levy was preparing himself for the International Piano Competition in Geneva, and he had suggested that I join him there for a few days.

"Geneva is full of competitors for the Concours," he wrote. "I'll try and find you a room at a *pension*. If you leave it till you get here you may be too late." He himself was staying in the apartment of a charming lady, Madame de Montmollin, who was private secretary to the famous jeweler, Cartier, and had a grand piano in her living room.

I journeyed by train along the lovely three lakes of Biel, Neuchâtel, and Geneva, and Philip was at Geneva station to meet me. As ever, he was great company. He played me his pieces for the preliminary competition and was one of the very few who passed. Great joy! Madame de Montmollin invited me to a meal and told Philip she was sorry I would be leaving, because she liked me, and because I "kept him out of mischief." He took time off to show me the charming Old Town and also the *Palais des Nations*, once the seat of the League of Nations, now part of the still young and idealistic United Nations. We left one morning early to travel cross-country by train, and then upward by another train, to visit Zermatt and Gornergrat. We were thrilled with the glorious landscape, the snowy mountain peaks glittering in the sunlight, and we clambered about joyously on the snow-covered hillsides. Returning to Geneva that evening we enjoyed a superb dinner at a restaurant on the island in the lake.

On the morning of my scheduled departure from Geneva I received a card, poste restante, from Dušan. It began: "My dear, dear one, how could I dream I would hear once more your loving voice!?" And so, rhapsodically, it went on, completely throwing me off balance.

When the time came to leave, Philip took me to the air terminal, and from there I went by bus to the airport. I sat in the airport lounge, reading and re-reading the card I had received from Dušan that morning, and fell to daydreaming about him. Half an hour after my plane to Rome should have departed, I began to wonder why my flight had not yet been announced. I thought I had better inquire. "Lady," said the airport official at the gate, "we kept that plane waiting for *ten minutes* while we tried to find the missing passenger. Where have you *been?*"

"I've been here all the time, I just didn't hear you," I said shamefacedly. "Oh dear, what am I going to do now? My friends are coming to meet me at Rome airport in an hour's time, and I won't be there."

"Don't worry," he said, "you can send a telegram. But I'm sorry, there are no more flights to Rome today. You can take one tomorrow evening at the same time. No, you won't have to pay any extra." This I did not understand, because it clearly was my fault that I had missed my plane, but I was grateful.

I telephoned Philip. "Guess where I am."

"Not still in Geneva!" he exclaimed, roaring with laughter. "I was just envying you such a perfect, clear evening for flying over Mont Blanc. Where on earth are you going to stay? I think the *pension* is booked up. Wait. Hold on a minute."

He returned to the phone. "Madame de Montmollin says you can sleep on her sofa in the living room." Saved. "And tomorrow," he said, "I'm taking you all the way to the airport to make sure you catch that plane!"

Queenie, with whom I had shared my first digs in Hampstead, and who had married a Roman, had intended to book me into an inexpensive hotel in Rome. She was not at the airport to meet me, as she was not only heavily pregnant, but also ill with flu. Instead, her husband, Enzo, as well as his sister and brother-in-law, all turned up and took me home to see her. They lived on the Monteverde Vecchio overlooking the whole city and the river Tiber. I was without suitcase, as my luggage was nowhere to be found. However, I felt confident that it would catch up with me, and I was not too disconcerted, although from then on I had to wash and iron my one and only dress and my underwear every day for the rest of the journey. Queenie's mother-in-law had prepared a delicious dinner for us, and the atmosphere was warm and friendly.

Finally Enzo took me to the hotel, which he, instead of the ailing Queenie, had booked for me. It was situated in a quaint old cobbled cul-de-sac and had been recommended to him, so he had not bothered to look beyond the pleasant-looking reception area. I had planned to be in Rome for five nights, and Enzo insisted that the first night be at his expense. He had already paid for it as a deposit and gave me no chance to refuse. We said goodnight at the reception desk, and then I went upstairs to my room, where a great shock awaited me. Had I not felt beholden to Enzo and honor-bound to stay the night, I would have left the hotel there and then, despite being a stranger in Italy, and having forgotten all my five-year-old Italian. The room was filthy, the bedding smelled stale and slept-in, and the adjoining bathroom floor was wet and covered in human excrement. There was no way of avoiding it, even on tiptoe, on the way to the lavatory or hand basin, and the bath was too disgusting to consider. I stuck it out in my room until five o'clock in the morning, then, unable to bear it a minute longer, I gathered my violin and overnight bag and crept out of the hotel, savoring fresh air and freedom.

I wandered about the quiet, lonely streets of the residential area where the hotel was located, waiting for a café to open and wondering where I would find a decent small hotel within my budget. Then I had an inspiration. I remembered that Petronel Davies, the young girl who had taken over Maggie's room at St. Peter's Square, had a friend who worked at the British Embassy in Rome, and she had given me the telephone number suggesting that I look her up. As soon as the offices began to open, I telephoned the Embassy and asked to speak to Veronica Page. To my relief she came to the phone. "I'm stranded in Rome," I said, and told her about the awful hotel I had escaped from a few hours earlier. "D'you happen to have a list of low-price hotels? I don't know where else to turn."

"If you don't mind sleeping on the floor, you can come and stay in our flat. I'm sharing with another girl. I know she won't mind. Come and have lunch with us, and you can give notice to your hotel afterwards. Do come," said Veronica.

I had fallen on my feet. Sleeping on a clean, cool floor was the best possible option in hot and sultry Rome. It was fun staying with Veronica and Kaye. They took me out on those evenings when I wasn't seeing Queenie and introduced me to my first pizza Napolitana— long before pizza had become commonplace in England—at an outdoor restaurant near the Trevi fountain. I even managed to practice the violin a little in the flat, in the comparative cool of the early mornings. During the daytime I went sightseeing on my own, armed with a pocket Italian-English dictionary and guidebook. There was so much to see, and except for the overpowering heat, I enjoyed it all.

"I can't tell you how grateful I am to you," I wrote to my mother, "for having practically forced me into taking this wonderful holiday."

Every morning Kaye checked with the airport for me, to find out whether my luggage had turned up. No luck. On the day of my departure, Queenie had recovered sufficiently to come to see me off. We discovered my suitcase at Scandinavian Airlines; it had been on an unscheduled trip to Stockholm. Nobody knew how it had got from Swissair to Scandinavian Airlines. Queenie's Italian was fluent, and she spoke earnestly to the luggage handlers, telling them to make sure that this time my suitcase would be loaded on to the right plane. "Yes, of course, don't worry!" they blithely said to her.

On the flight to Athens I sat next to a distinguished looking, middle-aged Turkish gentleman, who turned out to be a professor at Istanbul University. He told me a great deal about Istanbul and tried hard to persuade me to skip Athens and continue my journey with him to Istanbul. "I will show you around this wonderful city myself. You will find it very interesting," he promised, but I demurred. However, it seems my suitcase had other ideas.

When we arrived at the incredibly primitive Athens airport, I waited on the tarmac outside the plane with all the other passengers. One by one they picked up their suitcases and walked off to the terminal building a few yards away, until I was left behind, alone and without luggage. Night had fallen, all the taxis had been taken, and I felt vulnerable. Apart from the airport staff behind the counters, there was one solitary man, waiting for me. He introduced himself as a qualified tour guide, said he had been watching me from afar, and had passed up all the other potential clients in the hope that I would take him on as my personal guide. I asked one of the airport officials whether he was a bona fide guide and was told that he certainly was, but that if I employed him it would be at my own risk. I had to think quickly. I had only twenty-four hours—or so I thought—in Athens, and I wanted to see as much as possible. What better way than to have my own tour guide? He was clearly predatory, but I felt I could handle it. And so I said yes.

"First I will take you to your hotel," he said, picking up my little overnight bag; I held on to my violin case. "Then we will go and eat." His English was fluent, partly thanks to his having lived in Johannesburg for two years during the war. We walked to the hotel, which I had booked in advance through the travel agent. Then he asked if I would like to eat at a typical taverna, one that was not normally frequented by tourists, on the side of the Acropolis. He ordered a little of every typical dish on the menu, so that I might taste each of them, and he introduced me to retsina wine. Just as I was beginning to wonder what cost I had let myself in for, Mario announced, "Tomorrow you pay; tonight you are my girlfriend." I hoped he meant it as a joke, but I have to admit I was enjoying myself.

After the meal we clambered up the Acropolis, and I stood in wonder and awe, looking at the floodlit Parthenon. Finding our way there by the light of the stars he, unsurprisingly, made a pass at me. I had the perfect defence: that I had only just parted from the one

Mario and Eva at Athens taverna, 1956.

great love of my life, and that I could not possibly respond to any other man, my heart still bleeding with the pain of parting. He was able to respect this without losing face, but it did not stop him from making further attempts to break down my resistance the next day. In fact, my very faithfulness to the man I loved seemed to inflame him, and he decided I was the woman he was going to marry. None of this, however, distracted him from doing an excellent job as a guide, showing me in the short time available just about every important sight in Athens. He begged me to stay in Athens and marry him, and he absolutely refused to accept one drachma from me, not for acting as my guide, not for the meals we ate, not for anything.

At 5 p.m. we checked in at the El Al office to confirm my flight to Tel Aviv that night. "You should have checked in forty-eight hours ago," the El Al clerk said. "As you didn't, your ticket has gone to another passenger."

I couldn't believe my ears. "But I wasn't even *in* Athens forty-eight hours ago! How could I possibly have checked in! And the travel agent didn't tell me—*nobody* told me!" I was nearly hysterical.

Mario was jubilant. "There you are!" he said. "You were meant to stay in Athens and marry me!" This was all I needed to tip me over the edge.

"Mario, for pity's sake!" I shouted at him, "All my relatives in Israel are expecting me to arrive at half past midnight tonight; they'll probably all be there to meet me. They'll be mad with worry!"

Mario tried to calm me down. "Okay, so we'll send them a telegram. And I know a nice hotel where you can stay tonight, because your hotel is full."

"I'm afraid there isn't another flight to Tel Aviv until the day after tomorrow, and that's not a direct flight, it stops at Nicosia for two hours," the clerk informed us. "You won't be flying with El Al. We are fully booked. You'll be flying with Greek Airlines."

This was getting worse and worse. Mario gloating, yet trying to reassure me everything was going to be alright, my worries about a lot of relatives whom I had never met turning up at the airport and not finding me, my luggage still missing, and a feeling that everything had got out of control.

We did send a telegram, to the only pair of relatives whose address I knew offhand, but it arrived after they had all left to welcome me at the airport. In true Israeli fashion, they went off their heads with worry and upset, until they found the telegram and prepared once more to meet me two nights later.

Meanwhile, more drama in Athens. My hotel was indeed fully booked that night, and Mario did find me a room in another, similar hotel. I noticed him having a word with the room maid but thought nothing of it. He took me out for a meal and then a walk through the park in the center of Athens. The air was balmy, and the walk was pleasant. Every so often we would meet a group of his friends, and he would introduce me as his South African "Hebrew" girlfriend. Finally we returned to the hotel, and he escorted me to my room, where I found not one but two beds made up, with bedspreads taken off and corners folded back. Now I understood what he had been talking about to the room maid. I went berserk.

"If you think you are going to spend the night with me you are one hundred percent wrong! I thought I could trust you, and you've tricked me. I'm in such a predicament! How could you take advantage? It's dishonorable! Go away! Let me pay you what I owe you and go away! I don't want to see you again!"

He pleaded with me to forgive him and to stop being angry. "I don't like it when you're angry. I like it when you're sweet and smiling!" He promised to go home for the night and leave me in peace, and he asked the maid to close up the second bed. "I'll come back for you tomorrow, and after breakfast we'll go to Piraeus," he said. "I have a friend who has a speedboat there. He'll take us for a ride round the bay. You'll love it, I promise!"

I had laddered my stockings during our tour and had spoken of throwing them away. He was horrified at such waste and insisted we get them mended by a person who sat on the pavement doing invisible mending. I had no idea such work was still being done. This was the first thing we did before our trip to Piraeus. I was rather touched by his efforts to save me money when he refused to accept any of it for himself, and I was acutely aware that he might have been earning himself a tidy sum in the past two days, with other tourists. Piraeus was exciting, tearing through the bay in a speedboat, eating freshly caught fish on the shore, having my fortune told by a gypsy. Afterward we clambered about on the hilly outskirts of Athens, where the dry brush reminded me of the environs of Johannesburg.

The next day Mario took more time off work, in order to take me to the airport and find out what had happened to my suitcase. It had been on another unscheduled flight, to Istanbul and back, and I was assured I would meet up with it in Tel Aviv. He introduced me to the extraordinarily handsome pilot and the almost as good looking co-pilot of my plane, and had a long wait in order to wave goodbye to me from the tarmac when we finally took off. Perhaps he really meant what he said, because he wrote to me soon afterward to Johannesburg, begging me to let him come there to marry me.

The plane was full of passengers up to our arrival at Nicosia. Although we had several hours' wait there, as a transit passenger I was not allowed to leave the airport. Cyprus was at the time struggling for independence from Britain; the EOKA organization, closely connected with the by now imprisoned Archbishop Makarios, was fighting for union with Greece. But Cyprus was strategically important to Britain, which had declared a "State of Emergency"; British soldiers surrounded the airport, and the atmosphere was tense. I chatted with a couple of young soldiers, and they told me how much they hated having to be there. The woman who ran the canteen gave me a free cup of tea, as I had no Cypriot currency. Eventually, we flew off again, and I discovered to my amazement that I was now the only passenger. A great treat awaited me: I was allowed to sit in the cockpit with the two pilots, who explained how everything worked, and pointed out where we were when we approached land. Not until we began making the descent to Tel Aviv did I have to return to my seat in the cabin and fasten my seat belt.

Israel! The thought that I was about to arrive in the land of my forebears, which had at last achieved statehood during my lifetime—in fact, only eight years earlier—after we had suffered centuries of persecution as strangers in other people's lands, overwhelmed me. Added to this, I was to meet uncles, aunts, and a cousin of my own age, for the first time in my life. What excitement when I arrived, and what a heart-warming welcome. I felt at once that I belonged. For the first time in my life I was surrounded by close relatives other than my parents, not counting the one night in my grandparents' house in August 1936. My cousin Miriam had begun to work at the Israeli Consulate in Johannesburg during the latter part of my time in London, and my mother had come to regard her as a second daughter. Miriam had arranged her holiday at home so that the last few days would coincide with my visit, and she was to fly back to Johannesburg with me. She took me to a concert given by the Israel Philharmonic that very evening.

I slept in the flat of an aunt and uncle in Tel Aviv, and the next day we all drove up north, by way of Haifa and Mount Carmel, to Kibbutz Hazorea in the Jezreel Valley, in the shadow of Mount Tabor. This was where my mother's younger brother, Heini, now known by his Hebrew name, Naftali, lived. I was struck by the parched land, the hardship of kibbutz life, the long hours of hard work, the primitive huts in which the members lived, the simple food they ate in the common dining room, the clothes they shared and nobody owned. After the clothes came back from the laundry, they would be doled out to whoever approximately fitted the sizes. Nowadays Hazorea is a flourishing kibbutz, with lush flowers and trees, and common ownership of personal effects a thing of the past.

Heini was a pioneer and an idealist, and he became one of my favorite people in the whole world. He did his best to build bridges of communication and friendship with Israeli Arabs, later becoming an active member of the Peace Now campaign. He studied Arabic and spent hours translating from Arabic into Hebrew, well into his nineties. He came to see me in Tel Aviv the day after our visit, with a bunch of roses from Hazorea tied up in a wet rag, which I was to bring to my mother. They were still fresh when I arrived home in Johannesburg, and for several days longer.

After three intensely-filled days in Israel, Miriam and I left for Johannesburg. In the departure lounge of Lod—now Ben Gurion—Airport, just before taking off, I at last caught sight of my suitcase.

Part Four

☙ WORK, POLITICS ☙

Chapter Twenty-One
☞ JOHANNESBURG—OCTOBER 1956 TO MID-1958 ☜

The flight from Tel Aviv had been unusually long and eventful. Miriam and I sat companionably together. Our plane took off after midnight, and we managed to get some sleep. When we awoke in the morning we found ourselves flying over the Sahara desert. It was at the time of the Suez crisis, and the pilot had been obliged to make a detour via French Equatorial Africa, touching down at Fort Lamy and Brazzaville.

Just before Johannesburg, we flew into a violent storm. Our plane was tossed about relentlessly; most of the passengers were sick or screaming with terror. Miriam and I were determined to remain calm, though we did not manage to avoid being sick. "Please be calm, there's no cause for panic; don't worry, everything is under control," said the cabin crew, trying to reassure us. But when the pilot turned up at the Israeli consulate two days later, he admitted to Miriam that he and all the crew had been just as terrified as the passengers.

As we left the plane after landing, a large crowd of friends waved and cheered us from the viewing platform, but we were still feeling shaken and hardly in the mood for such a rousing welcome.

My mother tried so hard to make my homecoming happy. She had rounded up all my friends, including my beloved teachers, Pierre De Groote and Betty Pack, and we all made for our flat in Geraldine Court and had a party. There were masses of flowers, many welcoming letters and cards, an abundance of food and drink, gaiety, and excitement. And there were other surprises to welcome me back: a superior radiogram and a tape recorder from my mother—luxuries hitherto far beyond my reach—and a fancy gold ring with an amethyst from Fred Marcus in Cape Town. He had divorced Illa and had visited me once in London. "When I wake up in the mornings," he wrote, "I am happy that I live in the same world as Eva Schay." Ironically, there was a letter from Mario, but such disappointment: no letter from Dušan. Everybody seemed so glad that I was back, but my heart felt like lead.

Betty suddenly burst out, "Eva, do you love me as much as I love you?"

Dear Betty: she had arranged for me to play Bach's A minor Violin Concerto with her chamber orchestra, and at the first rehearsal I nearly disintegrated. There was now no longer any escape from the fact that I had to face life without Dušan, and the pain and longing were unendurable. I felt incapacitated by depression, and life didn't seem worth living.

My dizziness and faintness I put down to the altitude, no longer being accustomed to living almost six thousand feet above sea level. Listlessly, I dragged myself through each day, not knowing how to go on.

My mother and I sat in the back of a taxi, I no longer know where to, and she took my hand in hers and said, "You are so dear." I burst into tears. "Dušan must have said that to you," she said gently, and I nodded. It must have been so hard for her. She told me, to my surprise, that she had been ready to pack her bags and follow me to Yugoslavia, but there had been no question of that.

Soon after that first rehearsal I telephoned Betty. "May I come and talk to you?" I asked.

"Of course, you may," she said. "Something's the matter, isn't it? I knew it! Can you manage tomorrow at ten?"

She took me into her "pink room," her sanctuary at the bottom of the garden, and I poured my heart out to her, and my feeling that I could not go on without Dušan.

"Do you remember," I asked, "when you said that all I lacked was faith in God, and I scoffed? What did you mean by 'God'?"

"Not a man in the sky, if that's what you thought," she answered. "What I mean by 'God' is a pervading spirit, the Self that lives in the hearts of all. It's both within us and all around us, and is the source of all life and energy. It's Universal Consciousness."

Many years earlier she had studied yoga with an Indian guru—although how she had managed that, in racist South Africa, I never found out—and this had given her great strength. When Yehudi Menuhin, himself a great devotee of yoga, came to South Africa on a concert tour, they practiced standing on their heads together… Betty introduced me to several books on Raja and Jnana Yoga, which I devoured hungrily. Life was beginning to make a little more sense to me.

Betty had tremendous presence. Her dark, slanted eyes twinkled knowingly. She was humorous, powerful, generous, and a wonderful cellist. She gave me a simple mental yoga exercise to see me through, and I managed to give two creditable performances of Bach's A minor Violin Concerto with her orchestra. The first took place at the Priory in Rosettenville, the second at the Reps Theatre in Johannesburg.

Rosettenville was on the outskirts of Johannesburg, and the Priory was the home of an Anglican brotherhood, the Community of the Resurrection, whose headquarters were in Mirfield, Yorkshire. Father Trevor Huddleston, renowned for his anti-apartheid stand, had recently been recalled to England from the Priory, because his activities had embarrassed and angered the South African government. I had played at the Priory as a schoolgirl, with Joseph Trauneck's orchestra, during Father Huddleston's time there. He had been an inspiration for all of us who hated apartheid, and was the author of the book *Naught for Your Comfort*.

Father Matthew Trelawney Ross showed my mother around the Priory after the concert, and told her that I had played "in the spirit." She wasn't sure what it meant, but she repeated it to me proudly afterward. He was a fairly old man, an enthusiastic amateur pianist, and some time later we became friends. He loved his work with Africans and was heartbroken when he, too, was later recalled to Mirfield. I visited him there several times after my return to England, by which time Father Huddleston had become Bishop of Stepney.

It was only after the second concert, at the Reps Theatre, that it became obvious to my mother that I was ill. She had been out during the afternoon and found me asleep on my bed on her return. She kissed me awake, and I burst into tears. Then she felt my forehead, realized I had a fever, and called Dr. Lester, who still lived at Geraldine Court. He took a blood sample and assumed from the high blood titer—number of antibodies, I learned—that I had been inoculated against typhoid and paratyphoid fevers before my departure from England. Only smallpox and yellow fever vaccinations were compulsory, and I remembered quite clearly that I had avoided the typhoid inoculation, on the advice of a well-meaning friend. "In that case I'm sorry to tell you that you don't only have typhoid fever, you have one of the paratyphoids as well," said Dr. Lester. Now at last I understood why I had been feeling so dizzy and listless.

Typhoid never showed up in the numerous stool specimens my doctor sent to the Medical Research laboratory, but the blood titer kept increasing phenomenally, despite all the antibiotics with which he plied me. The pathologists were nonplussed, but I was greatly relieved that I was not a carrier of the disease, despite suffering from it. I racked my brains as to how I might have contracted typhoid fever, and all I could think of was that terrible hotel where I had spent my first night in Rome. I could not shake off a constantly raised temperature, and I lost weight, felt weak, dizzy, and nauseated for well over a year, but was never violently ill.

At last a letter arrived from Dušan, and I learned that several of his letters to destinations on my long journey homeward had never reached me. It was the only cause for heartache I'd had on that marvelous trip, although until I actually arrived in South Africa our parting had not truly become a reality to me. His letters were full of the love and longing that I myself felt, but they came infrequently, and I languished for him. Not all the letters that I wrote to him reached their destination either, and I sensed the same desperation in him as there was in me.

Pierre had written to me in London:

> Great changes have taken place here. The Johannesburg City Orchestra is no more. We've been amalgamated with the orchestra of the SABC, many of whose players have been weeded out. Michael Doré [who had been leader of the now defunct JCO] has retired and gone to live in Cape Town. Frits Schuurman [ex-musical director of the JCO] has gone to Durban. Bram Verhoef remains leader of the SABC, and I've been appointed sub-leader. We have no less than three regular conductors. The only really talented one is Jeremy Schulman, the musical director, who is getting on in years. It's not madly exciting, but something to aim for when you come back here.

However, there wasn't a single violin vacancy in the orchestra on my return, nor was there any other professional orchestra in the vicinity of Johannesburg at the time, so I had to wait.

At least this gave me time to recover some of my strength, while I waited for a vacancy to occur. Meanwhile, I was not idle. I practiced the violin assiduously, gave a few recitals, and formed a piano trio with Peggy Haddon, a lovely pianist, and warm-toned cellist Tam McDonald. We gave several concerts, and I also built up a successful teaching practice, despite feeling well below par most of the time.

Achim (on a visit to Johannesburg) and Eva, 1957.

In August 1957 I was invited to give an audition for the SABC. I took my courage in my hands and played that concerto most sacred to all violinists, the Beethoven. My playing was praised, but because of my lack of professional orchestral experience, I was put on trial until the end of the year.

I shall never forget my first rehearsal there, because of my encounter with three people who had briefly entered my life about ten years earlier, when I was sixteen. There was Anton Hartman, the young Afrikaner who had conducted the Johannesburg Symphony Orchestra during Joseph Trauneck's sojourn overseas. Hartman was now assistant conductor at the SABC, due to become musical director when Jeremy Schulman retired. (He was, incidentally, the first music student at Wits University to have won the Melanie Pollack Scholarship in Music, in 1951; my friend Bedana was the second, in 1952; and I the third, in both 1953 and 1954.) And there was "Ratface," my name for the timpanist who had made anti-Semitic remarks in Hartman's car after the concert at Alexandra Township. He was the last person I wanted to see. Now we were fellow professionals, playing in the same orchestra: how to avoid him? For weeks I dealt with the problem by simply walking past him, looking through him, not recognizing his existence, until one day he cornered me. He would not let me get away.

"You keep giving me the cold shoulder," he said. "No, please don't go. I beg you, please hear me out. I know why you're avoiding me. I remember that evening almost ten years ago. I remember only too well what I said, and I've never stopped regretting it. I don't know what got into me. I must have had too much to drink, and I was showing off. I've got nothing against the Jews; I've got nothing against *any* group of people. Most of my friends are Jewish."

"Ha! How often have I heard *that* before!" I said.

"No, but you must believe me," he begged. "It was a stupid, meaningless thing to say. You've no idea how much I thought about it, and how bitterly I regretted it. What you said made me realize one has to be responsible for one's words. I've honestly been careful not to say irresponsible things ever since. Please believe me, and please don't go on ignoring me. I can't bear it. All I ask is that you greet me and show that you've forgiven me!"

And so I did.

Lastly and above all, I was amazed to find myself face to face with the hero of the Johannesburg City Orchestra concert at our school ten years earlier, the principal double bass player, the fabulously handsome Willem van der Klaauw, looking more handsome than ever. Then I had scorned to be one of the immense crowd of girls who mobbed him. Now, on my very first rehearsal with the SABC Symphony Orchestra, although several yards separated us, we were positioned in such a way that we could look straight into each other's eyes. Every time I looked up from the music during the first half of the rehearsal, I found him gazing directly at me, as if trying to plumb my soul. I felt surprised, flattered, mesmerized.

During the rehearsal break I was surrounded by well-wishers, many of whom were aware of how long I had been waiting for this opportunity. All of them were sure I would soon become a regular member of the orchestra and said encouraging things to me. The women asked about my time in England, my studies, the concerts I'd been to, the celebrities I had met. The men just wanted to flirt.

Willem sat opposite and watched. Suddenly he got up, cut through the crowd, managed somehow to sit down next to me, and asked if I would be free to go out with him that very evening. I said I would go out with him only if he promised not to make it a late night, as I wanted to be in good form for the rehearsal the next morning. "Fine," he said, "We'll go out for a drive, and you can decide when to go home."

Dušan was the love of my life, yet for all his passion he had possessed incredible self-control and had guarded my virginity as if he were my mother—much to my chagrin. It was during the decade before the advent of the Pill, which seemed to change sexual mores overnight. Thanks to Maggie and Jenny I knew more about birth control than he did, and yet I shall never really know what held him back. I loved him to the very depth of my being, and it took me ten years to get over him.

Yet it took Willem just one evening to seduce me.

I did not even try to resist. It was bliss. He was skilled, gentle, and tender, and of course, I fell for him, and of course, he broke my heart. It was not exactly an affair; it became a disconnected series of delicious seductions, secret from the orchestra, secret from my mother. Yet strangely enough, he became my best friend in the orchestra, and there was practically nothing we could not talk about. He lived very near me, on the top floor of a tall, attractive block of flats, where he had brought me after our drive that first night. French windows opened onto a balcony with a fabulous view over Johannesburg. It was an ideal setting for seduction.

We often walked home from Broadcast House together. He was in the process of getting divorced after fourteen years of marriage, having married at the age of twenty-three, and I discovered quite a complicated, neurotic person beneath that smooth façade, behind those beautiful, penetrating blue eyes. He envied me the relationship I had enjoyed with Dušan and said that he had never felt so intensely about anybody, but that he was "irresistibly attracted" to me, felt at peace with me, and needed my love and affection.

And then he phoned me out of the blue and said, "Don't ever try to contact me. I don't want anything to do with you ever again." I nearly collapsed with shock. It was then that my mother realized the true nature of our relationship, and she had only sympathy for me. Willem disappeared for about two weeks after that, and I worried myself sick, until he turned up again and confessed to me that he had telephoned all his friends with the same message and that he had made a suicide attempt. We became friends again, and he said that I helped him, but I tried to untangle myself emotionally, realizing that there was more to this man than I was able, or even wanted, to handle.

I enjoyed working with the orchestra, particularly when artists from abroad played concertos with us or when we had a rare visit from a foreign conductor. One such was the young Italian conductor Pierino Gamba, who had been a boy prodigy, and who conducted everything from memory. He worked with us for several weeks. I remember the pleasure of playing Richard Strauss's *Till Eulenspiegel's Merry Pranks* and Falla's *Three-Cornered Hat* Suite with him.

"You and I are the only young people here," he began conversationally after a rehearsal.

I was still on trial, and my future in the orchestra unclear. "Have any of the three regular conductors asked you about me?" I wanted to know.

"No, why do you ask?"

I explained my position and said, "Would you put in a good word for me if they do?"

"I shall say you are very beautiful," he said.

"That's no good at all!" I exclaimed.

"And I shall tell them that you play even better than you look!" So I kissed his cheek, and he demanded one for the other cheek too.

My friend Philip Levy was back in Johannesburg and gave an excellent performance of Tchaikovsky's First Piano Concerto with us. Ivan Melman, a few months later, played Beethoven's Third Piano Concerto and the *Emperor* Concerto the following year. I felt proud of them.

In September 1957 the renowned harpsichordist and authority on the keyboard works of Domenico Scarlatti, Ralph Kirkpatrick, gave a series of three harpsichord recitals in Johannesburg. Just as Ludwig von Köchel had compiled the catalogue of all of Mozart's works, and his initial "K" had become the standard for numbering them—such as K551 for the *Jupiter* Symphony—so Kirkpatrick had catalogued all the hundreds of harpsichord sonatas of Domenico Scarlatti, and the standard for numbering them had become "Kk." Fred Marcus—he who had sent me the gold-with-amethyst ring from Cape Town—was on a visit to Johannesburg and took me to the second recital, where we witnessed an extraordinary event. The music critic of the *Rand Daily Mail* had, surprisingly, allowed herself to criticize Kirkpatrick's interpretation of a Scarlatti Sonata. After sitting down at the harpsichord, Kirkpatrick said, "Would Dora Sowden please leave the hall." We were transfixed. Could the accepted world authority on the works of Domenico Scarlatti really be so affected by a mere local review?

No one stirred. He then asked the ushers to escort Mrs. Sowden from her seat. Unbelievably, two ushers marched up to Dora Sowden; she quite properly maintained that she had as much right to remain there as anyone else. At length Kirkpatrick said, "I shall have to play in spite of the enemy in our midst," and launched into a magnificent performance.

During the interval, as Fred and I began to leave the hall after most of the audience had already gone ahead, we heard a scuffle on the stage. We turned round to look. Dora Sowden's distinguished writer husband Lewis, shirtsleeves rolled up, had gone to the dressing room, pulled Kirkpatrick out, and dragged him on to the platform for a fight.

In spite of this unrehearsed diversion, the second half of the recital was every bit as good as the first.

A new pupil came to me late that year, little eight-year-old David Miller, with a patch over one eye to make the other "lazy eyelid" work harder. His mother, Ruth, a poet, brought him to me. David and I got on wonderfully well, every lesson was fun, and he made speedy progress. His grateful parents invited me to their home many times. It was there that I met a very unusual person, a left-wing Afrikaner who believed in freedom and equality for Africans, as I did. His name was Jack Vermaak, and he was the brother of Lettie Vermaak, the beautiful principal viola in our orchestra, whom I had long admired. Jack and I had an exciting conversation, and he invited me to join the Congress of Democrats, the White wing, he told me, of the African National Congress. I was interested but needed time to think about it. And then I asked Walter Rothgiesser, who believed in those same ideals as sincerely as anyone, and he said, "For goodness sake, keep away from them! They are the same people who cheered when Soviet tanks entered Hungary last year." Then I realized that after learning of so much death and destruction, Walter had become disillusioned with the Communist Party and was putting humanity before doctrinaire politics, and I was glad. Yet I was no nearer to finding how I could contribute to the much needed political change.

At the Millers I also met Julio Bello, a young Portuguese from Lourenço Marques, who gave me driving lessons before my driving test and taught me how to cook prawns piri piri.

I have one momentous non-musical memory of late 1957: my mother and I in Joubert Park gazing up at the sky and watching in amazement the world's first artificial satellite, the Russian Sputnik.

In January 1958 I signed a contract with the SABC Symphony Orchestra. All the players received an annual contract, which was renewed each year. At last I could consider myself a full-fledged member of the musical profession. It had taken long enough. Yfrah Neaman was back on a concert tour of South Africa and was pleased with my success. Pierre continued to keep an eye on me and was always available if I needed advice or coaching. He seemed to get on well with Willem, who was an active member of the Musicians' Union. It was wonderful to be in the same orchestra as Pierre, but I was sad that Joyce, his wife, was ill with breast cancer. When she had told my mother about it during my absence in London, she had said wistfully, "It's what one always thought happened to *other* people!" She had fought it bravely, but it had returned.

Geisi, my erstwhile piano teacher, with whom my mother had kept in touch while I was away, was no more. Tante Ilse, too, had died, and we missed her badly. I played duets with my first violin teacher, Hermann Abramowitz, who still lived at Geraldine Court. By now I played better than he did, but he had left the musical profession and was working in a factory, stacking cases. It made me sad. I once reproached him for having robbed me of my self-confidence as a child, and he was shocked. "Surely you knew that I never meant it personally?" he said. He had no idea of the psychological damage he had caused, and there was no point in dwelling on it now. Mrs. Abramowitz had died during my absence, with my mother at her bedside. Their daughter, Joan, now sixteen years old, was following in my footsteps at Barnato Park School. She adored my mother, and I felt as if I had a little sister at last.

Playing in the orchestra I had many thrilling musical experiences. One was a performance of Beethoven's Triple Concerto by the Suk piano trio on their visit to Johannesburg. Ivry Gitlis came on a concert tour and gave a superb performance with us of the Brahms Violin Concerto. He struck up a conversation with me and said he would like to hear me play. I protested that I didn't play nearly well enough for him, and so he offered to give me a lesson. Warily I made my way to his hotel. In fact, he gave me two free lessons. They were all to do with relaxation and posture, and he said he had to keep reminding himself that I had come for a violin lesson and absolutely nothing else. "That's right," I said.

Jeremy Schulman, our musical director, was a stimulating musician and a joy to work with. He was always kind to me and told Pierre how well I was doing, but he used to have stand-up rows with the trombone players, who were always too loud for him. I cringed with embarrassment while the majority of the orchestra found it highly entertaining. The other two regular conductors, Anton Hartman and Edgar Cree, who hailed from England, were dull, but whenever a chorus was involved Cree would suddenly spring to life. It was clearly his métier and he shone.

It did not take me long to sense the atmosphere of dissatisfaction and unease in the orchestra. The quasi-fascist Nationalist Government controlled the SABC, and the directorship of the SABC in turn was highly political and authoritarian, without any sympathy for its orchestra. There was, for example, an occasion when we were due to broadcast a symphony concert, but discovered there was a fire in the hall adjoining ours, and smoke was seeping into our hall. Not unnaturally, we were unwilling to play until the fire had been put out. One of the directors came downstairs and pleaded with us to go ahead with the concert as planned: "The show must go on! If you play, we will be eternally grateful to you for your courage! Please, please don't let us down!" So, feeling like heroes and almost choking with fumes, we played. The following morning the managing director himself interrupted our rehearsal to say, "It has come to my ears that you actually dared vote against playing last night. Such behavior is unforgivable!" and went on railing at us in this vein. So much for "eternal gratitude."

I was told that not long before I joined he had threatened the orchestra: "We are quite capable of using Gestapo methods against you if necessary!"

Chapter Twenty-Two

On Saturday evening, May 24, 1958, I attended a concert at the home of a Mrs. Harvey. It had a large music room, which lent itself to such events. A superb African choir from a missionary church in Sophiatown, belonging to the Community of the Resurrection, gave the concert. Sophiatown was a non-white enclave in the outer suburbs of Johannesburg. I was struck by the outstanding musicianship of the African conductor, Michael Rantho. Where could he have had opportunities to learn; where did this remarkable ability come from?

A week later my trio gave a recital at the Jubilee Hall, part of the Bantu Men's Social Centre in Johannesburg, and who should come up to me after the concert asking for my autograph, to my amazement, but the same tall, imposing conductor, Michael Rantho. We exchanged compliments, and he asked if our trio would be prepared to play for his musical society in Sophiatown. "We usually listen to gramophone records," he said. "We are starved of live performances! It would be a great favour if you'd play for us. But I'm really sorry; we wouldn't be able to pay you; we have no funds."

We agreed willingly and played to a most attentive and appreciative audience. As I recollect, we played Haydn's *Gypsy Rondo* Trio, Mendelssohn's Piano Trio in D minor, and Dvořák's *Dumky* Trio. While we played the audience was completely still. There was tremendous applause afterward, followed by a lovely surprise: Michael's choir sang to us, and we were deeply moved. They offered us refreshments before we left. It was all graciously done. A few days later Michael Rantho wrote to me: "On behalf of our Musical Society I wish to express our gratitude for the wonderful concert you gave us. It was a great experience for everybody present. Please extend our sincere thanks to the other members of your trio. My wife and I would like to ask you, personally, if you would like to come to Sophiatown and attend Mass one Sunday morning, and afterwards have lunch with us at our house."

I felt enormously flattered. To be accepted socially across the racial divide was no small thing in South Africa. He later told me I was the only white person with whom he felt entirely comfortable, who, unlike even the Brothers from the Community of the Resurrection, was in no way patronizing. "You are the only really 'integrated' person I know," he maintained.

The political and social situation in South Africa made it almost impossible for black and white people to meet socially unless they belonged to one of the banned political parties, so this was a unique opportunity, and I was filled with a sense of adventure. However, there was a problem. At the time, the Group Areas Act was being implemented in Sophiatown, which was deemed to be in the midst of a "White Area." The largely black, with some Indian and some colored—mixed race—inhabitants, were being forcibly moved to new townships far outside Johannesburg. This would mean their having to get up at unearthly hours in the morning and take vastly overcrowded trains in order to arrive in time for work in Johannesburg. Sophiatown had been their home for generations, and their own houses were now being systematically destroyed. All around was destruction; people were fearful, angry, bitter, not knowing whose house was going to be demolished next, who would be the next to have to leave.

I telephoned Michael. "I'd love to accept your invitation," I said, "but I know that feelings must be running high in Sophiatown, and I'd feel nervous arriving on my own. Would you be prepared to meet me somewhere on the way, and we could drive in together?"

And so it was arranged that I would pick him up at a petrol station near Sophiatown, and we would drive straight to the church in time for Mass. In order to avoid misunderstandings, I told him that I was Jewish and had never been to Mass. The visit took a little time to organize.

Meanwhile, a great treat awaited me. The Vegh Quartet, whose playing had so enraptured me at Dartington Hall in 1953, came to Johannesburg on tour. They were Hungarian expatriates who had taken French nationality and were based in Switzerland. I hardly dared go to their first concert, in case it did not live up to my memory of this fabulous quartet. But it did, in every way, and when the concert was over I rushed backstage, unable to contain my enthusiasm. Only the first violin, my dream violinist Sandor Vegh, spoke any English. So I spoke to him, told him how I had admired their playing at Dartington Hall, and how thrilled I was to have heard them again.

"Where can we meet for coffee?" he asked me, to my astonishment and delight, in an artists' room brimful of admirers.

We arranged a time and place, and we talked for hours. Here was I, having coffee and talking with one of my greatest musical heroes, and it was not a dream. He asked about my life and music, and he told me of his experiences playing with Casals, with whom he'd had many disagreements about interpretation, at the Prades Festival.

"In the end the music won!" he said, laughing. "And I was invited to come back and play there every year."

He spoke of his ideas and ideals, expressing disgust with apartheid in South Africa. "If we'd known that they would not allow us to play to mixed audiences, we would not have agreed to come here," he said. "No, never! I wish there was some way for us to play to black audiences; I would feel better then."

"If you don't mind playing for a very small fee I think I can arrange a concert for you with an African audience at the Jubilee Hall," I said.

"We don't need a fee, we just want to reach these people," he said. "Can you really arrange it?"

He consulted me about the program, which music I thought would go down well, and whether they should wear lounge or dress suits. I said I thought it would be appreciated if they dressed formally, as they would do for a European audience, and as we had done. He asked me to introduce him to my African friends, as he, too, wanted to make personal contact with them.

Michael Rantho was beside himself with excitement when I rang and told him, and said he would arrange for his choir to sing to the quartet after the concert, as it had done for us. I had already told Vegh about the choir and how I wished he could hear it.

When the arrangements were finalized, Vegh asked me, "Will you come?"

"Yes, I'd like to, very much," I said.

"And can I hear you play?" I had been hesitant when he first asked me, but he persisted. "Yes? When are you free?"

We arranged a time for me to come to his hotel room. I wrote in my diary:

> I was so nervous that when I arrived there I was not merely trembling, I was shaking!

"But you are not going to play to a professor, you are going to play for a friend, a very old friend!" he exclaimed kindly. He took my hands in his to calm them; he made me sit down, offered me a cigarette, and chatted to me gently, until I felt at ease… "We musicians are complicated people," he said. "I too am complicated. And each of us is alone. But we have our music, and that will never let us down!"… He had stipulated Bach so I played him the Adagio from the G minor Solo Sonata, and he gave me a most thrilling lesson. He understood immediately my technical and mental problems. What a wonderful teacher! How well he puts things into words. I was there for two hours. After the lesson we sat down and talked again. "You are very talented," he said. "Yes, very talented and very interesting. You have a good sonority, good phrasing. But you are a flower that has not yet fully blossomed. You need the atmosphere of Europe. You need someone behind you to give you a push. You do not need a regular teacher, just someone behind you. Perhaps I have given you some ideas to work on, to think about. I hope I have helped you a little. But you cannot remain here—here you are isolated. If you like I could try to get you an orchestral job in Europe." He asked me to write my address in his little book. "Will you remember who it is?" I asked. "What kind of a man do you think I am?" he asked indignantly. "But you travel so much," I said, "and you meet so many people…" "I don't take down all their addresses—look!" and he paged through it to show me there were hardly any addresses at all. "There is Pablo Casals' address—it is almost the only one!"… My name in the same address book as Pablo Casals!

The Vegh Quartet concert at the Jubilee Hall was a great success and a heart-warming occasion.

From then on I became the quartet mascot. They asked me to come to all their concerts when I was not working, spoke to me in French, and treated me with great affection. Vegh made me promise to listen to their broadcasts, which I wouldn't have missed in any case, their playing was such an inspiration, and he said he would be playing especially for me. He invited me to come for a second lesson and found I had already taken much of what he had taught me on board. He repeated that I was very talented but added, "I would like to see Eva play without being entirely *inside* the music. You must remember that there are always *two* people in a violinist—the one who plays and the one who controls," and he quoted someone who had said that a good violinist is both Buddha and Maurice Chevalier: "For Chevalier to perform really well, Buddha must have distance. You cannot control when you are too close."

The quartet invited me to their farewell party, and the viola player gave me a photograph of the quartet and wrote on the back: "à Eva en souvenir du Quatuor Vegh, avec toute notre sympathie," and then they all signed it, and Sandor Vegh wrote "With my love and sympathie." He made me promise to think of him in a week's time, when he would once again be playing at the Casals Festival at Prades. It would be a broadcast performance; perhaps I would even be able to tune in to it. "I will be playing especially for you!" he promised.

Vegh Quartet and friends, with Sandor Vegh on the right..

I had not forgotten Michael Rantho in the midst of the excitement. He and I made arrangements for my visit to Sophiatown, and he met me on my way there, as we had agreed. I parked the car outside the church. Most of the congregation was already inside. As Michael and I entered the church all eyes were on me, the only white person there. Everyone looked extremely puzzled, and I felt uncomfortable, but I knew that Michael was highly respected, and his presence beside me was reassuring. Of the service itself I remember nothing but the people's incredulous stares. When it was over he took me to his home where his wife, Maureen, who had been preparing lunch, welcomed me shyly. After a while we all three relaxed and chatted easily.

In the afternoon Michael insisted on taking me around Sophiatown with his wife to meet all of their friends who were still there. Everywhere we went I was met with anger and hostility, and Michael explained again and again that I would hardly be there as their friend if I approved of what the government was doing to them; that I, too, was angry about it. Then they relented and smiled and invited me into their homes, so that when I left Sophiatown late that afternoon, I had a warm sense of having made many new friends.

The next day, during the orchestra break, I had tea with a group of colleagues, including one particularly unpleasant young Afrikaans Nationalist. He was spouting the usual garbage about "the natives" being no better than monkeys off the trees, to which I retorted that they were no less human than he or I.

"Ach! come on, Eva," he said. "Let's face it. You wouldn't sit down and have a meal at the same table as them, would you? Of course not!" He did not wait for an answer.

The following day I found an official letter in my letter-rack at the SABC. It said that my contract would not be renewed after the end of the year. I was shattered, bewildered. Pierre was furious; Bram Verhoef, the leader, was furious; François Bougenon, the principal second violin, was furious. They hadn't been consulted, and one after another stormed up to the office to demand an explanation. None was given, save that it had nothing to do with my playing. Willem tried to help me through the Musicians' Union, to no avail. A Belgian violinist, Clementina de Boeck, had a rather miserable lodger, also a violinist, who sat somewhere near me in the orchestra, and told her that my playing wasn't up to much. She invited me home with her, and we played Mozart duets together.

"But you are an artist!" she exclaimed. "He's not fit to clean your shoes! I'll tell him what I think of him. Not up to much indeed! I'm going to fight for you. They have no right to sack you. I won't let them!" Hilda Howitson, the cellist, also took up my cause, and between them they bombarded the management with questions and demands that I be reinstated, only to be met with grim silence.

After some weeks I received a letter from Father Matthew Trelawney Ross from the Priory in Rosettenville, where I had played Bach's A minor Concerto with Betty Pack's chamber orchestra two years earlier. "I'm so happy to be able to make contact with you at last, thanks to my friend Michael Rantho," he wrote. "It would give me so much pleasure if you would agree to let me accompany you at the piano. I could visit you in Johannesburg, but you would be most welcome to come here to the Priory if you could spare the time. It would be easy for you to come by car. I know that you have a car, because Michael told me that you drove with him to Sophiatown, *and that you were followed by the Special Branch*" (my italics).

I nearly hit the roof. Why had Michael not told me? Clearly this was why the SABC was threatening to sack me! I telephoned Father Matthew.

"Why did Michael tell you and not *me* that we were followed by the Special Branch?" I asked.

"Because he was embarrassed," he replied. "Obviously they must have thought it was a case of 'Immorality.'" (The Immorality Act had made sexual relations between black and white people a punishable offense.) "Because Michael was sitting in the front of the car with you like any white person. It's usual for black people to sit in the back of the car."

"I wouldn't dream of humiliating Michael, or *anyone*, like that," I said.

"Anyway, when you got out at the church they must have realized they didn't have a case," said Father Matthew.

But it didn't stop them making trouble for me, I thought.

Suzanne M. was a socialite on the board of the Johannesburg Musical Society and met all visiting concert artists, to whom she subsequently introduced me. She took me under her wing because my close relationship with my mother reminded her of hers with her mother, and touched her heart. She had married for money—and it was not a happy marriage—in order to put a roof over her own and her mother's head, and she was convinced I ought to do the same. To this end she introduced me to a little, round, middle-aged widower who lived in opulence in a villa in one of the wealthier suburbs of Johannesburg. I said, "But Suzanne, I can't possibly marry someone I don't love!"

"You've *been* in love and look where it's got you!" she replied. "It's time you were more practical. And anyway, I want to be able to come and visit you in this wonderful house!"

It didn't take me long to make it clear to Mr. L. that he was wasting his time on me. He took me out to lunch and declared he had given up all his girlfriends for me. I said in alarm, "For goodness sake don't! I'm *not* your girlfriend. I enjoy your conversation, I'm happy to have lunch with you, but that's as far as it goes." A year later he died, and the irony was that his entire estate went into liquidation. He was bankrupt. I wondered how Suzanne would have felt had her plans for me succeeded.

But I soon had reason to be grateful to her. Toni Georgiou was a visiting concert pianist whom she had taken on the usual rounds of lavish, lionizing parties. Later she brought him to our modest flat. He said, "But Suzanne these are *real* people! Why didn't you bring me here *first*?" My mother cooked a simple, tasty meal, and Toni felt sufficiently at home to bare his soul to us. He came from Salonika and was soon going to visit Belgrade. He came to see us a few more times, and I asked him, "Would you do me a very special favor and take a present from me to someone at the Belgrade Conservatoire?" He obliged willingly and left a book with a note for Dušan—who was away at the time—at the Conservatoire. I was overjoyed when Dušan wrote rapturously about a book that had turned up on his desk "like a miracle" from me.

Michael and Maureen Rantho were compelled to move to Orlando, an African township outside Johannesburg. They repeatedly begged me to visit them there. However, white people were not allowed to visit Orlando without a special permit, and it was difficult to obtain one. In the meantime, Michael was hungry for knowledge, and I lent him books, leaving them at a church in Johannesburg, where he would collect and return them. In particular, he was anxious to learn about religions other than the Christianity that he had learned from the Anglican missionaries, and I lent him a book on comparative religions. This cloak and dagger arrangement lasted until the end of the year, interspersed with telephone conversations.

I had to get away from Johannesburg and the SABC, which had become poisonous for me. Sandor Vegh was certain he could find me an orchestral job in Germany, but Germany was the one country I did not intend to live in. So it would have to be closer to home. I learned that there were no vacancies in the Cape Town Symphony Orchestra, so I wrote to Durban, and this time I was lucky.

I flew to Durban for an audition with Frits Schuurman, the Dutch conductor who had come over to South Africa with members of the newly formed Johannesburg City Orchestra and was now musical director of the Durban Civic Orchestra. There was only one violin vacancy, and I found myself in competition with a very self-confident young man who was already planning what he would do with the money he would be earning in the orchestra. However, "You have learned a lot in your one year with the SABC," Schuurman said to me. "I would like you in our orchestra. Can you start in January? Let's go straight away to get you a medical checkup, so that we don't lose any time."

"How wonderful to be treated like a human being!" I said.

"Was it as bad as that?" said Schuurman sympathetically. He was like a kindly grandfather, from whom I did not have to hide anything.

"It's in the bag!" I wired triumphantly to my mother, and I flew home the next day.

My two champions, Clementina and Hilda, had fought untiringly to get me reinstated. At length, Mr. Fuchs, the managing director of the SABC, summoned me to his presence. "After much thought we have decided to renew your contract after all," he said, no doubt expecting profuse thanks from me.

"I'm afraid I can't accept," I said. "I've already signed a contract with the Durban Civic Orchestra, as from January."

Clem and Hilda were delighted. Poor Pierre got the full force of Fuch's fury. I passed my more advanced violin students on to Pierre, and the younger ones to Clem. She was a lovely violinist and a warm, sympathetic person. I felt sure they would thrive under her tuition, particularly talented and sensitive little David Miller who had made such good progress with me right from the start. Now that I was leaving Johannesburg, I wanted to make sure David's violin lessons were left in kind, capable hands.

Clem, who had previously been a member of the Durban Civic Orchestra, urged me to make friends with the violinist Alfredo Galea. "You'll need him in any case," she said, "because he's the only violin maker and repairer in Durban and his work is excellent. He made my violin. It's a beauty, don't you think? But keep away from Paul"—a Belgian violinist she had known even before coming to Durban—"He's dangerous. Don't ever trust him."

Hilda said, "Be sure to make friends with Nancy Greig. She's the co-principal cellist of the Durban orchestra. She's a wonderful player and a wonderful person. Once you've made friends with her you'll have made a friend for life."

And so it was to be.

Chapter Twenty-Three
⌒ A Newcomer in Durban—1959 ⌒

Ever since I was torn away from Mallorca, I longed to live by the sea again. And here I was at last, living alongside the Indian Ocean. I felt liberated, walking along the shore at night to the sound of crashing breakers, watching the dark, rising tide and the white spume.

Literally moments before I left for Durban, a letter from Dušan had arrived, as full of love and passion as ever, sharing his thoughts on a new approach to student recitals, with news of a recital tour in France. It completely unsettled me and filled me with desperate longing. But the sea had a calming effect and made me feel whole again. I wrote:

> I could watch for hours and hours, and lose all sense of time and place. There is a mystery to the sea which I do not understand, but which seems to symbolise infinity, and the unity of all life, and all people; and Fate, against which we are powerless, which bears us in its arms. The stormier the sea, the deeper my tranquillity; life seems to have no more burdens—I know that I am, whatever happens...

All the same, my introduction to life in Durban was inauspicious. Even though I had been on frequent holidays in Durban, coming to live and work there was quite another matter, and I really did feel a complete newcomer. The manager of the Durban Civic Orchestra had arranged for me to stay for a week or so at the Connaught Hotel, a small family-run hotel near Durban's North Beach, to give me time to find suitable accommodation. While I was waiting to be checked in at the reception desk, a wizened little old lady told me she had just been knocked over on the beach and her diamond ring, her last valuable possession in the world, had been taken from her, together with all her money. I felt so sorry for her that I gave her a ten-shilling note—quite a large amount in those days. As soon as she left, a fellow guest came up to me to ask whether the woman had told me she'd been knocked down on the beach and had her diamond ring stolen. "She's caught me out with that story, too. Apparently she's been spinning that yarn to folks here at least once a week for the past year!" He might have warned me, I thought, feeling foolish.

The couple who owned the hotel took an interest in me because I was a musician. They had a teenage son, who, they told me, was a very gifted musician. "He's a wonderful conductor," they said. "We would like to give you a treat. We'd like to invite you to see him conduct an orchestra."

How could I not accept such an invitation? Besides, I was curious. Curiouser still, when the following evening I was taken, not to a concert hall, but to a small room in the hotel. There the young man in question had arranged low lighting and a gramophone, put on a recording of a Beethoven symphony, and with showmanlike gestures set about "conducting" it. I hardly knew how to keep a straight face.

January was the height of summer, and Durban was sweltering. "It's not the heat, it's the humidity," people would tell me. The only places that were air-conditioned, in my experience, were department stores and cinemas, and I often popped into department stores for no other purpose than to find relief from the heat. My little room at the Connaught Hotel was unbearably hot and stuffy, and I quickly began to look for other accommodation.

I found a pleasant furnished room with bathroom but no kitchen—only a small refrigerator and tea- and coffee-making facilities—in a smart modern apartment block, the San Francisco, overlooking the sea. I chose a room on the top floor—the twelfth—because I needed to be able to practice the violin without disturbing others, and I had learned that sound travels upward. There was also another reason. I had very quickly discovered that, if anything was going to drive me out of Durban, it would not be the heat or humidity: it would be the huge flying cockroaches that came in through the open windows, no matter how clean you kept your room. They had tentacles as long as their bodies; they were hideous, and I fancied I was more frightened of them than if I had come face to face with a lion. I thought they would not fly as high as the twelfth floor, but I was mistaken. One still, hot night I lay naked beneath the open window, hoping to catch any faint breeze that might come along, only to be awakened by a scrabbling sensation on my shoulder. A gigantic cockroach. I shook it off in horror and jumped up. It streaked away from me, then stopped and stared, waving its tentacles, and I stared back. We were equally frightened of each other.

There were days on end when no wind blew, but when it did blow in Durban, it was windier than anything I had ever experienced, and I remember once being blown right across the Esplanade, from one side of the road to the other. On the twelfth floor of the San Francisco, I was unnerved by the eerie howling of the wind throughout its lengthy corridors.

One half of the San Francisco consisted of rooms similar to mine; the other half consisted of self-contained flats, which I could not afford on my salary. There was a restaurant downstairs. All went well until I came down with a bad case of influenza. At first I could not eat, but after a couple of days I telephoned the restaurant with a request for a soft boiled egg and toast to be sent up to my room, which was met with "Not on our menu" and "We can't spare the waiter." Neither the staff of the San Francisco, nor anybody from the orchestra, thought to inquire after me. Not even Susan Leon, my desk partner, whose place I had taken at the SABC when she had left Johannesburg, and with whom I had now caught up in Durban. We were the two youngest in the orchestra and had already become friendly. But nobody rang. Debilitated and depressed from the flu, away from home and familiar faces, I felt lonelier than I had ever felt. In desperation, I telephoned Frits Schuurman, the conductor, and said, "I've been lying here ill with flu for the last three days. I haven't seen a single person and nobody has phoned to ask how I am. I feel like throwing myself out of my twelfth story window!"

"Oh my dear child, I had forgotten you were all alone here!" he said. "We should have thought. Hold on, hold on there! I shall send my wife over directly to see you."

His wife was the distinguished Czech violinist, Maria Neuss, a one-time assistant teacher to Carl Flesch. I had already heard her play the Dvořák Violin Concerto with the Durban orchestra. She came laden with fruit and flowers and saved me from my depression. She also introduced me to Barbara Lehman who worked in the orchestral administration office and had a flat at the San Francisco. Barbara and I spent many hours together in her flat while I was recuperating, sipping rum and Coca-Cola and gossiping. Maria and I became good friends, and throughout my time in Durban she gave me enormous encouragement as a violinist.

Work with the orchestra was varied: symphony concerts, which I enjoyed, particularly when conducted by Frits Schuurman, and the light classical concerts we were obliged to give in order to satisfy the city council, which was paying our subsidy. If you were a newcomer to the orchestra you automatically sat at the back of whichever section had a vacancy. Nobody was ever moved back, even if their playing had deteriorated. In the two years I was with the Durban Civic Orchestra, nobody left and nobody new arrived. We covered a large span of classical and romantic music, but we played hardly any modern works, which would not have gone down well in Durban. It was a bit of a backwater, but the relaxed atmosphere, the little courtesies there didn't seem to be time for in frenetic Johannesburg, the comparative lack of racial intolerance, as well as the ever-present sea, made life in Durban considerably more pleasant than in Johannesburg.

My mother, Joan Abramowitz, Clementina de Boeck, and Ruth Miller, David's mother, wrote to me regularly. David had spent a whole night sobbing for me after I had left, and Clem could do nothing with him.

"Dear David," I wrote, "I miss you too, but Clem is a lovely person, and her teaching method is not so different from mine. If you work for her as you did for me, I know you'll do well. You are very talented and have made a lot of progress. It would be such a pity to waste it. Besides, I am looking forward to hearing you play when I come home to Jo'burg on holiday, which will be quite soon."

He tried for a little longer, but then gave up. I'd felt sure Clem had the very qualities he would respond to, but he could not forgive her for not being me. "I wish you'd come back," wrote his mother. "David is inconsolable."

I kept in touch with them whenever I visited Johannesburg. My Israeli cousin Miriam, who was working at the Israeli Consulate, and I, had often met for lunch in town when I was working for the SABC, and now we saw each other again. She had married Bedana's cousin Aubrey Chosack: "I never knew it was possible to be so happy!" she said, and I was impressed. When I dropped in on the SABC Orchestra I was always warmly welcomed. I had cups of tea there with Willem van der Klaauw, who had meanwhile married for money. "What a fool I was not to make more of the time we had together! I was free then, now I am choking," he said, loosening his collar nervously. "Don't you feel it too? Your hands are trembling." I felt a little shaky, but I was determined to remain detached. Philip Levy, now permanently back in South Africa and great company as ever, was a steadying influence, always ready to make music with me and to cheer me up with stories, laughter, good food, and even once taking me to the circus. Gordon Vorster, whose artistic career was making huge strides, never failed to give me moral support; and so always, always did Betty Pack. I would stay with my mother when in Johannesburg, and occasionally she came down to Durban for the weekend to see me.

Yet it struck me as strange how in every new place I moved to I seemed to lead a completely different life, almost became a different person, and was surrounded by a host of new people whose lives I touched and who influenced mine.

In Durban I soon made new friends. I told Nancy what Hilda Howitson had said: "If you make friends with Nancy Greig you've made a friend for life!" Nancy was sixteen years my senior and a beautiful cellist. I listened to her broadcasts of Brahms cello and piano sonatas, and was enraptured by her warmth and expressiveness. She was the orchestra's subprincipal cellist, often led the cello section, and played several concertos with us, notably the Elgar and the Dvořák. Later, she was invited to play the Elgar with the SABC in Johannesburg. I was in awe of her, but I took my courage in my hands: "Nancy, I'm dying to play chamber music with you," I said. "Do you think you could organize a string quartet for me? I don't mind playing second fiddle, I just want to play!"

On Friday, January 16, we played string quartets at the home of the sub-leader of the orchestra. He played first violin, I second, but only for one evening. I had thought it was going to be splendid, but it was dreadful. His tone was excruciating. We didn't want to hurt his feelings by asking another violinist, so we waited, undecided what to do. After the Easter break we met for the first time at the tiny but charming seafront flat of our Hungarian viola player, Thilo Runge, and his wife, Berzhie, to play string trios. We had a wonderful time making music, followed by coffee and cake and pleasant conversation. We all enjoyed the evening so much that we met as regularly as we could after that, to play string trios and drink coffee in the cozy atmosphere of their flat.

I played piano trios too, with Nancy and Phyllis Millar, her pianist of many years' standing, and we broadcast Schubert's ravishing Piano Trio in B-flat from Broadcast House. Alfredo Galea, the violinist and violinmaker Clem had mentioned to me, gave a violin recital at the Durban Art Gallery on July 28, and I was impressed with his musicality. It was on that occasion that I first met an accomplished young Canadian pianist, Elina Templin, whose piano recital at the Art Gallery I attended a fortnight later. Two Sundays after that, for our first sonata rehearsal, I made my way to her home on the outskirts of Durban, close to the university where her husband, Carl, was a postgraduate student. The area was still wild enough for monkeys to be leaping about among the trees beneath which I walked on my way to their house. We had many opportunities to give recitals as well as broadcasts, and I felt I had really found my niche in Durban.

I asked Alfredo Galea why he had used a cello bow at his violin recital. "Oh you noticed!" he exclaimed in surprise "Well, I've always thought violin bows are too long, so I thought I'd use a cello bow instead. It worked, didn't it?"

"It certainly did," I replied.

Like Clem, Alfredo—Freddie—warned me against Paul, the Belgian violinist. In fact,

Freddie had two great, obsessive hatreds: for Paul and for Maria Neuss. I never got to the bottom of either obsession. He could be quite scathing about many people, and he didn't hide his feelings. But he was fond of me, said I was the only person in the orchestra he could talk to, and called me his "Bazuzza." I never knew what it meant, but it sounded like an endearment, the way he said it. Freddie must have been in his fifties at the time. He had gray hair and a well-cut face with the most unusual, glistening brown-green eyes. He had belonged to the Maltese community in Egypt, until Colonel Nasser had thrown them all out, leaving an embittered Freddie. Years later, a colleague in London told me that Alfredo Galea had moved to California, where he had won fame as a violin maker, and where she had actually bought one of his instruments.

Paul had a small group, the Baroque Players, made up of members of the orchestra. His harpsichordist wife, Jacqueline, played in it, as did Nancy. I was so busy avoiding him that for most of my time in Durban I missed out on an enjoyable aspect of music making. They gave regular concerts and broadcasts. He was quite good looking and also charming, but I had been thoroughly frightened off and kept well out of his way.

The Durban Civic Orchestra rehearsed and performed at the City Hall in West Street, Durban's main street. There was an art gallery nearby in Field Street, and I often visited it on my way to or from a rehearsal. I had an introduction to the owner, the painter Neil Sack, and his wife Fay, from friends in Johannesburg. The first time I visited, there was an exhibition of Chinese watercolor prints in a limited edition, and I fell in love with a painting of a Chinese goddess. I bought it and had it sent as a gift to my mother, and it graced her living room wall ever after. I often popped in at the gallery to look at the latest exhibitions and to chat with Fay, a lovely woman in her early thirties. She had black, shoulder-length hair, blue eyes, and pale, white skin. She and Neil had been married for ten years and were very much in love. Their temperaments complemented each other, Fay's calmness contrasting with Neil's flamboyance. "I know I'm a chandelier swinger!" he confessed. They frequently invited me to their home, with a sweeping view of the bay, from its situation high on the Berea. Fay did her best to marry me off to Neil's brother, Basil. He was nice-looking, pleasant, and affectionate, and for a while we regularly went out together, but we had very little in common, and I had to disappoint Fay.

After about six months of living on the seafront, I reluctantly moved up to the Berea where the air was just that bit cooler and more tolerable. From the San Francisco I moved—incredibly, it seemed to me—to the Los Angeles Hotel. Neil and Fay sent me a little pot of African violets to welcome me to my new home.

Despite my irreligious upbringing, I had always stayed away from school or work on Yom Kippur, the Jewish Day of Atonement, out of solidarity with my people. For the first time, this gesture seemed irrelevant to me, and I was considering going to work. Fay was dismayed. "Please, Eva, don't go to work, don't desecrate our holiest day. Come and spend the day with me. We'll be alone, and we'll fast together. It'll be good, I promise you," she said. And it was good. We spent a wonderfully tranquil day together, in memory of which I never again considered going to work on Yom Kippur.

Two months later, Neil and Fay suddenly went missing. They were not at home, and the gallery was shut. Disturbed, I made my way to Neil's father's shop, a gentlemen's out-fitters, and asked where they had gone. "You remember their maid was diagnosed with TB a little while ago?" said Mr. Sack senior. "Well, it seems Fay caught it from her, and they've flown to London to get the best medical advice."

It seemed a bit odd, yet it didn't occur to me to doubt Mr. Sack's word. Soon after, I re-ceived an ecstatic letter from Fay about all the sights she and Neil had seen in London and the plays and concerts they'd attended. I felt relieved and delighted.

On December 21, Basil telephoned me. "I'm sorry to have to tell you that Fay has died," he said.

I was devastated. "But I had a letter from her. She sounded so happy! Your father told me she'd caught TB from her maid. How could she suddenly be dead?" I asked, and I burst into tears of shock and grief.

"I thought you knew she had cancer," said Basil.

"How could I know, nobody told me! Why didn't you tell me?" I demanded.

He was taken aback, said he felt awful, told me they had been rather secretive about it, that she'd had cancer before, and that it had returned. In London she had undergone an operation for lung cancer, which had been successful, but then she'd had a hemorrhage and died. I felt outraged.

A little miracle happened. From that time onwards the African violet Fay and Neil had given me never stopped blooming. It seemed as if part of Fay was continuing to live in that flower. When I eventually departed from Durban more than a year later, I left it in Nancy's care. "You know I never was much good with plants," she wrote to me, "but I did try. I'm very sorry, but I seem to have killed off your African violet!"

Chapter Twenty-Four

☞ NANCY, POLITICS, AND THE MURDER OF FIGARO—1959 AND
1960 ☜

The move to Musgrave Road on the Berea was a happy one for me. Nancy Greig lived in a
block of flats just a few yards away from the Los Angeles Hotel, and a delightful new friend,
Yvonne Rentzke, whom I had met through my desk partner Susan, lived not far away in the
opposite direction, at a small hotel called Deansgate. Beyond lay Mitchell Park, where the
orchestra played light music on Sunday afternoons in the summer.

Yvonne, a South African of part Polish, part Spanish descent, was glamorous, blond,
and vastly entertaining. She enjoyed passing on beauty tips: "Wrap up your hair in a silk scarf
after washing it. It'll bring out the shine. And *don't* shampoo twice as it says on the bottle:
that's just to make you buy more shampoo! It isn't necessary, and it takes too much oil out
of your hair." She always had some exciting, romantic event to tell me about. "No, I can't tell
you over the phone," she would say, "I have to tell you with actions!" Then she would come
over and tell me her story "with actions," and we would fall about laughing.

My mother was surprised, on a visit to Durban, to see the two of us sniffing our wrists,
comparing perfumes. "You girls are so *feminine!*" she exclaimed. She had always regarded
perfumes and jewelry as foolish fripperies and was surprised to find her daughter had developed a taste for them. Yvonne introduced me to my favorite perfume, Shiaparelli's *Shocking*.
She was a devout Catholic but respected people of all religions. Exceedingly efficient, she
must have been an ideal secretary. She and Nancy became founding members of the newly
formed Progressive Party under Helen Suzman, who was for a long time its only represen-
tative in parliament. It gradually became a real force for change in South Africa, and Yvonne
contributed with much hard work.

The Liberal Party had almost been driven underground, but I had an introduction to
Professor Leo Kuper and his wife Hilda, who were active members. During my time away
studying in London, my pianist friend Shora had married a nephew of Leo Kuper. "Be sure
to contact them when you get to Durban. They are lovely people. I'll write and tell them you
are coming," she had said. They were a charming and courageous couple, and there were
many occasions of civil unrest in Durban when I feared they would be arrested. They openly
socialized with Africans, Coloreds, and Indians, which was far from usual in the unnatural

condition of apartheid in which we lived. I met people of all races and colors at their home, while the police invariably watched the house from across the road.

On Saturday, May 23, I was thrilled to meet Alan Paton, author of *Cry the Beloved Country*, at a party at the Kupers. He was the founder of the Liberal Party and at the time, its chairman. Hilda and Leo were very good to me, often inviting me to dinner, taking me on outings, and to see the latest plays. On Alan Paton's 56th birthday, they took me to a garden party at his home, held in his honor by the Liberal Party. He made a speech about what needed to be achieved, and I felt proud to be present and to hear in person the author of one of my favorite and most important books.

Eventually, in 1960, the Kupers decided to emigrate to the United States. I walked along the beach with Hilda, sad to be losing them, sad that South Africa would be losing them. "Our work here is done," she said. "The whole world's been made aware of the situation. Several countries are implementing sanctions, and in the end it'll be sanctions that bring this government to its knees." She was not far wrong, though it took another thirty years, as well as the strenuous work of anti-apartheid activists, for the change to come about.

In the United States, Leo Kuper went on to become a world authority on genocide, and he wrote a seminal work on the subject, *The Prevention of Genocide*, published by Yale University Press in 1985. He was the first to develop genocide studies as an academic subject in universities throughout the United States. Soon after he died in 1994, the Leo Kuper Foundation came into being, with the aim of finding ways to intervene and suppress genocide. Tragically, we have never seen the end of it. Nevertheless, I felt proud to have been numbered among Leo and Hilda's friends.

However, my deepest friendship was with Nancy. Everybody in the orchestra loved and respected her. She had charm and poise, seemed self-confident though reserved, and had a delightfully dry sense of humor. Above all, she was wonderfully kind, always ready to help where help was needed, and was never malicious. She made all her friends feel safe and cared for. As I gradually came to know her better, I discovered that she was actually quite diffident, full of self-doubt, softhearted to a fault, and prone to depression. What a contrast to my other great cellist friend, Betty Pack: flamboyant, self-confident, and in her own words, "sublimely happy." Yet in their different ways, both of them were able to spread happiness around them.

Nancy told me in her usually jokey manner that her mother had given birth to her on the kitchen floor of their home in Edinburgh. She was the youngest of four children, and when she was five years old her family emigrated to South Africa. She had very little formal training as a cellist. Her early career was spent touring with a Light Music band, until the pianist Phyllis Millar discovered her talent and persuaded her to have serious cello lessons with an Italian cellist who had recently arrived in Durban.

"There was so much I needed to learn," she told me. "The teachers I'd had as a child were pretty clueless. Now suddenly I had this marvelous teacher who taught me what music and playing the cello was really about. He had tremendous personality. I learned so much from him in a very short time. It was exciting, stimulating. And then, after six months, he was murdered, stabbed to death at night outside his home. Can you imagine? It was a dreadful shock. The poor man had come all the way from Italy, for his life to be cut short like this! Everybody who knew him was upset. We never found out who murdered him or why. It took me a long time to get over it. All I could do was try to build as much as I could on what he had taught me."

Despite her great ability as a cellist, she was never satisfied with her playing, always finding fault with her cello, with the quality of her sound production, which was superb, or some other aspect of her playing.

"Nancy," I said, "you're a *wonderful* cellist, yet you're never satisfied. Why do you torture yourself like this?" She shyly answered, "Because I want to be the best cellist in the world!" Did she really mean it or was she teasing me? I wondered.

One of her sweetest memories was of the day the war broke out: "I was standing on the City Hall steps when a soldier—a complete stranger—came up to me and handed me a rose." Many years later, she told me, he found her again, playing in the orchestra. He sought her out and said, "Do you remember me? I gave you a rose the day the war broke out!"

"How could I forget," she said.

I had left our car in Johannesburg with my mother, who had passed her driving test after me. Nancy had a little Renault Dauphine.

Nancy, cellist, 1960.

When she realized I was having difficulty settling down to practice at the hotel, even though most of the residents were out all day, she persuaded me to come down with her to the City Hall. There we would each find a room in which to practice, before or after rehearsals. There were no distractions, so it was conducive to concentrated work. She always parked her car defiantly in a "No Parking" spot in front of the police station but never received a fine. After we had both done a good afternoon's practice at the City Hall, Nancy often drove me down to the Mole, off the Esplanade, to have tea at the yacht club and watch the boats in the yacht basin below and farther out at sea. Sometimes we visited the Botanical Gardens, not far from where we lived, with its abundance of wonderful plants. I remembered my first visit to the Durban Botanical Gardens as a child, when my mother had treated me to tea and scones there. Monkeys had leaped down from the trees above us and stolen all our scones. I had been more delighted with this novel experience than if I had eaten the scones myself.

As the year wore on and summer came round again, the heat in the City Hall became overpowering. "You know there's a swimming pool in Medway Gardens next to the City Hall," said Nancy. "Why don't we go there early in the morning to cool down before the rehearsal?" That December we went swimming there for the first time. It was such a relief from the stifling heat. There was no air conditioning in the City Hall, and after twenty minutes we were bathed in perspiration again, but the swim was worth it for those first twenty minutes, and we decided to go there regularly before rehearsals.

When we had time off, we drove out to the Valley of the Thousand Hills, as green as anywhere in Europe, dotted with Zulu villages, and with bare-breasted Zulu women wearing skirts of colored beads. We visited the spectacular Oribi Gorge, taking a picnic lunch with us. We drove a little way up the North Coast, to Umhlanga Rocks, for tea at the Oyster Box Hotel, or down the South Coast to Amamzimtoti and Umkomaas. Life was more enjoyable and more relaxed than it had ever been in Johannesburg. "Lotus eating," as my friend Morris Kahn—another Durbanite I had met through friends in Johannesburg—called it.

Nancy was agnostic, as was I, but she recognized in me what she called a tendency to mysticism and introduced me to Aldous Huxley's *Perennial Philosophy* as well as William James' *Variety of Religious Experience*. We had intense conversations about the search for reality and for one's true self. When she found me gratuitously killing a small insect, she talked to me about Albert Schweitzer and his Reverence for Life. Any slight criticism was always done with the greatest tact and sensitivity. It was she who told me that General Smuts was the first to use the word "holism," for the theory that the whole is greater than the sum of its parts. This has since become common currency, as in "holistic medicine," which treats the whole person, rather than merely that person's symptoms.

Occasionally, the Durban Orchestra had to do some truly gruesome things. One of these was a week playing Mozart's sublime opera, *The Marriage of Figaro,* produced, rehearsed, performed, and finally murdered by an aging German couple who were wealthy enough to hire us for this annual event. He conducted; she produced it and sang the role of the countess, in English. At one point in Act Three of the opera, I could hardly believe my ears when I thought I heard her sing, "But vot ze hell?" I listened intently each night, and again the following year when we played the opera once more, but my ears always picked up those same four words. It was not until twenty years later, when playing *Figaro* in English translation with English National Opera, that I made out the Countess's words: "But where's the harm?"

A much happier operatic experience in Durban was in August 1960, when a group of Cape Colored singers, the Aeon Group, came with the Italian conductor who had trained them, to perform *Rigoletto* and *La Bohème* with us. They sang magnificently. One of the singers met Nancy and me outside the public library and asked if he would be allowed to go inside. Nancy said: "I don't see why not, but I'll go in and ask, to make sure." She came out blushing with shame and indignation. The answer had been "No."

The Pass Laws were a constant source of frustration and fear for black people in South Africa. If an African was stopped by a policeman and could not produce his pass, he could be thrown into jail without trial, sometimes never to be heard of again. In December 1959, a massive but peaceful demonstration against the Pass Laws was staged in Durban. Hundreds of black men marched through the city, while white people locked themselves in their homes, fearing violence. My colleagues begged me to cancel my rehearsal with Elina, at her home in the isolated university area through which the protesters were to pass. They were convinced there would be rioting, and that as a lone white girl, I would be torn to shreds. I felt such confidence in the good faith and discipline of the demonstrators that I ignored all advice. Determined to keep my appointment with Elina, I got off the bus at the nearest bus stop, violin case in hand, and began walking. Sure enough an enormous crowd of black men was marching, or rather jogging, toward me. I kept to the pavement on my side of the road and continued on my way to Elina's. Silently, looking straight ahead, they passed me—hundreds of black men—and went on *their* way toward the City Hall.

Chapter Twenty-Five
⌒ THE ROYAL BALLET IN SOUTH AFRICA—1960 ⌒

The Royal Ballet came to South Africa in February 1960 for a three-month tour, and the Durban Civic Orchestra was chosen to accompany it. Frits Schuurman called me into his office and asked how I would feel about playing on the third desk of first violins, next to Alfredo Galea. Susan Leon, my desk partner, was about to have a baby, and someone in the first violin section also had to remain behind for family reasons. He would like me in the firsts but knew that Freddie was not the easiest of people to get on with. I told him Freddie was my friend and that I got on famously with him, so that was settled.

John Lanchberry, the Royal Ballet's principal conductor, plus an assistant conductor flew to Durban a week ahead to rehearse with the orchestra. On February 3, we left by train for seven weeks in Johannesburg.

The majority of the orchestra stayed at the Carlton Hotel, but I stayed with my mother in our flat at Geraldine Court. Despite having to get used to working at 6,000 feet above sea level again—which was particularly hard on the dancers—and a grueling schedule of full-length ballets or triple bills that finished late at night, plus matinées, I managed to fit in a lot of chamber music. I roped in Clementina de Boeck to play string quartets with Nancy, Thilo, and me. She was wildly delighted. "Oh, it makes me want to go back to Durban!" she exclaimed. "I haven't enjoyed making music as much as this for a long time!" My former Johannesburg trio pianist, Peggy Haddon, played piano trios with Nancy and me. It was all sheer pleasure. I had a free day, and Betty Pack rearranged a whole day's teaching in order to be able to spend it with me. In my diary I recorded:

> We drove out to Little Roseneath together. It was a delightful day, in that complete mental and spiritual harmony we've enjoyed together in the past.

She and Nancy had known of each other as fellow cellists for many years, but now through me they met and liked each other and became friends.

The ballet was a great experience. I found Lanchberry tremendously stimulating to work with. He was one of those conductors who gave you energy, so that no matter how many times you had played *Swan Lake* or *Sleeping Beauty*, you still gave of your best, and it was always enjoyable. We also played *Giselle, Les Sylphides, Patineurs,* and *Don Quixote.* I enjoyed the modern ballets best: *Sweeney Todd, the Rake's Progress,* and *Solitaire.*

We played, not in a pit, but at the front of the stalls in the Empire Theatre, and had an excellent view. How we managed to play at the same time as watch is a mystery, but we did. Several great ballerinas danced with us: of them all, my favorite was Svetlana Beriosova, who alone had the qualities of expressiveness and poetry I had found in Margot Fonteyn. She was sensitively partnered by Donald McLeary.

On February 25, I noted in my diary:

> Tonight, Swan Lake with my favorite pair, Beriosova and McLeary. With them, Swan Lake is magic. Tomorrow is the opening night of Sleeping Beauty, with Nadia Nerina. We had a long rehearsal this morning, during which we rehearsed the Rose Adagio with four different ballerinas, and it was very interesting to compare them: Nerina, Beriosova, Beryl Grey and little Susan Alexander.

Then there were the younger up-and-coming ballerinas whom I admired: Elizabeth Anderton and Antoinette Sibley, whose twenty-first birthday we celebrated with a tea party given by the mayor of Johannesburg, for the entire ballet company and orchestra, at the tea gardens in the Zoo. The mayor welcomed us, and Antoinette gave a little speech expressing her pleasure at being among so many friends in such lovely surroundings on her birthday. It was a memorable occasion.

We gave just one matinee performance in Johannesburg for non-Europeans—mixed race audiences not being allowed—at the City Hall, and not at the Empire Theatre. I bought two tickets for Louisa, the part-time maid my mother had engaged while I was away in London. She had never seen ballet before, and she was so thrilled by the performance that she brought me a bunch of flowers the next day.

She was a lovely person. During my absence in London, when my mother fell ill, she had voluntarily made a bed for herself on the floor, next to my mother's bed, and remained with her until she recovered. She told us of the long, overcrowded train journeys from the African townships to Johannesburg every morning, and how on payday at the end of the week, the *tsotsis*—delinquents—would steal people's wages on the homeward journeys. She told us of the increasing talk she overheard of hatred of the whites and of the desire for revenge, which frightened her. When, on one occasion, my mother discovered that Louisa had been short of money, she said, "Louisa, why didn't you ask me for some?" to which Louisa replied, "The Missis is also sometimes broke!"

Beriosova left Johannesburg for London before the others, and we all felt bereft. It turned out that Lanchberry liked her best, too. "She's so easy to work with," he told a small group of us. "So musical and so pleasant. Always fits in, just one of the company, never creates a fuss—but all the best are like that. Fonteyn's the same. Beriosova's very emotional. I've seen her stand in front of a tree and weep because of its beauty! She's had to go back to London because she's doing a new ballet in April—*La Fille Mal Gardée*—a completely revised version. She's superb in modern ballets because she's so musical. She's just created a role in a brand new ballet, *Antigone.*"

Beriosova joined up with us again toward the end of April, in Cape Town, and we were delighted.

On Sunday, March 6, my mother, Nancy, Alfredo Galea, his wife, who had come from Durban to join him, and I went to the Johannesburg City Hall to hear a massed choir, composed of all the African choirs in the region, perform Handel's *Messiah*. Joseph Friedland conducted, with an *ad hoc* orchestra composed mostly of players from the SABC Symphony Orchestra, led by my beloved teacher, Pierre De Groote. Betty Pack played, too. Nothing like this had ever been done; it was an historic occasion. The soloists were not particularly strong, but the massed choir was outstanding, and one of the several choirmasters was my friend, Michael Rantho. I sought him out after the concert and had a moving reunion with him and his wife, Maureen. I felt sad that the law of the land prevented us from pursuing our friendship more freely.

The last two Royal Ballet performances in Johannesburg took place on Saturday, March 19, culminating in stupendous applause, balloons released from the ceiling, the audience showering the dancers with gaily colored streamers, and the dancers responding with masses of carnations. There were speeches, and there was a great air of celebration. The following evening we left for Pietermaritzburg, where we were due to give two performances.

I was not sorry to be leaving Johannesburg, but sad to be leaving my mother, who was soon to depart for a two-month trip abroad. She had spent many years saving up for this. Events in South Africa, together with my mother's fresh perspective from abroad, were profoundly to alter the course of my life once more.

The Royal Ballet opened at the Alhambra Theatre in Durban on Thursday, March 24. It was a gala performance, inaugurating the jubilee celebrations of the University of Natal. We were disappointed to be playing in a deep orchestra pit this time, unable to watch the ballet. Outside the theatre there were demonstrations by Africans, because as ever, they were being excluded. And as ever, I felt guilty.

On Sunday evening, March 27, Neil Sack gave a party for the whole ballet company at his marvelously situated house and garden in Durban. "I'd like you to come to the party, because you're a friend, but I can't invite the whole orchestra as well as all the dancers," he said to me. It was a wonderful occasion. I had an opportunity to chat with some of the dancers and learn about their lives. They were enchanted with the romantic setting, the tastefully decorated living room with its large picture windows, the heady scents in the glorious sloping garden and its view of the bay, the lights below, the starlit sky. But I missed Fay and felt sad for her children, who had been got out of the way and were spending the weekend with their grandparents.

The month that my mother began her overseas journey, March 1960, the Pan-Africanist Congress began a series of demonstrations against the Pass Laws. Hundreds of black men presented themselves for arrest by handing in their passes at various police stations throughout South Africa. The last of these was at a little town called Sharpeville, in the Transvaal, some miles south of Johannesburg. Thousands of peaceful demonstrators marched toward the police station to hand in their passbooks. They were entirely unarmed, but the police panicked and opened fire against them. The demonstrators, utterly defenceless, started running away, but the police went on shooting. Sixty-nine people were killed, many shot in the back as they fled, and hundreds, including women and children, were badly wounded. The whole world was horrified at what became known as the Sharpeville Massacre.

The African National Congress, headed at the time by Chief Albert Luthuli, a man of great stature and moderation, who was to be awarded the Nobel Peace Prize later that year, organized a stay-at-home day of protest and mourning on March 28. Several of the ANC leaders, including the young Nelson Mandela, publicly burned their passes. Some rioting broke out in the Cape, and the Government declared a State of Emergency. In its fear of a Communist takeover, the government had already long before suppressed the Communist Party. Now the PAC and the ANC were also banned. What next? The Liberal Party? Every movement, however democratic, and every person, however freedom loving, aiming to bring about black liberation, was labeled "Communist." It was a time of great turmoil, and it affected us all.

My mother wrote from London:

> My eyes have been opened. It is impossible to go on living in a country run by a criminal government. What has happened is too terrible. Now they have given themselves carte blanche to do whatever they please, without even parliament to hold them back. We're leaving!

For the first time in my life in South Africa, I had put down roots: I felt happy and at home in Durban. For the first time, I did not actually want to leave. But my mother was only echoing sentiments I had been expressing over a very long time, telling me of a decision I had been trying to persuade her to make for years. I was hardly in a position to refuse. However torn I felt, I knew she was right.

The last Royal Ballet performance in Durban took place on Saturday, April 9. On the same day, at the opening of the Rand Easter Show, a white farmer shot Prime Minister Verwoerd twice in the head. At 2:35 the following morning our train departed for Cape Town. My friends in the orchestra and I were agog to know whether or not he would survive, and we inquired as to the latest news at every station. It was rumored that Verwoerd's wife had already said, "Farewell my love." Nevertheless, he survived that particular assassination attempt, after careful surgery to remove the bullets. It seemed he was invincible and that "God was on his side." However, he did not survive assassination a second time, six years later, by a white parliamentary messenger, on the grounds that he was too liberal toward the black people. This was a great puzzle to those of us who saw in him the cruelest and most repressive Prime Minister South Africa had ever endured.

We arrived in Cape Town on Monday evening, had a seating rehearsal Tuesday lunchtime, and opened the Cape Town season of ballet with *Sleeping Beauty* on the same evening. On Monday, April 25, we gave the one and only matinee for non-Europeans at the Cape Town

City Hall. During the Easter weekend and on Sundays we had time to visit the magnificent Kirstenbosch Botanical Gardens; Stellenbosch; Kalk Bay, a pretty little fishing village; Seal Island; Cape Point, where the Atlantic and Indian Oceans met, swirling and wild; and Cape Agulhas, the southernmost tip of Africa. How beautiful the Cape was, with its purple mountains, its woods, its vineyards, and its dramatic coastline.

While we were in Cape Town I approached John Lanchberry about possible work in London. He told me that, apart from the harpist, the Royal Opera House, home of the Royal Ballet, did not employ women in its orchestra. This was the case with most of the large London orchestras at the time. "Anyway," he said, "the musical profession there is vastly overcrowded. Here you have a nice cushy job. Why risk leaving it for London?"

"Because of the political situation," I answered.

"Ah, now you're talking!" he said. "I can't offer you work with the resident orchestra at the Opera House, but I *can* promise you work with the Royal Ballet touring orchestra. Write to me when you know the date you're due to arrive, and I'll arrange it."

Jenny Welton had written me a long letter from London saying, "Last night I dreamt of you, but when I woke up you weren't here. *Why* aren't you here?"

I was able to write and tell her that I would be coming in the foreseeable future, and about Lanchberry's promise.

Nancy was miserable about my leaving, but unlike many of my other South African friends, she never for a moment tried to persuade me not to go. On the other hand, I tried hard to persuade her to come to London. "I've spent all my life here," she said. "South Africa is all I know. I don't have the courage to uproot myself and start all over again in a strange place, but I shall miss you terribly."

Once back in Durban, I told Schuurman of my intention to leave, though no date had been set yet. "But why, are you not happy here?" he asked.

"I love it here," I said, "but I'm fed up with living under a fascist regime."

"Where is there not Fascism?" he replied. But when he saw that my mind was made up, he said, "You will play the Bruch G minor Violin Concerto with the orchestra for your farewell appearance!"

Chapter Twenty-Six

⌒ LAST MONTHS IN DURBAN—LATE 1960 TO FEBRUARY 1961 ⌒

In the intervening months, life went on as before in Durban. I went back to my position at the back of the second violins, next to Susan Leon. Elina and I broadcast violin and piano sonatas from Broadcast House and gave recitals at the Public Library for the Durban Musical Society and for the South African Music Teachers' Association.

My friend, Morris Kahn, introduced me to Laura Cohen, a young widow with two small children and a large house. She was extraordinarily kind and was upset that I, a "Jewish girl," had been in Durban all this time without her knowledge, so that she had been unable to take me under her wing. She tried to make up for lost time with drives along the seashore and invitations to dinner.

My mother arrived back from her travels on May 24, and on June 3 she joined me in Durban. We talked endlessly about her newly formed decision to leave South Africa, debating, weeping, and finally putting off any final decisions as to when we would leave, until September. "I made inquiries in every country I visited," she said, "and it would be possible for us to emigrate either to Israel, the United States, or England. The choice is yours."

"If I go anywhere, I want it to be London," I replied without hesitation. "That's where my friends are, and where I've already been promised some work."

We agreed that I would go to London ahead of my mother, try to become professionally established, and find us somewhere to stay, while she would wind up her affairs in Johannesburg and sell her by now valuable accountancy practice.

For some time I had been beset by excruciating but undiagnosed abdominal pains, and just over a month after my mother's visit to Durban I underwent a major exploratory operation at Parklands Nursing Home. An inflamed appendix was removed, a biopsy taken from an inflamed right ovary, and a badly twisted right fallopian tube straightened out.

There was no keeping my mother away, though I now had two more "mothers" to take care of me, and all my Durban friends visited me, including two delightful new friends, Wendy Beckwith, a painter, and Rosemary Bamford, a junior lecturer at Natal University, Peitermaritzburg campus, where much later she became professor of theater studies and drama. They made me laugh so much on the first evening after my operation that I thought my stitches would break. Elina and Carl gave me, in advance, a whodunit to read while I was in hospital. I told them I didn't particularly like detective novels, but they said I was bound to like this one, it was so gripping, and so I accepted it. I read it all through the night after my operation, unable to put it down. The dénouement came on the very last page. It was missing; I nearly cried with disappointment. They had done it as a joke, and I wanted to kill them. By the time they produced the last page, I had lost all interest.

Nancy took me home with her when I was discharged and looked after me like an angel. I wished that she would always be there to take care of me whenever I was ill. But I was going away, and in any case she was sixteen years older than I, so the odds were against it. Laura came to see me and took me down to the beach many times during my convalescence. By the time I returned to work with the Durban Civic Orchestra, about a month after the operation, I felt fitter than I had ever felt since my return to South Africa nearly four years earlier, when I had suffered from typhoid fever.

On August 15 the orchestra went on holiday. Nancy and I left for a tour of Zululand: Eshowe, with wonderful brightly colored tropical flowers, lush plants, and magnificent trees; Empangeni, where the Zulu women openly disapproved of our wearing slacks as we shopped for provisions at the market; Mtubatuba, a small town surrounded by sugar cane farms; and finally, the Hluhluwe game reserve. We stayed in Hut Number 12, according to my diary. It was profoundly peaceful there, in a clearing surrounded by bushes and trees. All was silence except for the chirping of crickets and birdsong at dusk. Our African guide prepared dinner outside our hut; the cooking smells emanating from the wood fire were delicious. To our delight some warthogs paid us a surprise visit.

In the daytime our guide took us for drives as well as walks to see the many animals living in the wild—a herd of buffalo, giraffes, zebras, monkeys, mongooses, steenbok, bushbuck, kudu, and the incredibly graceful and beautifully marked impala. We were allowed to walk quite near to the rhinos—both black ones and white ones—as long as we were careful always to remain to leeward, so that they could not smell us. We saw hyenas, baboons, tortoises, crocodiles, eagles, lovely smaller birds, and many butterflies. After Hluhluwe, we went bird watching at St. Lucia Bay and saw miles of lonely windswept beach and white sand dunes, untouched and unspoiled.

We stayed at a guesthouse overlooking the river, run by a born-again New Methodist, who regaled us with tales of the various religious conversions he had undergone until he had finally seen the light. All through our first dinner there he spoke of the Coming of the Lord and the Last Day of Judgement, though, as I noted in my diary:

> …for all his preoccupation with the sinfulness of men he seemed strangely unaware of the moral problems besetting our country.

> After dinner he took us outside to watch the heavens. Never had we seen such a clear night sky, such a multitude of stars, overwhelmingly bright against its blackness. While our host held forth about the various constellations, those damned mosquitoes bit mercilessly at my legs and feet. I itched frantically for days after.

He told us to beware of sharks at the river mouth, and further along the river, to beware of the crocodiles amid the lush, subtropical vegetation. We spent my birthday at Mtumzumi. On our way back we stopped at Salt Rock and Shaka's Rock, where according to legend Shaka, the great Zulu king, had sat gazing out to sea. We continued via Umhlali, Umdloti, and Umhlanga, and finally arrived in Durban on August 28.

The following day I was on my way to Johannesburg and to decisions regarding my departure for London. Except for a few days in January, this was my last chance to see old friends and spend time with them: Hermann Abramowitz and Joanie; young David Miller and his parents; Gordon and Yvonne Vorster; Marion and Walter Rothgiesser; Philip Levy; Betty Pack; and Pierre and Joyce De Groote. Joyce was dying—*dying*—and Pierre could do nothing to hold her back. It was heartbreaking. It seemed to me I was forever having to say goodbye to people I loved, and I hated it. They all wanted me to stay; only Marion and Walter really understood my reasons for leaving.

I went to a couple of recitals with my mother, to hear Henryk Szerying and then the Carmirelli Quartet, and I listened to Nancy broadcast a cello recital from Durban. Philip had a marvelous story to tell of a recent concert tour. At one of his recitals in a small town in the Orange Free State, he had been playing Manuel de Falla's *Ritual Fire Dance* as an encore, when a fire broke out backstage, and he became enveloped in smoke. He swore he had not stage-managed it.

On September 10 I returned to Durban, and on Monday 12 the orchestra returned to work. Prime Minister Verwoerd had set a date, October 5, for a referendum on the future of South Africa, and tensions were heightening. The wording was: "Are you in favor of a Republic for the Union of South Africa? Vote Yes or No." In Durban, large banners had been erected across the roads, declaiming: **"Vote Yes and keep South Africa White!"**

Considering that we were outnumbered five to one, this seemed to me to be highly inflammatory: an insult to the majority of South Africa's inhabitants.

At the Los Angeles Hotel I usually sat at a table on my own for breakfast, but twice a year a young commercial traveler came down to Durban from the Orange Free State and sat at my table. Whether this was his idea or the management's, I cannot remember. He was of English descent but married to an Afrikaans woman, and he was more rabidly Nationalist than any Afrikaner I knew. He sat at my table during the run-up to the referendum, and the views he expressed made me go cold. I felt it was unsafe to express an opinion. It seemed to me that the majority of South Africans were not only afraid to speak, but increasingly afraid to think.

The Nationalists won their vote for a Republic.

On Sunday, January 8, 1961, I had my first rehearsal with the orchestra for Bruch's G minor Violin Concerto. I had been practicing hard for this in the sweltering summer heat. Everywhere was unbearable—my hotel room, Nancy's flat, as well as any of the rooms at the City Hall—until Laura Cohen offered me the use of her house. There I practiced in an open doorway, between two rooms with open windows, and there I occasionally managed to get a little breath of comparatively cool air.

The rehearsal went well, and all the members of the orchestra congratulated me, shouting "Bravo!" and "Excellent!" Paul, whom I had been avoiding so carefully for the whole of my two years in Durban, jumped up from his seat and exclaimed, "Very good—outstanding! You astonish me! All this time you've been quietly sitting at the back of the seconds, and you can play like that! You must play in my Baroque Ensemble. We are broadcasting Vivaldi's *Four Seasons* next Friday and I need you! Will you play with us?" I was happy to accept.

That morning I had crept into the City Hall with butterflies in my stomach, but by the end of the rehearsal I knew the worst was over. With such tributes from my colleagues I felt I had nothing to fear from the audience.

I had a second rehearsal on the morning of the concert, Sunday, January 29. My mother had arrived the previous evening. I wanted her to be at the concert, but her coming brought home to me very sharply that it was the beginning of the end of my stay in Durban, that I had to leave Nancy behind, and that an uncertain future lay ahead. Instead of looking forward to the concert, I wept half through the night. However, I took myself in hand next morning, and everything was under control at the rehearsal.

When I arrived at the City Hall in the evening I found bouquets of flowers, telegrams, and messages of goodwill in the artists' room. Jack Hayden, the orchestra's Roman Catholic double bass player, had lit candles in church and prayed for me. Neil Sack came around during the interval to wish me luck. Frits and Maria Schuurman popped in to encourage me, and according to my diary, "Frits stopped and looked at me as if for the first time and said, 'But you look a dream!'" I played in the second half of the concert, and I remained calm and confident up to and beyond the moment I stepped on to the platform, and all went well.

To my disappointment, Schuurman had undergone a hernia operation shortly before the concert and was not yet able to conduct, so the assistant conductor, Charles Denholm, conducted in his place. He was thrilled with the performance. When it was over the audience burst into rapturous applause, and when I'd finished taking curtain calls, the orchestra all came pouring into the wings, congratulating me and overwhelming me with praise, which was all the more surprising as on the whole they were a phlegmatic lot. By the time I got to the dressing room I found all my friends there, including the Kupers, who had not yet left for the United States, and now after all I was leaving too. There were a good many strangers from among the audience, all saying extravagant things to me about the great future that awaited me. I couldn't believe it was me they were talking about, knowing as I did that what lay ahead was simply to try to find work and earn a living.

Schuurman was waiting outside the dressing room. "It went *very* well," he said, "I am so glad, so glad! Aren't you happy?"

"I'm happy it's over," I said, but the next day I wished I could play it again, without the little flaws that I remembered, but which others seemed not to have noticed.

Laura Cohen threw a party for me after the concert, inviting all my friends, colleagues, and conductors. The next morning she popped in to see me before I left for work, and said she had spent the night weeping because I was going away. I suspected that Nancy had been crying, too, when I saw her, but she didn't admit to it.

Schuurman came down from his office during the rehearsal before the lunchtime concert—my last with the orchestra—to make a little farewell speech to me in front of them.

He said how glad he was of my success the previous evening, how sorry the orchestra was to lose me, and how they all wished me every success and happiness in England.

"I was so touched I was near tears," I wrote in my diary. "Wherever will I find such a kind and charming conductor again?"

After this, my mother and I spent a few days together in the beautiful and cool Valley of the Thousand Hills before briefly returning to Johannesburg. On February 16, I embarked at Durban harbor on the SS *Europa* of the Lloyd Triestino Line. At one end of the ship to see me off were my mother, Nancy, Laura, Wendy, Rosemary, Yvonne, Elina, and Paul, all bearing gifts; at the other end, still refusing to have anything to do with Paul, was Alfredo Galea, with more gifts. And there was I, dancing between the two ends, trying not to hurt anybody's feelings.

On the ship, to my delight and astonishment, I found my dear friend Clementina de Boeck with her three young boys. Clem was tired of emotional upheavals in Johannesburg and was returning to Europe to begin a new life there. They had embarked at Cape Town, and we were about to travel together up the East Coast of Africa, to Europe.

Part Five

 ENGLAND

Chapter Twenty-Seven

⌒ FAREWELL TO AFRICA—FEBRUARY TO MARCH 1961 ⌒

Clem was not the only person I recognized on the *Europa*. It was a pleasant surprise to discover Julio Bello, the young Portuguese from Lourenço Marques whom I had met at the Millers in Johannesburg in 1957, and who had given me driving practice before my driving test.

When I went down to the dining saloon for lunch and was shown to my table, I found myself seated opposite a personable young man, who introduced himself as Bobby Marks. He was an optician from England, now on his way home after spending some years in South Africa. A semi-professional pianist, he had played for the Allied troops in North Africa and Italy during the war, in the entertainment unit of the South African Defence Force, so he was not quite as young as he looked. He got on particularly well with children, and thus with Clem's boys, and he had a great sense of humor. At the same time, there was something whimsical and slightly melancholy about him. We became friends from the start. Clem and I played duets, and sometimes Bobby accompanied one or both of us at the piano in the saloon. Nancy had given me Gerald Durrell's *My Family and Other Animals* to read on board, and I laughed out loud as I read it, lying in a deck chair alongside Bobby. "Ridiculous affectation!" exclaimed Bobby. "How can a book make you laugh out loud!" There was no way to defend myself other than by making him read the book after I'd finished. He surprised himself by laughing as loudly as I had.

It was a wonderful journey. We made many stops on the way and had time to go ashore for several hours at a time to explore. We traveled up the Portuguese East African coast and berthed at Beira on February 18, two days after embarkation. Bobby, Julio, and I stepped ashore, Bobby linking my arm in his as if to claim possession. Julio took my other arm, and so the three of us proceeded ashore every time we berthed.

At Beira we had lunch at a magnificent hotel facing the sea. On the morning of February 21, we called at Tanganyika's capital, Dar es Salaam, where we entered the Governor's palace to look around after exploring the splendid gardens. A servant appeared silently as from nowhere, politely informed us we were trespassing, and sent us packing. That afternoon we stopped at the lovely spice island of Zanzibar, pervaded by a subtle scent of cloves, where we stood outside the Sultan of Zanzibar's summer palace, admiring it but careful not to repeat the morning's mistake. In any case we would have been prevented, as there were sentries guarding the gate. Coconut palms abounded, and the ground was thickly covered with countless coconuts. A little black boy shimmied up a tall palm to demonstrate how he'd picked one for Charlie Chaplin the previous year. We had not been able to persuade Clem to join us—she was saving her money for Egypt, as her boys had been learning about the pharaohs, the Sphinx, and the pyramids, and that was what they were looking forward to above all. I was sorry that she was missing so much of interest, but I could not prevail on her to change her mind. As for me, I was making the most of what came before, as I felt sure I stood no chance of being allowed entry into Nasser's Egypt, hostile as it was to Israel: my passport was stamped with an Israeli visa.

On February 22 we berthed at Mombassa, Kenya, for two days. We bathed in the incredibly warm sea, visited a lovely Hindu temple, and bought African woodcarvings from street vendors. Julio had been to Mombassa previously, and he led us through winding back streets to a bar he remembered, where we drank the most delicious iced coffee we'd ever tasted. In the evening we visited a nightclub, where a few male passengers from the *Europa* danced with local African women. This so upset a young girl passenger who had lived all her life in apartheid-ridden South Africa that she burst into tears and was inconsolable.

Three days later we anchored off Mogadishu, where for once we could not go ashore, and watched as disembarking passengers were being hoisted from the deck in a tall basket, three at a time, on to a tender that was waiting below. After two more days we arrived at Aden, hot as hell, dry and dreary. There were a few shops, overrun by chickens and goats. We watched as a caravan of camels bearing goods passed by. People stared at us in the streets. Taxi drivers competed for our business, promising to take us to "the oasis." We thought it had to be better than this, at the very least cooler, and agreed a price with the taxi driver. When we arrived at what turned out to be a sorry excuse for an oasis—a palm tree or two, a couple of mangy-looking camels, no water to be seen, and not at all cooler—he charged us double the price we had agreed upon. We protested, and he shouted angrily at us. A policeman strolled up and asked what the fuss was about, and we naïvely appealed to him for justice. Instead, he insisted that we paid the driver what he was asking. No doubt this was a double act they frequently played: Fleece the Tourist. I was glad to get away from Aden, its heat, and its hostility.

Finally, on March 2, we arrived at Suez. There we had the choice of either sailing through the Suez Canal, or of taking a tourist bus to Cairo and meeting the ship again the following day at Port Said. The customs officials boarded the ship and seemed to take an eternity examining all our passports. I felt distinctly nervous. As ill-luck would have it, Egypt had fallen out with Belgium the day before our arrival at Suez, and the sad irony was that Clem and her boys had to remain on the ship, while I, to my astonishment, was given permission to disembark. My heart bled for Clem, that this should happen after all her self-denial.

Once again Bobby, Julio, and I disembarked together, this time on Egyptian soil. We felt elated as the bus drove us to Cairo. There we were taken to a luxurious hotel where we were to spend the night. On arrival, registration forms were handed out to us, asking a number of, what seemed to me, impertinent questions. To begin with, we had to fill in our religion. What's it got to do with them? I asked myself crossly. I had visions of being murdered in my bed if I wrote "Jewish." Luckily for me Bobby was filling in his form ahead of me. When he got to "Religion" he blithely wrote "Methodist." If he's a Methodist, so am I, I said to myself. So I, too, wrote Methodist, and saved myself a sleepless night. We laughed conspiratorially, though I was sorry to be taking anybody's religion in vain.

We spent the evening at a nightclub watching belly dancing, a first for me. The next morning we took camel rides to visit the great pyramids at Giza, particularly the Pyramid of Cheops, and the Sphinx. We each had a *dragoman*—guide—dressed in what looked like a long striped nightshirt, to take care of us. As we climbed the great Step Pyramid in the burning sunshine, I repeatedly had to kick my *dragoman*, climbing immediately behind me. His wandering hands were even more persistent after we entered the pharaoh's tomb, and all along annoyed and distracted me from the awe I should have been feeling at these ancient historic sites.

Later, back in Cairo, we saw Tutankhamun in the Cairo Museum, golden and splendid. Finally, we went to a perfumery where we could buy lovely essential oils that went into the making of perfumes. We were shocked by the numbers of persistent beggars who importuned us in the streets, saddened by the poverty we saw.

That afternoon our bus drove us to Port Said via Ismailia, where, stopping to look at the view from a bridge, I accidentally dropped a pretty silver bracelet I had bought at a market in Cairo, into the waters of the Suez Canal.

We re-embarked at Port Said and now found ourselves in the Mediterranean Sea. I said goodbye to Africa, imagining I could turn my back forever on all its troubles. We sailed past the Greek islands and paid a short visit to Brindisi just above the heel of Italy. The last port of call was Trieste, but we had all decided to disembark at the preceding port: Venice. Clem and her boys went straight on to Belgium; Bobby, Julio, and I decided to stop in Venice for a few days. At the harbor, porters from the various hotels vied with each other for our business, tempting us with low tariffs. When we arrived at the hotel of our choice, the receptionist added a substantial amount to the price we had been quoted, for "tax." We pretended to fly into a rage and were finally given our rooms at the prices originally quoted.

Venice lived up to our dreams. The weather was wintry-cool but dry, and the sun shone through the clouds. The Piazza San Marco, with the Basilica at one end and the Doge's Palace at the other, was a vision of perfection. I drank blood-red orange juice at Harry's Bar in the Piazza. We took a gondola ride through the canals, enjoying the ancient palaces and villas, however decrepit. There were so many resonances: Vivaldi, Guardi, Canaletto, Turner, Henry James. Another gondola took us across to the Lido, with its grand hotels, home to the rich and famous during the season. But it was out of season now and deserted.

We left Venice on March 9. Bobby and Julio traveled direct to London, while I took a train to Switzerland. I shared a compartment with a desperate young Italian on his way home to Milan. He confided in me that he had suffered a nervous breakdown and had been in Venice in order to recover. He poured his heart out to me, and when we parted he insisted, despite my protestations, on giving me a number of pretty Venetian glass animals, to thank me for having listened to him. I wrapped them carefully in tissues, but by the time I arrived in London, I was sad to find them all broken.

In Switzerland, I traveled to Zurich, where I stayed at an attractive *Gasthof*, and I took a train to Winterthur to visit Gretl Gideon and her blind, ailing mother.

Finally, on Sunday, March 12, 1961, I flew to London, my new home, where I had spent over three-and-a-half happy student years.

Chapter Twenty-Eight

⌒ THIRD IMMIGRATION—MARCH 1961 TO DECEMBER 1962 ⌒

Jenny Welton, my dear friend of St. Peter's Square days, who had seen me off at London (now Heathrow) Airport four and a half years earlier in September 1956, came to meet me at the Airport. She took me home to the flat she now rented in a converted house in Thurlow Road, Hampstead, where she lived in a large attic room with her partner, Ross Pierson. Below this room were the kitchen, bathroom, and three bedrooms that she sublet to lodgers, of whom I was now one.

I well remember that first day back in London. Margaret Hayhurst—my friend Maggie, also from our time at St. Peter's Square—was there to welcome me. Between them—excellent cooks that they were—they produced an enormous lunch. I was amazed at the amount of food they could put away; they were disappointed at my lack of appetite. Ross, whom I had never met before, very left wing in his political views, launched an attack on me as a South African. I tried to explain that I had left South Africa because I fervently disagreed with its politics, but it didn't do me any good. He insisted on arguing with me, bringing forth all sorts of figures and statistics, which I didn't understand. Later Maggie told me she was sure Ross made these figures up as he went along and that it was hopeless to try to win an argument with him. He was fairly good-looking and had, I suppose, a certain charm. Jenny and he were mad about each other.

Jenny had good news for me. I had written to her saying that John Lanchberry had not answered any of my letters telling him when I was due to arrive in London, and she had bombarded the Royal Opera House with phone calls asking for Lanchberry's home telephone number. At first they had refused, quite properly, to give it to her, but she was so insistent that they had finally given in. She managed to reach him on the phone and demanded to know why he had not answered my letters, when he had solemnly promised me work with the Royal Ballet touring orchestra. He was apologetic and explained that he had been back home in Australia and had only just returned and found my letters. I was to phone him when I arrived, and he would arrange a meeting.

Besides this, I already had a job. I was to go to Newcastle upon Tyne the very next day, to play for a week with the newly formed Northern Sinfonia. At the time the Northern Sinfonia consisted of a small nucleus of players stationed in Newcastle, regularly swollen to full symphony orchestra size with imports from London. Later it became an excellent home-based chamber orchestra.

The train would be leaving from King's Cross station at 9:00 a.m. the following morning. My heart sank. I had less than twenty-four hours in which to become accustomed to my new home in the comfort of being among friends, before being thrown upon the mercy of total strangers. Where would I be staying? How would I have time to find "digs" between arriving in Newcastle, where I had never been, and the first rehearsal, which was scheduled for 3:00 p.m. on the same day, followed by another short one at 6:00 and a concert in the City Hall at 8:00?

"Don't worry, you'll be traveling with Isabel Smith, and she's bound to find you somewhere," said Jenny. "Oh my God!" she exclaimed, "I forgot all about Musicians' Union membership. You resigned when you left, didn't you? You're not allowed to play in an orchestra without being a member—or rather, the others aren't allowed to play with *you* if you're not a member. There's nothing for it. You'll just have to write to the Union today, apply for membership, and send them the subscription. I'll have a word with Isabel when I see you off tomorrow. Just make sure you avoid the subject with Betty Rajna—she's the union steward." Fortunately, Betty only thought of it halfway through the week. Isabel was very protective: "It's been taken care of," she said. And it was.

Jenny had another job lined up for me: a tour with the London Festival Ballet, beginning on April 15, which fitted in neatly before the coming Royal Ballet tour. Meanwhile, after my return from Newcastle, I could get in touch with Lanchberry. I was enormously grateful to Jenny for all the effort she had put into finding me work, and at the same time I felt frightened and homesick. Coming to live and work in England was quite a different matter from my carefree life here as a student. "Real life" had finally arrived, and lotus eating was definitely a thing of the past.

Newcastle was a nightmare. I longed for the warmth, light, and spaciousness of Africa; I missed its star-studded night skies; I missed Nancy dreadfully; and everybody I came into contact with seemed alien to me. It wasn't that they were unkind or excluded me in any way; I just didn't understand them.

From the station, Isabel phoned some theatrical digs she had seen advertised, for those of us who had no pre-booked accommodation. There was no time to go there and inspect them before the day's work was done. A large group of us—three young women and eleven young men—arrived at the house that evening in time for dinner at 11:00 p.m. It was among a row of identical, anonymous-looking houses, in a dreary residential area, with not a landmark in sight. We had piled into taxis, address in hand, too tired to notice where we were going. I had no idea of the locality we were in. Our host and hostess had gone to the trouble of cooking an enormous meal of soup, followed by meat with a huge amount of vegetables, all boiled to the point of tastelessness. We had hardly eaten any lunch, and I was ravenous, so I tried to get the food down while holding my breath. A girl called Gillie sitting opposite me kept raising a forkful to her lips, sniffing at it with a look of distaste, and lowering her fork again without eating. I completely lost my appetite and gave up. Some ghastly stodge was served up for pudding. Our host and hostess were hurt that we didn't eat with more enthusiasm.

Then came the bathroom routine. There were no other guests in the house, but we were fourteen, with only one bathroom between us. I was accustomed to having a bath or shower every day, but I realized I could not monopolize the bath, looked forward to having my turn, and made do with a strip wash at the handbasin. The next day, to my dismay, I found a large carpet, dye seeping out of it, soaking in the one and only bath. And there it remained, presumably to prevent us from using too much precious hot water. But the worst ordeal was the bedroom. We three women were put into a large room with three narrow single beds. We had flannelette sheets and pillowcases, a new experience for me. They were damp, impregnated with human body odors, and had clearly not been washed at least since the previous lodgers had slept in them. Gillie lay on her back and wrapped her woollen scarf around her neck and mouth, right up to her nose, to avoid the smell. For some reason, this only intensified the horror for me. I decided I had to get out of this place, whatever the cost. The men laughed at us and said that if we'd had to endure National Service in the army as they had, we wouldn't be so fussy. Their teasing did not make us feel any better.

As it happened, Gillie had a relative in the area with whom she could stay, so she had a means of escape. Liz—the third girl sharing our room—and I decided to look for a hotel, but there was only one gap in our schedule, Wednesday morning, when we had the time to do this, as we were working and traveling so much all week. We did, in fact, find a reasonably priced hotel that Wednesday and moved on the same day, assuring our disappointed hosts that we did not expect a penny of the week's rent returned. It was far too cheap anyway. They would have done better to charge more and raise their standards of hygiene.

The hotel was also bleakly penny-pinching—I wondered if this was a leftover from the hardship of the war years—but at least it was relatively clean, and there were some trees lining the street.

To add to my general misery, South African Prime Minister Verwoerd attended a Commonwealth conference in London that week, in the hope that South Africa might remain a member of the Commonwealth despite becoming a republic, and he had stormed out of the meeting in anger because the other Commonwealth members would not accept the principle of apartheid. Now the last vestiges of restraining influence that Britain had provided would disappear. Despite having turned my back on South Africa, I found that I still cared deeply.

On the other hand, I enjoyed the work. The standard was high, and we had some good soloists, including Gina Bachauer at the piano in Middlesborough and violist Cecil Aranowitz in Newcastle. We spent most of Thursday rehearsing at different locations for a television broadcast on Friday, and in between we gave a concert for schoolchildren. We rehearsed all day Friday from 9:30 a.m. at Tyne Tees television studios for a live transmission at 9:30 p.m. On Saturday, we gave another concert in Newcastle, our third that week. It had a large catchment area; people came from far and wide. Our last concert, on the Sunday, took place in Sunderland.

The one thing that sustained me all week was looking forward to being with Jenny on my return to London, and to picking up our old affectionate friendship. But it was not to be. We had both changed and seemed unable to adapt to the changes we found in each other. I spent far too much time dashing around, catching up with every single friend from my student days who still lived in London, as well as seeing my new friends Julio and Bobby, and people to whom I had introductions from South Africa, including the pianist, Bruno Raikin, who had given me such welcome encouragement many years previously in Johannesburg. He and I formed a regular sonata partnership and gradually developed a great friendship. Bruno had been Paul Robeson's official pianist on his tour of Prague and Warsaw, and he had huge admiration for Robeson, both as a singer and a person. I introduced Ignatius, my African tenor friend, to him and they worked together for several years. Bruno said that although Ignatius—who by now wanted to be known by his African name of Bejen—was a tenor and Robeson had been a bass baritone, he had very similar qualities and was a joy to work with. (Some years later Ignatius sang the whole of the title role of Verdi's *Otello* to me, with Bruno at the piano. It was overwhelming.) I somehow expected to see Jenny, who was at home all day, in the evenings, after all my other engagements, but that was always the time when she wanted to be with Ross. I wonder now at my utter block-headedness.

But there were other reasons why Jenny turned away from me. She told me that she associated me with the unhappiest period of her life. I felt dreadfully hurt, because I remembered it as the happiest period of my life, in which she had played such an important part. Jenny had been a most faithful correspondent during my years in South Africa, and from everything she had written to me, the unhappy things that had happened to her had occurred after my departure from London. Yet I had to accept that this was how she now felt. I asked her why, in that case, she had gone to so much trouble in helping me find work.

"Look at me," she said. "I had a few small orchestral jobs, not enough to set me off on a career. I started too late on the viola, and I couldn't catch up. So I gave up trying, and now I'm copying music for a living. It's soul destroying work. I couldn't bear that to happen to you!"

So she still cared about me, despite not being able to stand me. I was too needy, and she was unable to cope. She, Maggie, and I arranged to go to a few concerts and plays together, but whenever we met, having arrived from the different places we had been to during the day, it grieved me to see a shadow of displeasure cross her face.

On Thursday, April 13, Jack Lanchberry left a complimentary ticket for me at the stage door of the Royal Opera House, to see a mixed program of modern ballets. We met for drinks afterward at the Nag's Head to discuss my joining the Royal Ballet touring orchestra. I was to be in the first violin section, as was also the case with the Festival Ballet and the Northern Sinfonia, to which I was frequently asked to return. Rehearsals would take place at the Crush Bar in the Royal Opera House, beginning on May 29, followed by a four-week tour. There would be another, longer tour starting on September 25 and ending on December 9. We talked about the ballets and the dancers I had seen. He complimented me on my judgement, and we had a pleasant time together.

But first, there was the Festival Ballet tour and having to get used to traveling on interminably slow Sunday trains, so that one would be available for rehearsals at theaters on Monday mornings; cramped, often dirty backstage conditions; cold, uncomfortable digs; and dull, frugal meals that were all one could afford on one's meager salary. The musicians in the orchestra seemed a pretty weird lot to me—perhaps I seemed just as weird to them—until on later tours I got used to them and came to really like some of them. The culture shock I had not experienced in England as a student had caught up with me at last.

To my great relief, Achim arrived from the Philippines to visit me, and as I was on tour, he came up to Bradford to join me for about a week, before going to Paris on a business trip. At last, I could be with someone I cared about.

I felt even more out of harmony with the members of the Royal Ballet touring orchestra, some of whom appeared to me to be completely mad, but I made one lifelong friend in it: clarinettist Daphne Down. She tried to influence me not to be so critical of everybody. We went on marvelous cross-country walks wherever the tour took us, and with the advancement of spring the weather improved, blossoms appeared, the land turned many different shades of green, I managed to find better digs, and life began to seem more tolerable.

In Glasgow, I stayed in the home of Farquharson Cousins, a gifted horn player in the BBC Scottish Symphony Orchestra, whom I had met on a brief visit to Glasgow in 1956. He was an eccentric but attractive man, one quarter Native American, his Scottish missionary grandfather having married an American Indian squaw, as Farquharson would proudly tell all newcomers. He had filled his house with young musician lodgers and one middle-aged violinist, a warm-hearted, motherly woman called Margaret Lawson, who was everybody's confidante and comforter. Farquharson often quarrelled with her, and later would leave an apple on her pillow to make friends again. His house was beautifully situated on the green, leafy, tree-lined banks of the River Kelvin, and its heart was the kitchen, which took up the whole of the basement, where everybody met to cook, eat, and converse with each other.

Toward the end of my stay there I was having tea in the kitchen with Margaret Lawson and a nice-looking young cellist from Cornwall called John, enjoying the cozy atmosphere and Margaret's comforting presence. They were discussing deputy string players and Margaret said, "I don't like those Jewey players from London." My heart stopped. Good, kind Margaret of all people. I felt betrayed. What should I do? I remained silent until it was time to part. Then I said, "Before we part there's something I have to say. I seem to have been here under false pretences. You've been very kind to me, all the time not realizing that I am Jewish."

"What nonsense!" said Margaret, "I don't have anything against Jews. I don't care what you are! I have lots of Jewish friends."

"You said you didn't like 'those Jewey players from London.'"

"Well, but I didn't mean specifically Jewish people. It's just a type of people who come from the East End of London. They don't even have to be Jewish."

"Then why refer to them as 'Jewey'?" I interrupted.

John came to Margaret's defense, saying she merely meant certain loud-mouthed types, she didn't mean Jews, and she really was no anti-Semite. We parted in an uneasy truce.

The following morning when I came down to breakfast I found John deep in conversation with Farquharson. "Here's the very person," said Farquharson, "I'll leave you to it."

"Oh Eva," said John, "If only you knew how I admired you yesterday. You were so brave, and I've been such a coward. All my life I've been afraid to admit that I'm Jewish. When people asked me outright if I was Jewish, because of my dark coloring, I'd say it was because of my Celtic blood, as I came from Cornwall. Now I feel I've got to tell all my friends that I'm Jewish—starting with my fiancée!" At that point Margaret came and joined us, so he had to start with her. "I always knew it," she said.

I had to move away from Jenny's, partly because our downstairs neighbor kept complaining that my practicing disturbed her, partly because of the coolness between Jenny and me, though we went on seeing each other occasionally. Then Jenny announced that she and Ross were taking pottery lessons and intended to move to Spain and try to make a living out of pottery. I was astonished that they were prepared to throw their left wing principles to the wind and live in fascist Spain, Franco being still very much alive then. And I felt abandoned by the one person who had repeatedly begged me to come back, the one person I still cared for most in London. Yet they were having such a struggle to earn a living that I could hardly blame them. However, much as they loved Spain, it didn't work out. They ultimately returned to England, Ross doing Union work, Jenny teaching violin and viola. Later she turned to painting, under the name of Jenny Knowland, her mother's maiden name. We lost touch.

The Republic of South Africa became a reality on May 31, 1961. I was fortunate in that I had arrived in England while South Africa was still a dominion, so that I had no longer than a year to wait in order to take out British nationality. My mother was not so lucky. By the time she arrived in London in October 1961, South Africa had left the Commonwealth, and she had to wait the full five years before she could become naturalized.

In order to economize, my mother and I lived together, first in a large room in Warwick Road, Earl's Court, then sharing a room in the flat of our dear friend Gessy Gathercole, an anti-apartheid activist in exile from South Africa, whom we had met years earlier through Walter and Marion Rothgiesser. This was in Hoop Lane, Golders Green, just a few yards away from the crematorium, with hearses passing by our window every morning. Eventually we rented a flat in Hendon. Nancy came for a visit in March 1962, and stayed with us until her return to Durban in early June. I continued to play with the Royal Ballet. We had a memorable week at the Bath Festival, during which Yehudi Menuhin, with the cellist Maurice Gendron, accompanied Margot Fonteyn in the solos from *Swan Lake*, Act Two. There followed a tour with Ballet Rambert, more Festival and Royal Ballet tours, and just a few other freelance dates in between.

It was at the end of one of these tours that I found my mother waiting for me at Brent—now Brent Cross—Station, barely able to contain herself; she had terrible news to impart. A letter from Johannesburg, from the Millers, had arrived that morning. They had given David a toy radio as a birthday present, and during the night, curiosity as to how it worked had got the better of him. While his parents were asleep he had got up, taken the radio apart, and electrocuted himself. David, my beloved pupil, was dead.

We were both devastated by the news, but then a strange thing happened to me. I found that I responded with a quite uncharacteristic enthusiasm to everything that crossed my path. Colors were much more vivid, trees more beautiful, people more wonderful than I had ever experienced them. It was as if, for the space of about a fortnight, David's spirit had somehow entered into me, and I was seeing everything through his eyes, experiencing everything through his unquenchable enthusiasm, his sense of wonder. If anyone had told me of such a thing happening to them, I would have dismissed it as fanciful nonsense. But it happened to me, and I cannot explain it, any more than I was able to explain why my little African violet in Durban continued to bloom uninterruptedly for over a year after my friend Fay, who had given it to me, had died.

Chapter Twenty-Nine
⌖ A CHANGE OF COURSE—1962 TO 1965 ⌖

What began as a lifesaver had turned into a dead end. The time had come to give up the endless ballet tours. Daphne Down, my Royal Ballet clarinettist friend, and I, had a long, heart-searching telephone conversation toward the end of 1962, during which we both decided to take our courage in our hands, turn down the next tour, and hope to build up enough freelance work in London to earn a living. I was persuaded to advertise for pupils in the local press, which I found demeaning, as in the past I had always been recommended by word of mouth. Nevertheless several good pupils came to me through the *Hendon and Finchley Times*. One of the mothers advised me to write to the excellent South Hampstead High School for Girls, part of the Girls' Public Day School Trust, and I was fortunate enough to get a part-time position there. The girls I taught were intelligent, though few of them seemed to be particularly gifted, musically. I got on very well with Jean Middlemiss, head of the music department. All the members of the music staff were congenial, and I had the added pleasure of playing chamber music with them at school concerts.

After a BBC audition I frequently worked as an extra or deputy with the BBC Symphony Orchestra at the time when Pierre Boulez was its musical director, and I participated in wonderful performances of Mahler symphonies as well as Schoenberg's *Gurrelieder*. The Royal Philharmonic Orchestra offered me work as an extra and deputy soon after it first opened its doors to women. Paul Collins, a fine violinist and friend of Jenny Welton, gave me work in several West End musicals that he led. The first of these was *Half a Sixpence*, with Tommy Steele, at the Cambridge Theatre. On the evening of October 29, 1964, Paul and all the players sitting ahead of me had put in deputies in order to start playing for a new show, *Robert and Elizabeth*, at the Lyric Theatre, Shaftesbury Avenue, where I was soon to follow them. It was based on the story of the Brownings, with Keith Michell and June Bronhill in the title roles. Meanwhile I found myself leading the little *Half a Sixpence* orchestra at the Cambridge Theatre, with some solos to play. The orchestral management was the same as that of the English Chamber Orchestra and happened to be in the theatre on October 29. The next day they telephoned to offer me work as an extra with the ECO. Some of my best musical memories are of that time, particularly of the young Daniel Barenboim conducting and divinely playing Mozart piano concertos with the ECO, transporting one straight to heaven. This was genius, quite out of the ordinary. Subsequently, when he was engaged, and later married, to Jacqueline du Pré, we were treated to a double dose of genius, he conducting, she playing the Boccherini, Haydn, Schumann, and Elgar cello concertos.

Emanuel Hurwitz led the English Chamber Orchestra at the time, partnered by Kenneth Sillitoe. Manny Hurwitz was a marvelous violinist, a marvelous leader, and a delightful person. He also led the Melos Ensemble, whose performances of the Schubert Octet and Beethoven Septet I relished above all others. Subsequently he became co-leader of the Philharmonia Orchestra and led the Aeolian String Quartet, with impeccable style and ravishing tonal beauty.

I decided to have some lessons with Manny, and he assured me that I had more than enough ability to play in any orchestra. Unfortunately he didn't realize that, however well I played my prepared pieces at auditions, my sight-reading nearly always let me down. I would see a lot of black notes, be seized by panic, and my mind would freeze. On a train journey to Bournemouth to audition for the Bournemouth Symphony Orchestra, I found myself in the same compartment as another of Manny's students on his way to audition for the same violin position. He succeeded; I didn't. When I told Manny, he was appalled. "But you're a much better violinist than he is!" he exclaimed. "I thought it would be a walkover! What on earth happened?"

"I played alright until it came to the sight reading," I said, "and then I went to pieces. I messed up completely." Fortunately I enjoyed the freedom and variety of life as a freelance player, and I liked the balance between playing and teaching. Not all the work was equally satisfying, and it was unpredictable; I never knew where I was going to be from day to day, and I was forever waiting for the phone to ring. But when it rang it was always with a surprise, sometimes an exciting one.

Nevertheless I gave two good auditions while Manny was with the Philharmonia. One was at the Wigmore Hall where the Philharmonia was holding two full days of auditions for one first violin position. Manny, who was not on the audition panel, said he'd been told that I had played exceptionally well on the first day of auditions and would have got the position, had not someone else played even better on the second day. That was the one orchestra in which I would have dearly loved to play. The other audition was for the BBC Welsh Symphony Orchestra, which did offer me a position, but after all, I wanted to remain in London. For both of these auditions I played the Prelude to Bach's Solo Partita in E and Chausson's *Poème*, and the second audition resulted in a fair amount of work with the BBC Welsh as an extra and deputy.

I enjoyed those visits to Wales. The BBC was situated in the Llandaff district of Cardiff, near the lovely cathedral with its Epstein sculpture of Christ; the BBC canteen had beautiful, open, green views from its large picture windows; and the members of the orchestra always treated me with friendliness and warmth.

However, there had been many hurdles. Immigration had not been easy, though I suffered none of the hardships my parents had experienced, and I was not fleeing for my life. After South Africa, I valued especially the freedom of thought and of expression I found in England. But for a long time I suffered an underlying depression: once again my life had been dislocated and my self-confidence shaken. I was fearful of what lay ahead, deeply sad at the many good-byes I'd had to say, afraid of losing my mother, afraid of death itself. I often awoke at night in a frenzy of fear of dying. Added to this I was acutely conscious of the injustices, terrors, and tragedies the world over. I felt as if I was carrying all these burdens on my shoulders, and the world seemed an altogether terrible place.

Morris Kahn, my Durban friend, was now living in a London flat, part of a converted house on Haverstock Hill, Belsize Park. His landlady lived in the same house, and he used to say to me, "You must come and play with my landlady! She's a marvelous pianist. She studied with Edith Vogel. She's really good. I know you'll enjoy it." I was happy playing with Bruno Raikin, with whom I continued to play over the years, but eventually I did as Morris suggested and telephoned Jane Blenkinsop. Our first meeting was in December 1962. I was strongly drawn to Jane. She had a creative approach to music making, and it was a joy to play with her. At first we rehearsed as often as twice a week, but we talked almost as much as we played. I told her how depressed I felt about life, about the world, about man's inhumanity to man.

She said, "But you've got it all wrong! Life is wonderful, and the world is full of beauty. Think of a tree in blossom, or a new green leaf, or a rainbow; think of the workings of the human body, how *amazing* it is; think about people, how there's always somebody extraordinarily brave and kind, who is prepared to give up his life for others. It's all miraculous, can't you see that?"

"I know you're right," I answered her, "but in order actually to see life that way I'd have to turn my mind right around. I don't know how to do that."

"You should learn to meditate," she said.

"But that's what I've been wanting to do! I just didn't know how to go about it. I've tried to learn to meditate from books—with some success—but I know it's best to find a teacher."

"How funny," said Jane. "Here I've been stalking you, and all the time it's what you've wanted to do!"

On January 7, 1963, I went with Jane to be initiated into a method of meditation, which had its origins in India, and which literally changed my life. Within a couple of weeks I lost my fear of death and my depression, and to my surprise I discovered that, underneath, I was actually a happy person. I kept pestering Jane that I wanted to learn about the philosophy behind the meditation, and Jane kept holding off.

Less than a month later, after we had been making music and were sitting down in her kitchen for coffee and a chat, I said, "You know Jane, how I've been going on about wanting to learn about the philosophy. Well, I don't feel it's important anymore, because I suddenly realize the answers are already there inside me."

"That's what I've been waiting to hear!" she exclaimed. The very next day she telephoned me with an invitation to come to one of the groups at the Study Society, with which I have remained connected ever since.

We were urged not to accept any ideas we didn't understand or agree with, only to accept what rang true. I remember being surprised and disappointed that, although for the first time in my life I found myself with people who were, incredibly, looking in the same direction as I was, I found a few of them as irritating as anyone I'd met in the world out-side. Then to my relief I heard it said, "We have to learn to live with each other, and it can be quite difficult. All of us have different histories that have made us what we are, and we're not here to criticize each other." It was a kind of release to hear those words, to become free simply to accept the other person: another new idea for me.

I was happy, more centered, more aware, and stronger than I'd ever been. There is an entry in my diary dated August 19, 1963:

> I awoke with a period pain but was too sleepy to do anything about it. I thought if I ignored the pain sleep would win, but after about an hour the pain had won and I was wide awake. I tiptoed past Mummy's room feeling warm and secure know-ing she was asleep in there, wishing it could always be so. In the kitchen I filled the kettle, lit the cooker, and sat down on a stool, waiting for the water to heat up for my hot-water bottle, to ease the pain. Outside, the sun was just beginning to rise. There was a stillness and charm in the atmosphere and suddenly I was overcome with a feeling of peace, and of awareness of being part of it all—the stillness, the sweetness, and the life that was asleep beneath it. There was no fear, everything was good and beyond the devastation of time. I was happy simply because I was aware. One was unhappy because one was unaware of the happiness underneath. One was afraid because one forgot that eternity was *now*. I filled my hot water bottle, went back to bed, and decided to read a little before turning off the light…

I turned the page and had the extraordinary experience of seeing the identical thoughts and feelings I'd just had, mirrored in Dostoevsky's *The Possessed*—a book I had until that moment found disappointing, distasteful, and difficult.

On November 23, I wrote:

> I am almost surprised that the world is still spinning on its axis, so rocked and shat-tered are we all by the assassination, yesterday, of President Kennedy.

My next entry, on December 4 reads:

> After that, I could not indulge in too much self-pity when I received the announce-ment of Dušan's marriage. And yet I *was* shaken. Pain, a sense of loss and bewil-derment had me by the throat.

The seven years since Dušan and I had parted had not been without emotional involve-ments, and yet there had remained an underlying hope that one day we would be together again and "live happily ever after." On November 30, 1963, I received a letter from Dušan telling me that he had been married two days previously in a civil wedding, and that on the day he was writing to me, there was going to be a church wedding:

> For such a purpose I think it is better to start off with a lot more common sense. Anyhow, it doesn't change anything concerning my relationship with someone dear to me…

Oh but it does, I thought, and ignored his questions about my life. I sent him my good wishes, together with Aldous Huxley's *The Perennial Philosophy*. It is an anthology of mystical experiences from varying traditions across the world and across the centuries, showing the same truths underlying them all. It had made an enormous impression on me when Nancy first introduced me to it in 1959, and I felt certain it would appeal to Dušan. However, I refused to reply, when he wrote again, to his further queries about me and my life. It would have been too humiliating to tell him the truth, that I still loved him above all other men, that I was not prepared to be turned into "the other woman," and that I felt devastated. The only thing that kept me going was the meditation. From meditating twice a day for half an hour at a time, I needed to go deep into myself again and again throughout the day, for days, weeks on end. And so I survived.

I discovered that the stiller I became, the deeper I went, the closer I came to others and to the underlying unity in which we are all joined. It seemed to me that I also began to see the hidden meanings behind religion and wished I could have discussed this with my father. I suspected it was the literal acceptance of the scriptures that he had rebelled against, and that if he had seen them more in terms of allegory and symbolism, behind which lay great riches of meaning, he would not have rejected them out of hand.

I wrote:

> I am aware of a "place" inside me where there is no confusion, only simplicity and clarity. All it bids me do is to remember it, to stay connected.

I have not always remembered when I have needed to in the years that followed, far from it. But when I have remembered, help has always come.

Chapter Thirty
⌇ A New Beginning—1965 to 1967 ⌇

On January 23, 1965, after an evening out with friends, I arrived home late at night to find a note from the police to say that my mother had been in an accident and was in New End Hospital, Hampstead. I rushed to be with her and found a bleeding, smashed piece of humanity. The surgeon who had operated on her informed me of the extent of the damage and of what he had done, but warned me that she might not survive, and that if she did, she would be forever wheelchair-bound. She had been crossing the road earlier that evening on a zebra crossing when a car had come speeding around the corner, throwing her in the air, and she had crashed to the ground several feet away. Both her femurs were smashed, an ankle broken, a shoulder dislocated, her face torn, her forehead cracked, and her whole body bruised, swollen, and bleeding. Both her thighs now had metal pins through them holding them together; both her legs were now in traction, one raised, with a thick nail hammered through it at the knee, one stretched flat along the bed. She was already awake after the operation, with a strong dose of morphine against the pain, and she actually joked with me and assured me that she would survive. "Trust me," she said. "You know what a fighter I am!"

Two days later I wrote in my diary:

> The look of pure joy, the radiant, loving smile on my mother's face when I visited her in the hospital this evening, the third time in this endless, aching day, was like sunshine breaking through clouds. At that moment, I knew that she would pull through, for though her body has been so pitifully smashed, her self is intact. And she is *the* most valiant fighter.

The surgeon was an angel. I have no doubt at all that he saved her life. He must have worked to the limit of his strength and ability to put her together again that night, but it didn't end there. Indomitable though my mother's spirit was, there were times when even she could no longer bear the pain-filled, immobile months and the attendant discomforts and illnesses she had to endure. Then he spent hours at her bedside talking courage into her, urging her not to give up.

After six and a half months of visiting her in hospital I took her straight to Bad Ragaz in Switzerland, where she bathed her poor limbs in the thermal baths and had physiotherapy. Far from being wheelchair-bound, she was able to walk with the aid of a stick, having discarded her crutches. Everyone was amazed at the progress she had made, given the extent of her injuries. Her lifelong friend Gretl as well as Achim joined us there.

We decided that the time had come to give up living in rented accommodation and to buy a flat on the ground floor, as climbing the stairs to our first floor flat had become an ordeal for my mother. We eventually found an inexpensive flat still in the process of being built, in a small new block of flats in Golders Green. On the strength of my work as a musician we managed to get a mortgage, and between us we scraped together enough savings for a down payment. We moved into our new home in mid-April 1966. This was the very first home we had ever owned. It was clean and new and had central heating, and we were delighted.

A lady of about my mother's age, another German-Jewish émigré, began to gradually move her belongings from the house she was selling nearby into the ground floor flat across the hall from us, and she made friends with

My mother at 65.

us. Every time she brought something to her new home-to-be, she would stop and chat. Her name was Gerry—with a hard G, short for Margarethe—Mayer. She finally moved into her flat in August, shortly before my mother and I were about to pay a return visit to Bad Ragaz. When I saw her arrive, I offered to make her a cup of coffee.

"That's not necessary, all my cooking equipment is ready to be used," said Gerry, "but I can't make out how to work the waste disposal unit in the kitchen sink. Would you come and show me?"

While I was showing Gerry how it worked, in walked her son, Henry, who had come to help her with the move. I turned round from the sink and saw a tall, handsome man with hauntingly expressive eyes. There was immediate, tremendous attraction between us, and I knew that I had met my fate.

Henry was too honorable to deceive his then-current girlfriend, and it was to be another three months, during which I occasionally saw him through a window when he was visiting his mother, before that relationship played itself out. Then he asked Gerry to invite my mother and me to tea, which she did on November 30, 1966. Conversation flowed easily and already then we had lively debates. I found he had an enormous sense of history. His voice was irresistibly rich and warm. With remarkable prescience he invited me, on my one free evening, to a performance of *Madam Butterfly* at Sadler's Wells Theatre, for which he already "happened to have" two tickets.

Like my parents, Henry's parents had left Germany in 1933, the year Hitler came to power, with Henry, originally Heinz, aged eight, and his little sister Ilse, aged five. Unemployment was rife in Britain at the time, and immigrants were not welcome. However, Henry's father, having invented a tubular lamp with filament, had found a firm prepared to open a small factory to make these lamps in England. In this way he was in a position to offer employment, which gained him and his family entry into Britain. Unfortunately when war broke out in September 1939, the factory was closed down; he lost his source of income, and Henry's mother had to keep the family going by taking in lodgers and badly paid sewing work, just as my mother had done in South Africa. Then to make matters worse, Henry's father was interned as an "enemy alien," while ironically, Henry was in the Officers' Training Corps at school, being trained to shoot. He fought every way he could think of to get his father released, writing to the Home Secretary, Members of Parliament, the camp commandant, doctors, and the press.

He'd been fortunate in winning a scholarship to University College School, and he was forever grateful to the masters and headmasters there for fostering his ability to think for himself, in fact allowing him to become somewhat of a maverick, fearless of the opinion of others. His sister went to South Hampstead High School for Girls, the excellent sister school to UCS, where I became violin teacher so many years later.

Ilse's school was evacuated during the war, as were most other London schools, but UCS remained in London. Henry and his mother lived through the Blitz, of which he had many horror stories to tell, including being bombed out of their home, but he spoke admiringly of how the British people just carried on with their lives, whatever they had to endure. At sixteen, he himself had to go before a tribunal to decide whether he should be interned, but it was decided that he did not represent a threat to the security of the state. At eighteen, having early developed an enthusiasm for ships, he would have liked to join the navy, from which, as an "enemy alien," he was debarred, but amazingly he was given an apprenticeship in a "reserved occupation," designing and building motor torpedo boats for the rest of the war, with Vospers at Portsmouth, a high security area.

From a successful career as naval architect, much of it in the Far East, Henry had made a complete change following the breakdown of his marriage and had turned to mental health social work at Tower Hamlets in London's East End. That was where he was working at the time we met. I was playing in *Robert and Elizabeth* and found him waiting for me at the stage door every evening, ready to drive me home or take me out for a meal or dancing at a night club. He was dashing and romantic and swept me off my feet.

We went for walks in Regent's Park where he told me how, after the breakdown of his marriage, he had made a serious suicide attempt. "I thought it would be better for our little three-year-old son, Simon, not to be torn between two warring parents," he said. This struck me as a strange sort of rationalization, but I held my peace. "I made *so* sure it would work," he continued, "so I was astounded and furious to find myself waking up in hospital!" He described to me, convincingly, how he had gone about trying to take his own life. "I thought, even in this I've failed!" he said. "But then it occurred to me that perhaps after all there *was* a God, that he'd intervened, and that he had a purpose for me. I'd never been a believer before. I began to talk about these things to the male nurse in charge, who happened to be a Methodist. We had many conversations. Then he brought along his minister. It was the first time anybody had spoken seriously to me about religion. My parents had a laissez-faire attitude toward religion, and I knew nothing at all about Judaism. My father thought I ought to learn some Hebrew for my bar mitzvah and hired a private tutor, but I was bored and managed to persuade him to take me rowing on the Serpentine in Hyde Park instead. When my father discovered what was going on, he dismissed the tutor, and that was the end of my Hebrew lessons *and* my bar mitzvah. Anyway, soon after I came out of hospital I converted to Christianity. In my enthusiasm I became a lay preacher and started studying for the ministry—but I became disillusioned with the infighting inside the church. After all it was just like everywhere else. I decided I could do better helping people as a social worker. And then I got involved with social psychiatry and with mental health."

He gave me all sorts of reasons why he was not going to ask me to marry him. (*"Why's he talking about marriage?"* I wondered. *"We've only just met!"*) But on New Year's Eve, just one month after his mother's tea party, he announced, "Before I say what I'm going to say, I want you to know that I'm not drunk!" He paused, and then, "Will you marry me?"

Although I couldn't bear to be parted from him and had been counting the hours when we would be together again, I foresaw problems and suggested living together for a trial period first. "If you're talking of a trial period you're already thinking of leaving," said Henry. "No, I want total commitment or nothing."

"There are things we need discuss," I said.

"Say yes first, and we'll discuss them afterwards," he insisted, and so I did, because I didn't want to lose him. He was wildly happy and told everybody in sight that we were going to be married.

With Henry I had a sense of homecoming, of kinship. I had never imagined I would marry someone who was not a musician, but Henry had such charm, such magnetism and warmth, that I found him impossible to resist. Besides, there was something in his face that reminded me of my beloved father, for whom I'd never stopped looking—although their personalities were entirely different. I was convinced of the sincerity of his conversion and urged him to keep up his connection to the church, but not to expect me to participate. He continued to hold to Christianity, but drifted away from the church.

Our marriage took place in the registry office at Hampstead Town Hall on March 22, 1967. Only our two mothers and a friend each—in my case, my pianist friend Jane Blenkinsop, who, not long after, married an Egyptian and went to live in Cairo—were present as witnesses. Plus Leo, an alcoholic social work client of Henry's, who had got wind of the wedding and walked all the way from Tower Hamlets in order to be present. Afterward we had lunch at The Spinning Wheel restaurant—since vanished—in Perrin's Court, Hampstead.

A little later, as my brand-new husband and I were walking up Hampstead High Street together, who should be walking down it toward us but my dear, estranged friend, Jenny Welton. I introduced them to each other. She seemed glad and excited and asked for our address. When we arrived home—Henry's rented flat in Chalk Farm, where he had built our wooden marital bed with his own hands and where he carried me over the threshold that day—there was a telegram waiting for me: "Congratulations stop he is gorgeous stop love Jenny," and our once beautiful friendship was renewed. She remains one of my closest—and, after all, most affectionate—friends.

Gerry was the ideal mother-in-law: loving, caring, and discreet, knowing

Henry and Eva's wedding day, March 1967.

never to interfere. She said I reminded her of her daughter, Ilse, who had married young and had gone to live in Australia. Sadly, only a few months after our wedding she suffered a massive heart attack while visiting friends. For a week she was in intensive care at St. Mary's Hospital, Paddington. We visited her anxiously every day. On July 24, 1967, she was taken off the danger list. I went to see her that afternoon while Henry was at work. Suddenly she clutched my hand, burst into tears, and said, "I have always loved you!" I said, "Gerry, why are you speaking like that? You are out of danger now!" But she died later that night.

Gerry inspired great devotion, and her friends were devastated by her death. Henry comforted them at the funeral, not really aware of his own loss until we were camping at Grafham in Surrey some time after, when he was suddenly overwhelmed by grief and broke down, and it was my turn to comfort him.

In her will Gerry left half of her flat to Ilse and half to Henry. After much deliberation we decided to move into it, taking out a mortgage for Ilse's share. It was a blessing, later, to be living so close to my mother when she became increasingly frail and needed my nearness and my help. In the meantime, she went to art classes, took up oil painting, put an easel in what had been my bedroom, and turned it into her studio. She also attended classes in English literature, and from her I learned to understand some of the finer subtleties in the writings of Henry James, Virginia Woolf, and James Joyce.

Henry doted on Simon, his son. A series of disasters had led to their complete estrangement for ten years, which caused Henry much suffering. It was to be twelve years before

I met him, by then twenty three years
old and soon to be married. There was
so much of Henry in him that I took
to him immediately. My mother loved
him too. I have a memory of us all sitting on the lawn outside our flat a few
years later, my mother and Henry on
canvas chairs; Simon, his wife Val, baby
Kate, and I on a blanket spread on the
grass. Kate had just learned to stand,
and Simon was trying to encourage
her to take a few steps. She hesitated,
looked as though she was about to try,
then changed her mind and sat down.
Plop. "Coward!" said Simon conversationally, and my mother was enchanted. He had inherited Henry's
zany and loveable humor.

    However, the years without his fa-
ther, as well as his mother's bitterness,
had left their mark on Simon and led

*My mother in her early eighties, taken by surprise by Henry,
as she was striding out.*

to some outbursts on his part, which
threw Henry into fearful emotional turmoil,
and there were long periods when he refused
to see his son. I desperately wanted to heal
the breach. I loved and missed Simon, wished
I knew Val better, and felt deprived of seeing
Kate grow up. She already had two grand-
mothers, so they called me Grandma Eva, but
I had little opportunity of being a grandma.
Besides, they lived in Nottingham, a journey
of over two hours from North West London,
so even in good times we saw each other infrequently.

    After many years Henry had an inspira-
tion. He asked Simon to come and see him
alone and to agree not to leave until every issue between them had been discussed. They
would have to be perfectly open about their
differing perceptions of what had happened
during the first thirteen years of Simon's life,
and if necessary, agree to differ. I went down
to see Jenny, now living on a barge in Kent,

Henry and Simon.

and Henry asked me not to return home until he telephoned to say that they had resolved their differences.

They never fell out again.

Kate and Henry.

Val Mayer.

Kate.

Chapter Thirty-One
☞ My Years with ENO—1968 to 1998 ☜

"Gone to Cardiff—back day after tomorrow" came as a shock to Henry on his return home one evening early in our marriage. He had been visiting clients, and I had been unable to reach him at the office. Mobile phones and e-mail had yet to be invented. So I left a note. As a freelance musician I had to be prepared, at short notice, to play in out-of-town concerts. Henry pleaded with me to find a regular job, so that he would know where I was likely to be at any given time.

On August 22, 1968, I auditioned for Sadler's Wells Opera at the Coliseum, just at the time of its transition from Sadler's Wells Theatre to the much larger and centrally situated London Coliseum. To avoid confusion it was later renamed English National Opera. Mario Bernardi, the conductor, followed me out of the audition room. "Are you free?" he asked, "I would very much like to have you in the orchestra!" It was during Bernardi's last year as musical director, and his sensitive conducting of *Madam Butterfly* was a revelation to me.

At first I felt uneasy in the orchestra during rehearsal breaks. The musicians all gathered in little cliques, from which I was excluded, with the exception of an unprepossessing trumpet player who insisted on walking to the underground station with me after my first rehearsal, because he was under the mistaken impression that I had been "making eyes" at him from the opposite end of the orchestra pit. Only Ruby Hurn, the sub-leader, thought of introducing herself to me, adding, "Welcome to the orchestra!" I always remembered that gratefully and made a point of similarly welcoming newcomers. Gradually I came to be accepted by the others and made some good friends, and eventually I learned to treasure the camaraderie of orchestral life.

Charles Mackerras, whose Handel, Mozart, and Janáček performances were beyond compare, followed Bernardi as musical director. He was knighted during his time with us. His dynamism enlivened every opera he conducted, and he worked with some wonderful singers: Janet Baker, Felicity Lott, Ann Murray among them. In all the years I was with ENO, I think we probably played Bizet's *Carmen* more frequently than any other opera, and nobody, but nobody, was able to bring such intensity of emotion to the closing bars as Charles Mackerras.

At first I found him intimidating, but he turned out to be very human. One morning, while attempting to get out of bed, my feet became entangled with the bedclothes, and I fell onto the floor, laughing. Then I stopped laughing. The pain was exquisite. Henry rushed me to hospital to have an X-ray—I had cracked my coccyx.

"There's nothing we can do, it can't be reached," the doctors told me. "Just rest your back as much as possible. It'll take a long time to heal."

"Will I damage it if I go on working?" I asked.

"No," was the reply, "it'll just take even longer to heal."

I decided to continue to work as usual and took a soft cushion to rest against while playing. After the coffee break during a rehearsal a colleague sitting behind me tried to help me adjust my cushion. Mackerras, waiting to begin, asked sarcastically, "Are you *quite comfortable* now?" and I answered, "I'm sorry Sir Charles, I've cracked my spine"—it sounded better than "my coccyx."

The next day, as I approached the stage door, I met Mackerras deep in conversation. He turned aside and said to me, "Did you say yesterday that you'd cracked your spine?"

"Yes I did," I replied.

"And I mocked you, I *mocked* you! You must have felt awful!" he said.

The company toured the provinces for many weeks each year, until eventually several good provincial opera companies sprang up and our visits were no longer required. Henry and I hated those long weeks of separation, though at least we knew that the rest of the year's performances would be in London, which was not the case with the other London orchestras. My first tour after joining the orchestra began with three weeks in Glasgow, starting on November 11, 1968. Farquharson was a little cross with me for having married someone else—he wrote, to my surprise, that he had hoped I would be beside him to brighten his middle years—and recommended that I stayed with his friend Robina, rather than in his house. She lived a few houses away from him along the river Kelvin, and I was happy and comfortable there. But by the second weekend Henry and I were both out of our minds with separation anxiety and had a terrible row over the phone. I felt it could not remain unresolved; we had to sort it out face to face. So I went back to Robina's after the show to pack an overnight bag and told her I was taking a sleeper train to London and would return on Monday in time for *Rigoletto* that evening.

The flat was empty when I arrived home early on Sunday morning. No Henry. I went cold with apprehension. Could he be having an affair?

The phone rang. "Henry! Where are you?"

"I'm at the airport. I felt I had to see you, we had to clear things up, so I booked a plane ticket to Glasgow. Then I thought you might go out and I wouldn't find you. I wanted to make sure you'd wait for me. So I rang your landlady, and she told me you'd taken the overnight train to London. I'm coming home right away!"

When he arrived home we laughed so much that our row was completely forgotten. The following Friday he took a train to Glasgow to join me for the weekend, staying with me at Robina's. She asked what he would like to do while I was playing in *Don Giovanni* that evening.

"I'd like to see the Gorbals," he said. "I keep hearing how poor it is. There's an awful lot of poverty where I work in Tower Hamlets. I'd like to be able to compare it."

So Robina, her husband, and Farquharson took him to the dog track that evening. After the performance they came to collect me at the King's Theatre, minus Henry.

"Henry sends his regards," said Farquharson. "He wasn't able to meet you because he's in hospital. We have to take you there. They want to ask you whether he's been on any drugs."

He was in the Glasgow Royal Infirmary, and it turned out that he was in no state to send me his regards. He had fainted in the Gents; strangely, he had fallen over backward, cracked his skull, and was unconscious. I sat by his bedside all night, not knowing whether he was going to live or die. Suddenly he came to, puzzled and indignant, and said, "What's going on here anyway?"

By morning, though badly concussed, he was lucid enough to give me a list of people in London who had to be notified of his absence. I telephoned my mother, only to have her friend Kay answer, "Don't worry, Eva, your mother's being looked after, she'll be okay!"

"What are you talking about, Kay, why are you there?" I asked.

"Oh I'm sorry, didn't you know? She slipped in the hallway. The floor had just been polished. Much too highly polished. She's dislocated her shoulder, and she's had a slight heart attack so they're keeping her in hospital."

I did not continue the tour to Nottingham the next day.

Henry was supposed to remain under observation in hospital for at least ten days, and assuming that my mother was being well cared for, I had every intention of remaining with him in Glasgow. However, he was determined to get home as soon as possible, and managed, after a great deal of persuasion, to get the doctors to allow him to return home after only five days, with special transport arrangements and a letter to his GP.

It took several months for Henry to return to normal. His sense of taste and smell were completely distorted, he became frighteningly irascible, refused to follow his doctor's advice, and suffered perpetual headaches. Eventually both he and my mother, whose condition had been worse than I'd been given to understand, recovered. It had been a difficult time.

Whenever I went on tour after that Henry would drive up to see me, unless he was on call for emergencies over the weekend. He would leave early on the Saturday morning and invariably arrive just as I was waking up. We would go for long walks or exploratory drives, and together we made lasting friendships with some of my landladies. This was how he met my friend Maggie, of my student days in St. Peter's Square. She had meanwhile married cultivated and attractive Geoffrey Musset, an architect, and they had moved up north when he'd become a partner in a firm of architects in Liverpool. Whenever the opera tour took us to Liverpool, I would stay with them and their three delightful children, in their large Victorian house and garden in Birkenhead. After their return to London, we saw a lot more of them. Henry had a high regard and liking for Geoffrey, and Maggie was, and is, my closest London friend.

There was a tour to Edinburgh that stands out in my memory. A number of us string players were put up at a small, pleasant, private hotel. The entire cello section stayed there, including their new leader, John Catlow. I knew nothing about him, and he knew nothing about me. I had just moved into my room when I decided to go down to the reception desk to make an inquiry. John had arrived before me and was speaking to the receptionist, discussing the needs of each of his cellists in such a caring way, making sure they were all properly looked after. I stood some distance behind him, wondering at his evident goodness and a certain innocence of demeanour, a naïveté that I found touching. I thought to myself, he's just like *The Idiot*.

John turned around and said to me, "I know, just like *The Idiot*."

I was astounded. "How could you possibly know I was thinking that? How did you know I read Dostoevsky?"

"I didn't," said John. "It just came into my head."

We must both have been tuned into the same wavelength.

We often laughed about it, called each other teasingly Prince Myshkin and Nastasia Filippovna, and sometimes, during intervals, discussed nineteenth century Russian literature.

A highlight of that time was Wagner's *Ring* cycle conducted by Reginald Goodall, who coached a wonderful cast headed by Rita Hunter, Alberto Remedios, Norman Bailey, and Derek Hammond Stroud. The production, by Glen Byam Shaw and John Blatchley with stage design by Ralph Koltai, was simply magnificent, with a timeless quality I have never seen equalled. Goodall, or Reggie as we called him, was a frail, elderly little man, so shortsighted as to be almost blind. His conducting arm kept disappearing below the desk, so that to begin with we were lost in confusion; yet he was able to make magic with us as no one else could.

I know of no other conductor who was so averse to applause. He regularly crept into the orchestra pit with us, hoping the audience would not notice him, but the moment he stood up to conduct, small though he was, the audience always broke into thunderous applause. He looked irritated, annoyed, as if the applause had shattered a very special atmosphere. And then he would smile at us and make a sweeping inclusive gesture with his arms, as if to say, "Forget all that. Now you and I enter another world altogether.

Another highlight was Hans Werner Henze's opera, *The Bassarids*, conducted by the composer. It is based on Euripides' *The Bacchae*, which Henze set to an English libretto by W. H. Auden and Chester Kallman. A tremendously powerful opera, it expresses the conflict between rationality and control represented by Pentheus, King of Thebes, and wild, uncontrolled passion and ecstasy represented by the god Dionysus. The performance was unforgettable in its intensity. At the end of the run Henze threw a lavish party for us all.

We played several avant-garde operas, and it took some getting used to the harshness of the sounds. One was Penderecki's *The Devils of Loudon*, based on a study by Aldous Huxley of actual events in early seventeenth century France. I remember a small group of us in a coffee bar near the Coliseum stage door complaining bitterly to the young conductor, Nicholas Braithwaite, about the sounds we had to produce and the audience had to endure. He patiently explained how the harrowing story justified the sound effects, and he made them much more acceptable to us. It is a story of political manipulation, witch hunt hysteria, sex-crazed nuns in the confinement of a convent, exorcism, and accusations of sorcery, leading to the execution of an innocent man. It was one of our great performances, with Josephine Barstow powerfully expressive in the role of the central character, Sister Jeanne.

For me, being part of the musical-theatrical scene was incredibly exciting. Life was not only confined to the orchestra pit, but to the sights and smells and activities backstage, the gradual transformations taking place from the initial orchestral rehearsals, then rehearsals with principal singers, then with the whole cast, seeing productions taking shape, the costumes and stage props, up to the dress rehearsals, often with invited audience, sensing the interaction with that audience, and finally with the first-night and subsequent audiences.

The company was invited to Munich as part of the cultural activities alongside the summer Olympics in 1972. We left for Munich on September 1 and gave two performances, on September 2 and 3, of Benjamin Britten's *Gloriana*, an opera about Queen Elizabeth I, which he had written to celebrate the coronation of Queen Elizabeth II. It was a great success in Munich, both with audience and critics. Only one thing marred the occasion—the efforts of the Baader-Meinhof Gang, otherwise known as the Red Army Faction, to sabotage a performance with heckling, on the grounds that opera was "elitist." We had already come across a Red Army Faction rally in the street. I was repelled by their hooliganism; for all their supposedly left-wing ideology, they seemed to me no different from their Nazi predecessors and made me feel sick at heart. What I only learned subsequently was that they had received terrorist training from Yasser Arafat's Al Fatah movement in Jordan in 1970.

In September 1970 a conflict had begun between King Hussein of Jordan and Palestinian guerrilla groups that attempted to overthrow him, ending with the expulsion of thousands of Palestinians from Jordan in 1971. Hence the name, Black September, the parent organization of which was Al Fatah.

We returned to London on September 4, and I felt a gray cloud of depression hanging over me. I didn't know what was causing it, but I could not shake it off—until I passed a shop window with newspaper headlines about the massacre of eleven Israeli athletes and a German policeman, by members of Black September at Olympic Village on September 5. There was no doubt in my mind that some sort of premonition, brought about by the nasty atmosphere I had encountered in Munich, had caused my depression. The whole civilized world was horrified by the massacre, and I was grief-stricken.

Many years later I met a middle-aged German woman at a party. Somehow our conversation led to Munich, and I mentioned having been there with ENO at the time of the Olympic Games and that members of the Baader-Meinhof Gang had heckled us. "Did they really do that?" she asked, with a little guilty giggle. "I used to belong to them. We thought we knew the answer to all the world's troubles. We were so arrogant. Now I'm a Buddhist and realize we knew nothing at all."

I have a happier memory of our week-long visit to Vienna with Mackerras in 1975 when our production of Gilbert and Sullivan's *Patience* at the Theater an der Wien drew such praise from the critics as "English National Opera can show Vienna how to play operetta." That, in the home of operetta, was high praise indeed. We also played *Gloriana* at the Volksoper and had plenty of time for marvelous sightseeing.

Mackerras left ENO as musical director in 1978, but he was frequently invited back to conduct. One evening in January 1993, I was deputed to go to the conductor's room in the interval to ask him to add his signature to a retirement card from the orchestra for my friend Susheela Devi. "Sush leaving!" he exclaimed. "The orchestra will never be the same again!" and duly signed the card. It was the last performance of Janáček's *The Adventures of Mr Brouček*, and as he passed Sush on his way out of the orchestra pit, he gave her a kiss and handed her his baton. She has treasured it ever since.

Mackerras was succeeded as musical director by Sir Charles Groves. Opera was not really his métier, and he didn't remain with us for long. But I had reason to be grateful to him for, together with Hazel Vivienne, head of music staff, he initiated a series of lunchtime recitals open to the public, in the Terrace Bar of the London Coliseum, and invited members of the orchestra and chorus to apply as soloists. I felt excited. This was my opportunity to get back to some solo playing. My friends and colleagues in the orchestra thought it sheer madness to risk performing solo at my place of work, but I went ahead and applied. Sir Charles suggested Ernest Bloch's *Baal Shem* Suite. I practiced hard on the next tour, until I felt I knew it so well that nothing could go wrong. Besides, I was in love with the music. By now I knew that my past performing disasters had partially been due to under-preparation, leaving too much to chance. I obtained permission to bring my own pianist, Bruno Raikin. On the day of the performance I felt confident, played well, and received much praise. At the time Hermann Abramowitz, my first violin teacher, was, to my great distress, dying of kidney cancer in Johannesburg. I wished so much to please him and wrote to him about this modest success, thanking him for having laid the foundations. "I am proud of you," he replied. At last.

Bruno and I continued to play together in public, at relatively minor venues. Henry said, "One would think you were preparing to play at the Festival Hall, by the amount of work you are putting in!" No matter—I never felt more alive than when we were working on interpretation, preparing for a performance, and striving for excellence. Bruno died in January 2005 shortly before his 93rd birthday, and I continue to miss him as pianist, friend, and confidant.

With Mark Elder, ENO's youthful and dynamic musical director for nearly fourteen years, there were unforgettable tours: six weeks in the United States in 1984, and four weeks in Soviet Russia in 1990, on the invitation of President Gorbachev himself. It was the last year before the breakup of the Soviet Union.

One of the operas we took to the United States was Jonathan Miller's brilliant production of *Rigoletto*. A wonderfully imaginative producer, he transported the action from the sixteenth century court of the Duke of Mantua, to Mafia-ridden Little Italy in the New York City of the 1950s. For me, this made the story much more convincing and absorbing. Before we left London, we had bomb threats by some outraged New York Italians who thought, mistakenly, that we were casting aspersions on their community, but we went ahead, and the opera was a great success.

I shared a room with my friend Adrienne Sturdy throughout the tour. We stayed in the French Quarter of New Orleans for one week. Every evening after the opera Addie and I and one or two others from ENO went to hear jazz in Preservation Hall. The atmosphere was exciting, different from anything we had previously experienced, and the music hugely enjoyable. We met some other jazz musicians and invited them to a performance of *Rigoletto*. They enjoyed it enormously and were struck by the fact that the discipline of ensemble playing was equally important in both fields of music with which, respectively, we were involved.

What I remember most about our visit to Russia—apart from all the marvelous sightseeing we did and the fancy ex-KGB hotels we stayed in—was Nicholas Hytner's delightful production of Handel's *Xerxes,* stylishly conducted by Sir Charles Mackerras, with a superb cast including Ann Murray, Yvonne Kenny, Leslie Garrett, and Christopher Robson; Benjamin Britten's haunting *Turn of the Screw*, based on the short story by Henry James; and Mark Elder's brilliant and inspiring conducting of Verdi's *Macbeth*. In London, he also gave magnificent renderings of all the great Verdi operas; Shostakovitch's *Lady Macbeth of Mtensk*; Strauss' *Salome, Der Rosenkavalier and Arabella*; Tchaikovsky's *Eugene Onegin*; Wagner's *Lohengrin*; Debussy's *Pelleas and Melisande*; and so many others.

It was a wonderful time.

Chapter Thirty-Two

⁀ LIFE WITH HENRY ⁀

Life with Henry was a huge adventure. There was never any room for complacency, because owing to his mood swings I was flung from the heights of bliss to the depths of misery again and again in a matter of minutes. Ours was a stormy marriage, with violent clashes of temperament and dreadful, soul-searing rows. We shouted things at each other from which it seemed impossible to recover, yet recover we did, and despite everything our love prevailed and grew deeper as the years went by. Henry was faithful, romantic, and devoted, but he was also deeply insecure and became demonic when in the grip of one of his black depressions. I did not know how to cope and became frightened and angry, and he for a long time expected me to leave him. But I always believed in the core of him, in his basic goodness, and I adored him.

Only in our little boat did peace and tranquillity always prevail. There he was in his el-

Henry on Ardmair.

ement, and I happy to share in his pleasure. Before *Ardmair*—named after a favorite place in Scotland where we had camped and rowed and where Henry had caught fish—came into our life, our holiday accommodation had always been a tent. We even took our tent to the Yorkshire Dales when I played in the Harrogate Festival with the English Chamber Orchestra. I would arrive at the concert hall every evening wearing muddy boots and a long black evening dress, black court shoes in one hand, violin case in the other. In our A-pole tent I practiced Mozart's G major Violin Concerto, cross legged and careful to bow toward the peak and not hit its sides with my bow. Suddenly I noticed a row of boots peeping through the bottom of the tent…

In those early days I used to take my violin on holiday with me. One amazingly hot summer in the Scottish Highlands we camped on a tiny plateau above the sea at Elgol on the Isle of Skye. Henry was sunbathing below on the beach, while I practiced the violin outside our tent, dressed in a bikini. I'd attached some music I was studying to the opening of the tent with a clothes peg. Suddenly I had the same eerie sense of having an audience. I turned around and found myself surrounded by a semicircle of attentive looking cows.

Ardmair, despite its small size and outboard motor, was perfectly seaworthy. We spent many weekends in the Thames Estuary and also enjoyed a holiday in Skapa Flow in the Orkneys. When I was on tour in Bristol, Henry towed her there and anchored on the River Avon. When not on tour Henry would sometimes sail alone upriver on the Thames on a Saturday, if I had a performance that evening, and I would drive to wherever he had arrived with *Ardmair* on the Sunday and join him there.

This peaceful pleasure came to an abrupt end after many years when, on April 3, 1990, the boatyard where *Ardmair* was having her bottom scrubbed caught fire, and every boat including *Ardmair* went up in smoke. We felt utterly bereft. We had bought *Ardmair* as an

Henry, seadog, 1980s.

empty hull, and Henry had fitted her out so beautifully that she was renowned up and down the Thames. He had put so much of himself into her that he hadn't the heart to get another boat with the insurance money. I thought we would be able to pay the bills at last. Instead, he poured it all into our communal garden, which had been badly neglected. He knew nothing about gardening, and so he bought books on the subject, which he studied assiduously, bought gardening equipment, topsoil, plants galore, leaky hose, a sprinkler, a lawn mower, and more, until he turned the garden into a paradise. He would wake early every morning, open his eyes, and say, "Dig, dig, dig," fill himself with painkillers against the peripheral neuropathy that made his legs ache, and go out and dig. Whatever Henry turned his hand to, be it sailing, becoming a Yachtmaster, tending plants, breeding tropical fish, making tapestries—or building a beautiful little clinkered wooden dinghy with both a sail and oars, as tender to *Ardmair*—he studied and carried out to perfection. He named the dinghy *Cockle*. Sadly, it was in the boatyard together with *Ardmair* and suffered the same fate.

Henry's garden from our kitchen window, taken by Richard, Henry's Australian nephew, his wife Karen with Henry and Eva in the garden.

At one time we had five tanks of tropical fish on our living room windowsill. Henry had owned tropical fish in the Far East and had learned how to take care of them, how to keep the water clean, each tank a perfectly balanced small ecosystem. He had special fish food for each tank. The fish bred and thrived. It was fascinating to watch how the cichlids cared for their eggs, both parents carrying them to a different hiding place every evening, and after the eggs were hatched, how they would continue to watch over their young. This was in contrast to the behaviour of live-bearing fish whose offspring had to be protected by a horizontal barrier underneath the mother as she dropped them through an aperture, to prevent her eating them. We watched for hours, spellbound.

Shortly before we were due to be married, Henry and his mother had taken me aside, saying, "There's something we feel we have to tell you."

Henry said, "I had a breakdown when my first marriage ended. I was diagnosed as a manic-depressive psychotic. I suffer from endogenous depressions and…"

"What nonsense," I thought. *"Psychotic! They're being melodramatic."*

"And he's horrible when he's depressed," added Gerry. "We felt we had to warn you. You must never take it personally if he's nasty to you."

"Easier said than done," I said, "if it's directed at me!" But I wasn't worried; apart from his always spending more money than he earned and being heavily in debt, I hadn't noticed anything amiss. This wasn't surprising as he was buoyed up by the novelty and excitement of being in love.

Henry continued to be in love for the rest of his life, but as the novelty wore off, old habits of thinking and behaving returned. Often he would take offense where no offense was intended. He could sulk for days, sometimes weeks, on end. He looked for reasons to quarrel and would goad me until, however much I tried to stop myself from reacting, I would lose control and end up screaming at the top of my voice. Mrs. L. who lived upstairs on the second floor would telephone my poor mother and exclaim, "Mrs. Schay, I think your son-in-law must be murdering your daughter!" Then he would refuse to speak to me because I had once again screamed at him. For days, sometimes weeks, he would not speak to me. He would rebuff any attempts at reconciliation from me. I had to learn to wait until he was ready to make the first gesture. And yet when at last he was released from the iron fist of his depression, and he relented, happiness would return to me in a flash. Nobody in the world had the power to make me as angry, frightened, or miserable as he did, nor had anybody else the power to make me as happy.

He would have liked to have my company twenty four hours, seven days a week, and many of our rows centered around my not spending enough time with him. We'd be in the midst of a screaming match when he would shout, "I'm in love with you, you silly woman, don't you understand?" On my occasional nights off we might go to a concert or a play, or spend some time with friends. But when I stayed alone with him at home, he would say, "You've no idea what a difference it makes, you being here with me." Yet no matter how much time I spent with him, it never seemed to be enough.

Henry was a magnet for children and animals, and whatever his mood at home, was unfailingly kind and sensitive toward his clients—unless he was so incapacitated by depression that he had to take time off work. I once met an elderly brother and sister in his care. "Your husband is a wonderful man. There is no one like him. You are married to a prince!" they declared.

In many ways he was a marvelous husband. He was remarkably tolerant of my violin practice—in our small flat there was no escaping it—and tolerant of my lack of domestic skills. I was no cordon bleu cook, but he encouraged me, often said, "Thank you, that was a good meal," and frequently did the washing up. If he thought my playing sounded good, he would say so, and he insisted that I underestimated my ability as a violinist. He was good with his hands and lost no time over doing repairs, putting up shelves, hanging pictures. Unlike many husbands he always noticed what I wore and often complimented me. If I had somewhere to go where parking was a problem, he would offer to take or fetch me, or both. He was an opera-lover and came to many performances at the London Coliseum. When he was well he was protective, tender, proud of me, and enveloped me in love.

But when he was not well I spent much of the time walking on eggshells, not knowing when I would inadvertently upset him, when the next angry tirade would come. He never ever laid a finger on me in anger, but his words cut into me like knives. Often I left for work emotionally in shreds, and terrified, on my way home, of the cold reception awaiting me.

Eventually I reached breaking point. I had to get away. On Friday, November 4, 1977, with a heavy heart, I went to see Mr. Laurence Litt, a divorce lawyer highly recommended by Addie, my recently divorced friend in the ENO orchestra. I wanted to know what my legal position would be if I moved away for a while. After closely questioning me about my feelings for Henry, Mr. Litt said, "You are far too attached to your husband to leave him, even temporarily. Go for a long walk on Hampstead Heath and think about your feelings. Don't do anything rash. Ask your doctor to prescribe some tranquillizers to help you deal with the situation," and he refused to charge me for the consultation. What an extraordinarily nice man, I thought, and always remembered him with gratitude.

I had told Henry I was thinking of a trial separation. The following Monday, November 7, he left for work while I was still asleep. When I got up I noticed something different about the fish tanks on the window sill. The varying drums of fish food, which Henry normally kept on the shelf next to the windowsill, were now carefully placed on the tanks above the fish for which they were suited. This was clearly an unspoken message to me, that from now on the fish would be my responsibility, and that I was to be sure put the correct food in each tank. That meant he was not going to be around. It could mean nothing else. I went cold with fear. When I telephoned Henry's office he was out visiting a client. I had a free morning before an overtime afternoon rehearsal and was able to get an emergency appointment with a doctor—not our usual one—at our surgery that morning. I told her of my fears that he might take his life, as he had attempted to do after his first marriage had come to an end. "He's just trying to frighten you," she said. "I should ignore it. Go to work and call his bluff."

With an uneasy mind I made my way to the Coliseum. What was I going to do if he wasn't at home when I got back? I hoped fervently that I had misunderstood why the fish food had been moved, that it wasn't a message at all, and that he would be at home as usual. But he wasn't. I picked up a photograph of Henry and drove to the nearest police station, told the sergeant in charge of Henry's probable state of mind and of my fears, gave him Henry's photo, a description of his car and number plate, and begged him to send out a search party for him

"It's a bit pointless, isn't it—he could be halfway to Scotland by now," said the police sergeant.

"He's hardly likely to take the trouble of driving all the way up to Scotland if he's about to kill himself," I said. "He's much more likely to be in some quiet spot north of London. Please, please don't waste any time, *please* look for him and his car, please help me!"

Only after my return from the police station did I discover a note in our letter box, where I hadn't thought of looking earlier. It began, "By the time you read this it will be too late… Please don't blame yourself; it has nothing to do with you, and everything to do with the fact that my whole life has been a failure…"

It was well after midnight when the police phoned. They had found Henry, unconscious in his car, in a quiet area at the back of Scratchwood service station. He had taken a full bottle of sleeping tablets together with brandy and had fallen asleep with the brandy bottle half finished. They had taken him to Edgware General Hospital and said they would meet me there in the car park. I was jubilant, picked up Henry's letter, and drove to the hospital. Two policemen approached me and spoke to me severely. "This was no suicide gesture, this was for real. *If* he wakes up he's going to be very angry that we interfered, so be prepared!" Menacingly, they said, "If he doesn't survive we shall want that letter."

"That's alright; I have nothing to hide," I said and dashed up to his ward. He was deeply unconscious, but he was alive, and that was what mattered. I sat by his bedside for hours, willing him to wake up. When daylight came I drove home, made breakfast for my mother, and asked her to come over so that I could tell her what had happened.

"Why didn't you wake me and tell me?" asked my mother, woefully upset.

"You need your sleep. I can't afford to lose you too!" I replied.

I returned to Henry's bedside and did not leave it until his eyes opened, two full days later. His first words were, "You wanted me to do it."

I was aghast. "I *never* wanted you to die!" I said "Never, never! But you've often told me about 'total separation therapy'—how it could help couples realize what they meant to each other…work out what to do to put the marriage right. We *had* to break this pattern of incessant rows. Marriage guidance didn't work. I thought it might help if I went away for a while."

The hospital refused to discharge him before he gave an undertaking to see a psychiatrist. He agreed, on condition that I went with him, which I was only too glad to do.

At home, my friend Addie came to see him. "I wanted to set Eva free," he said to her.

"Eva only wanted to be free from your domination," she said. "If you'd succeeded in killing yourself, she'd have been dominated by you for the rest of her life."

The most effective help the psychiatrist gave Henry, besides a whole year of talking therapy, was to prescribe antidepressants. The change was dramatic, as if a great storm cloud had lifted from Henry and enabled him to be himself: the wonderfully attractive, loving, and kind person I had married.

My mother died on February 13, 1984, nineteen years after her near-fatal accident in 1965. Toward the end she became extremely ill and bore it as bravely as she had everything else in life. I was with her when she died, and there was so much warmth and love between us, and my heart was so full that at the time it did not feel like a parting at all. Yet I could not bear to listen to music for a year after she died, apart from when playing, and that was hard enough. I had to force myself to keep my eyes open and not allow myself to fall asleep at work, though at night I could not sleep for the recurring mental pictures I had of her in her last illness. Henry gave me enormous, loving support.

She had asked to be cremated, with a Reform Jewish service, and that is how we met Rabbi Charles Emanuel, who came the next evening to ask me about her life and character,

My mother aged 82.

and the following day gave a eulogy that, according to her English literature classmates who came to the funeral, brought her back to life for them. It was a marvelous service. A week later he came to see us again, and Henry told him about the spiritual wilderness he felt himself to be in. His early enthusiasm for Christianity seemed to have evaporated, and he felt lost. After a long discussion, Charles gently persuaded us to come to a service at the North Western Reform Synagogue. "If, after a few services you find you're a better Christian than you were before, good luck to you!" he said. Henry could not resist such a soft sell. The upshot was that we both became members, despite my agnosticism. Henry returned to his roots and became a devout, though not uncritical, Jew.

Henry took early retirement some months after my mother died, in 1984. He had long dreamed of selling our home and buying a yacht, small enough for the two of us to handle, but big enough for us to be able to get away from each other, if such a thing were possible. We would live on our yacht, sail to wherever the fancy took us, leave "this awful climate," and follow the sun. Unfortunately he had omitted to tell me of this dream. He simply expected me to know, and to share it with him. It was romantic and beautiful, but I had no intention of giving up work with ENO and life in London, and his health was such that not to be within reach of a hospital was a terrifying prospect. Just at this time he had to have an emergency operation to remove a kidney stone in his ureter. The pain was so overwhelming that he had fainted while waiting in the X-ray department. What if we had been at sea? It didn't bear thinking about. Yet he was deeply disappointed in me and fell into an abyss of depression. In my fear for him I agreed to his plan, but that was not enough for him: I had to genuinely want it, not just go along with it for his sake. We eventually saw another psychiatrist, one for whom Henry had developed great respect in his years as mental health officer, when they had often worked together. After a number of consultations he was convinced that Henry's problem lay in a chronic chemical imbalance in the brain and that he should be taking antidepressants for the rest of his life.

To compensate for not having a yacht, Henry lined our living room ceiling with wooden panelling, which, he said, made it seem more like a boat. He listened to CDs of Mahler and Bruckner symphonies, which suited his mood, listened to broadcasts of current affairs, absorbed himself in history, both in books and on television, and was endlessly fascinated with wildlife programs.

Life was always good when he was taking antidepressants; catastrophic whenever he rebelled and decided to do without them. I have never known anybody with two such distinct personalities: one charming, wise, deeply compassionate, warm, and loving; the other cruel, hateful, and with a terrible sense of emptiness and worthlessness. The two sides did not seem to know each other at all. We continued to have terrible rows. Sometimes, as I was shouting at him, I would see the expression on his face change from ferocious to utterly vulnerable, and my heart would break. Oh why did I not stop then and there, throw my arms around him, and tell him that I loved him? Perhaps because I knew he would not believe me at that moment and would push me away—and partly, I have to admit, because I was too far gone. Eventually our GP persuaded Henry to go on taking his antidepressants indefinitely, "for Eva's sake," and life became wonderful for us both. I look back now with only deep love and endless longing.

The time came when I reluctantly had to retire, although up to May 1998 I continued to play almost full time with ENO on a freelance basis. When that was about to come to an end, although I still went on being asked to deputize now and then, Henry whisked me off to Barcelona and the Spanish Pyrenees, to take the pain away. He had so much sweetness in him.

I was happy at last to have the time to play string quartets with fellow professional and retired professional musicians, and to get to know this most glorious repertoire of all. And at last to spend more time with Henry, who had been waiting for so long to have me to himself. We traveled a good deal and those were nearly always adventurous, happy times, away from the stresses of everyday life.

As he grew older, Henry became more affable, anxious not to waste our precious time together in discord, and to get over disagreements as quickly as possible. He became enchanted with the antics of little children, could watch them for hours, and he recovered his sense of humor. On one occasion, waiting to leave the garage where our car had been serviced, I noticed him joking with a couple of ladies and reproached him afterward for holding them up. "Why shouldn't I share my funniness with them?" he asked, and I was completely won over.

All the same, Henry was often in misanthropic mood, people made him tired, and he withdrew from them, yet even then they were drawn to him. Without effort, his presence would dominate a room. "He had a kind of natural authority," one of my friends has said. "There was something about him—wise, like a rabbi—you couldn't forget him—and he could also be very funny."

He often said to me, "I know why I love you, but why do you love me?"

"If I could give you a reason, *then* you'd have cause to worry," I said. "Reason doesn't come into it."

"You're mad!" said Henry.

But I would frequently find him gazing at me, and when I asked him why, he would say, looking at my ageing face with the eyes of love, "You are beautiful. You grow more beautiful every day. You are more beautiful than when I married you."

Or he would say, "Thank you."

"Thank me for what?" I'd ask, and he would answer, "Thank you for being."

Sometimes he would creep up behind me when I was working in the kitchen and kiss the back of my neck and tell me how much he loved me, or say, "I'm so fond of you that it hurts!" And I would just as often tell him that I loved him and that he was the handsomest man I knew, which was the truth, but which he found hard to believe.

"It's not what I see in the mirror," he'd say. "I have to believe the evidence of my eyes."

I see his beautiful face in my mind's eye. I can almost touch it. I love the feel of him, the look of him, the marvelous bone structure, the lovely skin, and above all the depth of soul in his eyes. It's a spiritual face. It's the most beautiful face in the world for me.

I wanted him to live forever, but for over a year his health had been deteriorating rapidly. We had managed to enjoy a ten-day holiday in Madeira just before he fell seriously ill with a urinary tract infection on July 14, 2006. He lost the use of his legs, he couldn't eat, and some of the time he was delirious. He was admitted into the Royal Free Hospital on July19, and was in and out of hospital for three months, trying repeatedly and sometimes successfully to discharge himself. He told me he wanted to come home so that when he reached out his hand in bed at night he would find mine responding. Now I know that he will never again reach out his hand for mine, nor my hand find his when I reach out.

When I said, as I was about to leave after many hours in the ward with him during the last week, "I love

Henry in cable car, Madeira, June 2006.

you so much!" he answered, "That's the one thing I'm certain of." What amazing progress from the bad old days when he was so unsure of me that he constantly expected me to leave him and drove me to the limits, to test my constancy! Oh how good it was to hear it! He said several times, "If I recover I'd like us to go back to Madeira," and I promised him we would. But it was not to be.

Little by little his entire system broke down. Sometimes he appeared to make progress, and we would hope for recovery, and then he would get worse again. On Friday, October 13, I had an early morning phone call from a nurse in his hospital ward. "Your husband is very ill," she began.

"I'm coming straight away," I said.

When I arrived I found half a dozen doctors around his bed, trying to work out where the site of his latest infection was and what to do. "I don't know what the fuss is about," Henry said. "I feel fine!"

Dr. Chadwick, the consultant, asked me to step into the passage with him and told me how serious Henry's condition was. "We're doing everything we can for him, but he is extremely ill. I'm sorry to have to be so blunt, but I believe he may not survive the day. Is there any close relative who needs to be informed?"

"He has a son by his former marriage, with a wife and daughter, up in Nottingham."

"Anyone else who needs to know?"

"The rabbi," I said.

"Well get on the phone and talk to them both quickly. Shabbat is approaching."

I sat by Henry's bedside all day, holding his hand. He had grown painfully thin, but his emaciated face, with its deep set eyes and hollow cheeks, looked more beautiful to me than ever. Over and over he raised my hand to his lips and kissed it. I kissed his forehead, his bony cheek, and sometimes lifted his oxygen mask for a moment to kiss his lips, and he kissed mine. He wanted so badly to drink, but his throat muscles had suddenly stopped functioning and liquid would go straight into his lungs, so he was on a saline drip. I tried to give him relief by sponging his mouth with little water-soaked sponges on sticks. Later the hand kisses turned into drinking from an imaginary glass, until he said with a sigh, "I can't drink any more!"

By evening Simon, Val, and Kate had arrived. He talked quite a lot with Simon. Some of the time he was lucid, and sometimes his mind wandered. And suddenly, "I've been so rude! I don't know why! I'm so angry with myself and so ashamed. I was rude to Kate three times in a row!"

"No you weren't," said Kate. It was true, but he had been rude to many other people in the past, without it apparently bothering him in the least. It was as if he was trying to "make peace with his Maker." He knew he'd been rude to somebody, and wanted to make amends. He insisted he'd been rude to Kate.

"Anyway we forgive you," said Simon.

"No, that doesn't help—there's no excuse. I can't forgive myself," he said.

Eventually Simon, who was in quite an emotional state, said, "We're going for a little walk now; we'll come back later," and Henry said, "Please not tonight. I'm very tired; I need to rest. All of you please leave me alone to rest." So they returned to Nottingham, and Henry waved goodbye to Simon as they left.

I asked for a room where I could stay the night. Of course I didn't sleep. I kept bobbing up to see how Henry was, at the far end of the high dependency area, with a soft light shining on him so that he was clearly visible from the nurses' station, but curtained off from the patient opposite. Fortunately the bed next to him was empty. From the nurses' station I saw his body convulsively fighting for breath, and I kept my distance so as not to disturb his rest.

At 4:30 a.m. something made me go right up to his bed. His eyes were closed, so he didn't see me. With every exhaled breath he whispered, "Eva…Eva…Eva…" I waited, listened carefully to be sure I wasn't mistaken. He went on saying, "Eva…Eva…" I kissed his hand, his lips, and said, "Darling… Sweetheart… I'm here. I'm Eva. I'm right beside you. I'm not going to leave you," and he said softly. "I have found you." Oh, thank God, thank whatever made me go up to his bed and answer his call. Those were the last words that I heard him say. I went on holding his hand, and sometimes he raised my hand to kiss it again, and I poured endearments on him.

In the afternoon, Rabbi Charles Emanuel, who had become a good friend since the time of my mother's funeral and had given Henry much emotional support during his illness, rang. "Do you think Henry would appreciate a visit?"

"I don't think he's in a state to appreciate a visit," I said. "But *I* certainly would."

Not long after Charles arrived, at 4:00 p.m., Henry breathed his last.

Charles' eulogy was particularly moving and real because he did not pretend Henry was perfect. "He was not an easy man," he said. "He could be argumentative, and sometimes he was wrong! But he was a caring and compassionate human being." He spoke of his integrity, strength of character, individuality, and was able to say repeatedly and from the heart, "Henry was my friend." Henry had asked for his ashes to be buried as close as possible to my mother's. Simon came with me to witness the interment and to help choose the plant to grow above the ashes—a camellia bush with deep crimson blooms, opposite my mother's, which has white blooms.

After about a fortnight I expected him to come back, and for over a year I felt shock wave after shock wave every time I realized he would never return. I felt I had lost my moorings, alone in a vast ocean, despite all my friends rallying around. Such grief was beyond anything I had ever experienced.

And yet, what happiness to have known such love.

Eva, September 2006.

Epilogue
❧ Revisiting Mallorca, South Africa, and Germany ❧

Exile is about loss: Loss of homeland, loss of family, parting from friends. It is about practical, mental, and emotional adjustments. It is a journey through grief, fear, bewilderment, and loneliness; a sense of being cut off from the surrounding society, a longing for the familiar, nostalgia for the past, and finally, acceptance—sometimes even gain. Ultimately, exile is a state of mind. In order to come to terms with my exile, I felt the need to return to the lands from which I had come.

And so, in June 1999, I paid a return visit to Palma de Mallorca, together with my husband, to try to find the house where I had spent those first happy years of my life. There stood the Castell de Bellver crowning the wooded hill, and just below the hill, the Calle Santa Rita, the street where *Pension Schay* had stood. The house had disappeared, and in its place stood a small block of flats in a derelict garden. I felt hugely disappointed. But the setting was just as I remembered it after sixty-three years, and that was thrilling. We clambered about on the hillside and viewed Palma and the Mediterranean Sea from above. In among the trees the sounds of the cicadas and birds, the scent of the pine trees, evoked nostalgic memories. The seafront with its many high rise hotels was unrecognizable, but what we saw of rural Mallorca looked mercifully unspoiled.

Henry on train in Mallorca.

Strangely, nobody spoke of the Civil War or of the Franco years. They seemed to be covered in a deep blanket of silence, as though they had never happened.

Nearly two years later, in January 2001, I returned to South Africa for the first time in forty years, again together with my husband

Great changes had taken place. After twenty-seven years' imprisonment, for the most part on Robben Island, Nelson Mandela had been freed in 1990. Apartheid was dismantled, democratic parliamentary elections were held, and in May 1994, Mandela, as leader of the majority ANC party, became South Africa's first black president. He resigned as president in 1999, having chosen Thabo Mbeki as his successor. There were still many inequities in living standards, much unemployment, and a huge increase in violent crime, but the bloody revolution the world had expected had not happened. Both Mandela and Archbishop Tutu had done tremendous work on reconciliation between black and white. Nevertheless, from all we had heard, there was much frustration among Africans that promises to improve their living conditions were taking too long to be fulfilled. We found a new South Africa very much in a state of transition. But in the short time we were there, we were struck by the apparent lack of resentment, the courtesy, goodwill, and touching friendliness we encountered from all the Africans and the few Indians we met, wherever we went. On the whole, the different ethnic groups still appeared to live in separate enclaves, with a certain amount of mutual mistrust and nervousness, but they came together in the workplace, on the sports fields, in shops and restaurants, in a seemingly friendly and courteous way.

We found a wonderful burgeoning of indigenous culture. It had always been there, of course, but it was more self-aware now, more creative, and full of vitality.

My beloved friend Nancy Greig had suffered a stroke, and Henry had urged me to go to see her in Durban. Then my Durban friend Yvonne, now married to Sinclair Stone, issued an oft-repeated invitation to us to come to stay with them in Umkomaas, in what is now called kwaZulu Natal. It is about sixty kilometers south of Durban along the coast, with a view of the sea and surrounded by lush subtropical vegetation. "I'll drive you to Durban as often as you like to see Nancy, every day if you wish," she had said, "But you must leave a few days for going on Safari." And so it was arranged. Nancy was living in a nursing home, frail and unhappy at having lost her independence. She was able to put misery aside, while together we relived the good times we had enjoyed in the past.

Durban had changed from the compact, attractive city I remembered to a vast urban sprawl. Instead of sultry January weather it was cool, with more rain than sunshine—although it did warm up after a few days—and to everyone's amazement there was snow on the distant Drakensberg. We sat on the veranda in the evenings with Yvonne and Sinclair, and during an electric storm watched as lightning turned the whole sky white. The large cockroaches, which had in the past been such a torment to me, had largely been brought under control, and I was lucky enough not to meet a single one. Even the small ants had changed their habits; instead of climbing into sugar bowls they were now chewing the plastic coverings off electric wires.

On our way home we stopped in Johannesburg for a brief three days, to visit my remaining relatives, as well as my father's grave. There was hardly anything I recognized. We stayed with Joan Abramowitz, my first violin teacher's daughter, now Joan Blackburne but still Joanie to me, and her husband, Hugh. They lived in a housing complex called Wendywood, situated in Sandton, a suburb that had sprung up long after my departure from Johannesburg. We had to drive past security guards to enter and leave Wendywood, and again to enter the vast shopping complex of Sandton City, where what I had known as "town" had moved. Emmy and Ernst Wenger, my father's cousin and her husband, whom I had so rudely sent packing at the age of eight when they had paid me a sickness visit, were still in the home they had lived in all their married life. But now their beautiful garden was hidden behind high walls; people seemed to be imprisoned in their own homes. Berea, where my old school was located, Hillbrow, where we had lived for so many years, my old playground Joubert Park, and the "town" I remembered were all "no-go areas" now. The British Foreign Office had even published a warning to visitors to Johannesburg to avoid these dangerously violent areas. Joanie told us that organized crime and international drug syndicates were causing much of the violence, which the police were unable to control. I felt disoriented, as though I had come to a completely strange city, one that bore no relationship to my past.

Joanie drove us to West Park Cemetery, where my father lies. As we got out of the car I noticed that Henry's face wore a rather solemn expression. I said, "Why the long face?" and he answered, "We are going to visit your father's grave."

"I haven't come here to be maudlin," I said tetchily, "I've only come to see if his grave is well-tended."

Henry knew me better than I knew myself. The simple gravestone was just as I remembered it. The moment I stood in front of it great sobs unexpectedly took me over; they seemed to well up from deep inside my body, completely out of my control. It felt as if there was no end to them. I had not realized how much grief had still been stored in me.

Shortly after our return to London, I visited my mother's hometown of Laupheim for the first time since that one fateful night in 1936 in my grandparents' home. I met the curator of a new museum in Laupheim tracing the history of the Jews in Germany. The seriousness of her and her colleagues' research, and their determination to set the record straight, impressed me. Altogether my encounter with younger Germans in recent years has shown their desire to face squarely a past for which they could not be held responsible and that filled them with horror; a desire to make amends insofar as that was possible and to build bridges. I am aware that this is not the case throughout Germany, but it has certainly been my experience. It could not have been more different from the hostility or denial I found among Germans in the early years after the war.

The following year, in January 2002, my husband took me to visit parts of India where he had been so happy, including his place of work, Mazagon Dock, in what is now called Mumbai, where he was fêted with great honor. It was a wonderful experience.

After World War II we all thought that humankind had learned a lesson and that genocide would and could never happen again. Yet since then, heartbreaking horrors have been perpetrated around the world again and again: wars, dictatorship, civil war, terrorism, starvation, victims without number, and a never-ending stream of refugees. I wonder whether, some fifty or sixty years later, those who have survived will be looking back too, recording their experiences of being strangers in other lands, of the hardships they suffered, of the sense of dislocation they felt, and of the gradual adjustments they were able to make to their new lives.

Many years ago when my husband and I were visiting friends in the Lake District, our hostess asked us how we now felt, having been immigrants to this country. I stopped to think and replied a little sadly, "I feel like a Displaced Person." Henry said without hesitation that he simply felt British. But it was not as simple as that. In the year 2000 he felt compelled to drive alone to Berlin, his birthplace, to try to understand what had taken place, and to come to terms with the fact that he was not one of the six million who had perished.

It was only during my husband's last illness that I suddenly realized that I was truly no longer in exile, nor had I been for a number of years, for I had found my home at last, in Henry. And when the time is ripe, I hope to find again that oneness in which we all have our being, and which is beyond time and place.